Real Estate Essentials

A GUIDEBOOK FOR BROKERS, BUYERS, AGENTS, AND SELLERS

P. Johan Sekovski

ISBN: 0999454404

ISBN 13: 9780999454404

Pangea Press: Monument, Colorado

Table of Contents

Many thanks to:

My wife Heidi, whose eternal patience with me is nothing short of a miracle. Beyond that it was she who first encouraged me to get into real estate many years ago when we lived in Stevenson Ranch, California.

My kids, who put up with me being holed up in my home office, writing and writing and writing.

My parents Nick and Lisbeth for instilling in me a love of home, building, and landscaping. As immigrants they taught me the keen value of a firm work ethic. Getting up early to throw newspapers, long hours weeding the garden, cutting down trees, pruning bushes, mowing the lawn, cleaning out the chicken coop, and shoveling snow all taught me mental toughness, tenacity, consistency, determination, and focus. You taught me many things through your words and by your actions, but I think one of the greatest is the love and value of working hard at something.

Paul Banas of Banas Mortgage in Williamsville, New York, for always being supportive and giving me my first chance many years ago. I was honored to landscape your new home. You told me, "There is no such thing as job security. Security is your ability to produce." That along with many other bits of wisdom have never escaped my mind. Thank you, Paul. And yes, thank you, Nancy, for without you being the best elementary school teacher a kid could ever have, I would never have met Paul!

Mike and Carol Licata for your friendship of many years. You were the first people Heidi and I met who were involved in real estate and you made a big impact on us. Thank you Mike for encouraging me to write. Thank you Carol for your never-ending support.

Judy Brinkman, who was my earliest imprint of what a sharp real estate agent looked like. You made a massive impression on me as a young boy. Your smile, warmth, kindness and elegance has been something I have never forgotten.

Fran and Lori Pyle for being the picture of support and friendship. Thank you Fran for our endless phone conversations about life, family, and work.

Glenn and Beth Allen, Randy and Brenda Kerls, Ron and Sandy Archer for believing in me and encouraging me to write. You are all true friends and thanks for not rolling your eyes when I kept saying the book would come out "soon."

Lori Moran, whose shoulders my entire incompetency falls upon. Thank you Lori for not only your brilliant work that enables me to thrive but also for just being you. You have felt like family to me since day one. Thanks for getting me and understanding my humor and sarcasm. You're awesome my sister.

Kelly Pecqueur, though we haven't known each other long, I feel I have known you for a lifetime. You bring a sense to me that we're not the weird ones, they are!

Jennifer Holms, whose warmth, kindness, and great attitude brightens up the office.

Stephanie Hayes for just being a total boss at Unified Title! I'm so glad that Lori Moran referred me to you. I have enjoyed every step of the way and deeply appreciate your attention to detail, great attitude, and fun-loving spirit.

Lisa Key for being a great part of the Unified Title team and always being ready to help and serve. More Starbucks coming! And yes, you're awesome. Just in case you don't hear it enough.

Daniel Osinski for being a fellow Polack even though my family isn't Polish! I felt a friendship with you from the moment we met.

Brian Cooper for the amazing team you have built and for the gentle servant leadership you portray. Unified Title has locations throughout the state of Colorado.

Mike Ferry for inspiring and motivating me since we met in 2002. Your impact on real estate is immeasurable. Thank you for your leadership and consistency.

Michelle Williams (TreasuredPages.com) for a great cover. Thanks for all your hard work and friendship over the years.

Chris Behan, owner of Pillar to Post Home Inspections, for being a great guy from my hometown of Buffalo. Glad we met. I appreciate your professionalism and congeniality. You are a super pro my friend.

And, of course, a great big thank you to all my clients. Your trust in me is something I don't take lightly. I am humbled that you ask me to represent you and negotiate on your behalf. It truly is a privilege.

Chapter One

Why People Hate Real Estate Agents

There are some things that are exactly common among all humans regardless of our differences. You don't even need to be an expert on Maslow's hierarchy of needs to understand this. At the very basic level, all humans need to eat, sleep, and have shelter. Shelter. Home. A place to hang your hat. We all need a place to call home. It is something that touches us all. Some of us prefer an urban loft, while others want dozens of acres out in the country. Some want maintenance-free patio homes in quiet, gated retirement communities, while others want big houses with big yards in bustling neighborhoods. Whatever our preference one thing is a fact, and that is we all need a home. Since this is such a basic and fundamental need for humanity, you would think people would love the process and the people involved, but they don't. Well, some people may enjoy aspects of the process itself, but many have negative opinions of the agents in particular.

Real estate agents, used-car salesmen, and retail
Real estate agents are held in such a lofty view by the general public that they are second to last place next to, you guessed it, used-car salesmen. I say men because most women are smarter than to work at such places. Think about that for a minute. In trust, competency, and likability, the general public in the United States places real estate agents just above the

all-time most disdained person, the prototypical used-car salesman. This is a really huge disconnect. Homes and cars. Here are two things that most people find completely necessary, and yet they despise the people selling them and have significant frustration with the entire process. Why is this so?

Much of this is stereotype, but stereotypes originate somewhere in historical fact. Regardless of the current stereotype somewhere, somebody at some time acted a certain way often enough to give people an opinion of such actors. Over many years those opinions become entrenched in the public mindset. It is a fact that the kind of person who is trying to sell you a used car at some corner car lot with a string of light bulbs hanging from poles is most likely going to fit your low expectations and align with previous bad experiences. Even large new car dealerships are not immune. It's just part of the car selling and dealership culture. Perhaps at some point, you may be pleasantly surprised, but odds are you won't.

Unfortunately, real estate agents have accomplished the same feat. They, through their unprofessionalism, incompetency, greed, and lack of skill, have become a sideshow, a Saturday Night Live skit, a stereotypical joke. Because of this reality, there is tremendous distrust and even more noteworthy a dislike, disdain, and even contempt of real estate agents. Want to part a crowd like Moses at the Red Sea? Just announce you're a real estate agent at a party. It's like mosquito spray for humans. They are instantly repelled. You will find yourself alone drinking margaritas in the corner as you check your e-mails on your smartphone.

When I go shopping and I don't care if it's for a pair of jeans or a new car, I and every other living human hate being approached by the typical drone of a so-called sales person asking the same old tired and excessively worn-out phrase, "Can I help you?" I mean how many more years must we labor under the same taxing, predictable, and meaningless cliché? Is there no better way to engage with potential customers, and if not are such workers even necessary? All of us respond to the uncomfortable but predictable social choreography in the same predictable manner. "No thanks. I'm just looking." Interpretation? "Bug off loser. You're bothering me."

I've been at car lots and can actually feel my muscles tensing up as I spot out of the corner of my eye the trench coat-wearing sales guy with a bushy mustache sauntering in my direction. Think about this disconnect. People love that new car smell. They love having a new car whether it's brand new or pre-owned but new to them. It's exciting having a new car. It's a dream come true for most people. However, getting there is usually a nightmare. Between awkward salespeople and a tortured process that has them running back and forth to their manager in order to approve aspects of the deal, most people just hate the whole thing. Nothing to say of the hours wasted in playing this game.

One of my favorite humans on the planet is Marcus Lemonis. On his show *The Profit*, he speaks often about the three fundamentals of any business: the people, the process, and the product. When purchasing a vehicle, the product is desirable, the people are mediocre at best, and the process is broken and truly horrible. Can no employer actually hire fun, energetic, skilled employees who know how to engage with people instead of roaming the lot or store like zombies? I mean we may as well have programmed robots whistling about if we're just going to be saying the same thing over and over again. It makes me wonder why some stores even hire anyone at all. *Death of a Salesman* was not only great theater; it's actually fact. In most places companies could save fortunes by clearing out their stores of all zombie employees. That style of the so-called sales is indeed dead. Many companies have not understood the difference between sales and just being an order taker.

This is why grocery stores along with Walmart and Home Depot all have self-checkout options. Chase bank is doing away with tellers and replacing them with kiosks as is McDonalds and Shake Shack. I write articles on LinkedIn, and I have written extensively about the impact technology has on our economy. In this regard many companies are figuring out that they don't need certain types of employees. I don't mean this to be hurtful, but you have no job security if a member of the general public can do your job with zero training. Dragging a box of pasta across a sensor isn't rocket science. Neither is depositing a check or ordering fast food.

Do we really need help finding a pair of jeans? You walk in, find your size, try it on, and buy them if you like the fit. No need for anyone to "help" you. You're not a child. Though they blame Amazon, I think one of the real reasons there is less foot traffic in retail stores is because people have grown weary of the process and the people involved. Maybe it made sense a hundred years ago when men wore derby hats and suits in public and ladies wore white lace gloves, but that time is long gone. Maybe "help" in retail was the appropriate and courteous cultural thing to do, but now? Absolutely not. In our casual culture of well-informed buyers with limitless ways to shop, such an outmoded method is just silly.

That's why the car industry freaked out when Tesla announced they didn't need traditional dealerships. It instantly revealed the antiquated and obsolete method most car companies use to sell their vehicles. I mean I'm at the point now in my life where I just want to go online, find the car I want, select color and package, and click "purchase." Think about how efficient that is instead of wasting impossibly long hours at a local dealership. My cousin has been buying cars on eBay for years. He loves it. He lives in Colorado and recently purchased a vehicle from Florida online. The semi pulled right up to his house and unloaded his new car. Nothing to it. People just don't want to waste time.

The retail and auto industries need to go through a massive revolution and actually tap into what people want instead of cranking out the same undesirable nonsense year after year. Seriously, is there no one out there in retail who can be the least bit creative when training sales agents? Must we tread along like some grotesque version of a heavy footed Frankenstein? Our current techniques, models, and methods are entirely antiquated and obsolete, yet nobody seems to have the least bit desire or passion to create a superior model. To the one who does, the spoils and profits will be immeasurable.

The same is true in real estate. "Thinking of buying or selling? Call me!" Seriously? That's the best you can do? Wow, let me stop writing, so I can clap my hands in thunderous applause. The real estate industry is so entrenched in outdated methods, jargon, and slogans that it's up there with retail and auto sales. Oh sure, most real estate companies are aggressively pursuing technology and slick websites with all the bells and whistles, but they continue to attract and retain the same tired, low-skill people. Ask around for a testimony or review of any interaction with a real estate agent. Ask around or recall yourself how your last transaction went or your last three transactions went. Odds are it was less than amazing.

Some people might say what a great agent they had and how wonderful he or she was. Congrats! That is definitely the needle in the haystack. For the vast majority of people, they have such nightmare stories that they defy logic. Virtually everyone I encounter has had a negative experience. In the world of opinion and stereotypes, the general public has a picture of what a real estate agent is. Then based on that picture, they create expectations. Low expectations. When people have repeated negative experiences, they lower their expectations until they reach very low levels. Like ranked just above used-car salesmen, for example.

That's why some restaurants fail. If people continue to have a negative experience, they won't come back. They'll dine elsewhere. In business, any business, you just can't continue to disappoint your prospects and actual customers and think you can prosper. It just doesn't work that way. That's why there is an 85 percent turnover rate of real estate agents every five years. The failure and dropout rate for real estate agents is exactly the same as for small businesses. It's because people get into real estate for all the wrong reasons, are poorly trained, have little if any actual business and negotiation skill, don't understand high-level sales and marketing, lack competency in communication and customer service, and are overall flops. People don't realize they are a 100 percent commission earner and an independent contractor which means if you get into real estate, you are running your own small business. Well, most people have never run their own small business so we are surprised when they fail miserably at real estate?

Real estate for some agents is like airport food. The reputation of many restaurants in airports is not good. Service is usually subpar, and the quality of meals is forgettable. Why? Because the culture of airport restaurants has historically been a lazy one where they know they will most likely never see the customer again. If there is no repeat business, then why bother being excellent? It's a horrible mentality, and it's the same in real estate. For most agents they will never deal with the same client again, so they just don't put as much effort into things. It would be different if they were selling soap or bottled water, but because in their minds it's a "one and done," they just don't care too much. Smart agents work hard for everyone, because they know people talk and recommend great agents, and that people eventually move again, but we're not talking about the smart ones in this chapter. That comes later.

So many real estate agents!
The problem is there are *so* many agents out there that they have literally flooded the industry, and that's why there is such a negative opinion in most people's minds. It seems like everyone and their sister, aunt, broth-er-in-law, and grandma has a real estate license. You can't hardly swing a dead cat without hitting a real estate agent. Sorry, I have no idea what that means. For the record I have never seen anyone actually swinging a dead feline, nor have I ever engaged or endorsed such behavior should it actually exist. As a matter of fact, we have always had cats. We love cats. We have Persians. They're expensive cats. That should prove our allegiance and affection! Don't call PETA. Cats notwithstanding there are just *so* many agents in every single town, borough, hamlet, village, and city. I blame the industry itself. I blame the greed and shortsightedness of local, state, and national governing bodies as well as real estate broker-ages and companies. They all make money on fees and dues, so clearly the more people you have paying said fees and dues, the more profitable you become.

It's actually unfair and frankly sad because new real estate agents are actually set up. They think they can earn fortunes and so they jump into real estate. Nobody tells them the truth. All the governing bodies at the local, state, and national level, along with the brokerages are all excited for them. They're excited because they all collect fees and dues from every agent. Therefore the more agents, the more profit. Nobody apparently cares if these people succeed, have any actual potential, or are well trained. They are just released on the general public. If they fail, the governing bodies don't care because there are hundreds of thousands of new rookies eager to take the bait. This isn't a cynical perspective; it's reality. The industry is less concerned with producing competent and lasting professionals than it is with earning profits generated by flooding the market. So in a sense, the industry itself sets agents up to fail.

Can you imagine how much better it would be if everyone was just truthful? "Oh hello person considering being a real estate agent. 85 percent of agents fail and drop out within five years, so let's just get that out of the way before we talk any further. Do you have the skills to be part of the 15 percent that makes it? Do you have significant experience running a small business? Do you have a good CPA that can coach you on the tax and deduction strategies for your new small business? Are you good at record keeping? Do you understand sales, marketing, prospecting, lead follow-up, and business development at a high level? Are you an exceptional communicator? Do you have a proven track record at being great at customer service? Do you possess the temperament, emotional stability, intelligence, personality, and attitude to remain positive in the face of struggle, hard work, and setbacks? Do you have the appropriate capital reserves to run your new little small business? Are you committed to dedicating the 40, 50 or 60 hours a week it takes to run your small business? Are you prepared to work evenings and weekends if necessary? Are you good at time management? Are you dedicated to getting a coach, attending seminars, reading extensively, and doing whatever it takes to improve your skills? Yes or no?"

If it was a firm yes then the person should be allowed to move forward in real estate. If it was a no, then perhaps that person should think about doing something else because in less than five years they will be anyway.

So why not cut to the chase? Why not be honest with people and really tell them the truth about the industry?

But no. Nobody tells anyone the truth. Everyone just smiles and rakes in the dues and fees. I am amazed at the low level of people this industry attracts. I mean if you can pay some money and pass a test or two, you're in! You're a bona fide real estate agent. In real estate there is virtually no barrier to entry. No other industry has such a low threshold. You can't just jump into medicine or psychological therapy. You can't decide one day to wake up and be a home builder. You can't tomorrow become a computer programmer or financial analyst or stock broker. Most careers or professions take a serious commitment of time, money, and education before you are cut loose on the general public. Not so in real estate, though. Just got out of the military? Stay-at-home mom? Bored retiree? Conduct home parties selling candles, plastic containers, cosmetics, or frying pans? No experience in business at all? No proven history knowing how to negotiate? No economic education? No problem! The real estate industry welcomes you with open arms; well, that is as long as you pay your fees and dues! Many of these people go from selling items at home parties under $30 to selling homes worth more than $300,000. How can selling $30 worth of candles possibly prepare you for much higher numbers that require significant business, communication, and negotiation skills? At home parties all you have to do is bake muffins, brew some fresh coffee, and take orders. While perfectly fine for some people, this is not exactly high-level business.

Not only is there virtually no barrier to entry, but once people become licensed, there is no accountability. Yes, of course, there is accountability in the legal and ethical sense. If an agent messes up a transaction, overlooks some important details, or is involved in fraud, certainly they and their broker could possibly end up in a world of trouble. What I am talking about is performance accountability. The actual production statistic for real estate agents nationally is less than four transactions a year. Think of that. Would you want a surgeon to operate on you if she only did four operations a year? Would you want a mechanic to work on your car if he only replaced parts on four cars a year? In real estate, as long as you can pass the initial exam, do some continuing education, renew your license, and pay all corresponding fees and dues, you are free to roam around town telling people you're an agent. No governing body cares if you do one deal a year or one hundred. You are an agent. If you took a sales position for a major corporation, you would be held accountable for your sales production. If you underperformed or if key clients went elsewhere, your job would be in jeopardy. You couldn't just float along indefinitely with low numbers. You would have to produce. You would have a quota. You would have standards. You would have mandatory goals. You would have to grow your portfolio. You would have to build a wall around your customers and make sure they were happy with your service. You would be fully accountable.

No such mechanism exists in real estate. There are no standards and no accountability for low or no production. The nonexistent threshold and lack of performance accountability cause the real estate industry to be a magnet for dabblers, hobbyists, underperformers, part-timers, and weak agents. They are using real estate to make a little side money. They are not making a commitment to the craft or making it their priority, and this lack of skill and commitment translate into a sloppy engagement with the general public. Such sloppy engagements create a negative perception with low expectations in people's minds.

Saturation and Commoditization

Supply and demand dictates price. Pretty standard stuff in the economic world. High supply with low demand creates low prices. Low supply with high demand and prices surge. Scarcity creates high prices. That's why diamonds are expensive, and that's why homes on the beach are expensive. The issue with saturation or high supply is that prices are driven down because products need to be sold. Companies don't make money with shelves overloaded with products collecting dust. Companies make money moving inventory. In high saturation areas of our economy, price is always driven down to the lowest tolerable levels, and the quality of the entire process becomes mechanized because of limited perceived value.

When price levels hit rock bottom, things often become commoditized. When something is commoditized, it means it is like corn, copper, or silver. These commodities are all the same any way you slice it. One ounce of copper is not better than the other. They are all virtually the same thing. In such situations the only standing issue is price. If the perception is that a bushel of corn is the same as any other bushel of corn, then whoever sells the cheapest bushel will win. In other words the quality of the entire process diminishes, and everything degenerates into a battle for the lowest price.

Since there are in every American town a glut of real estate agents and since so many of them are subpar, there is a perception in the public that they are not worth their pay. Therefore, the public will begin to demand lower prices for real estate services, and since most real estate agents are weak, they are more than happy to provide a bargain. And so the entire industry unravels, while the poorly skilled, the newcomer, and the weak agent allow prices for their services to be driven into the ground.

Competition, in the minds of many, is no longer based on quality of service, negotiation ability, competency, or skill but on rock-bottom price. Once public perception is changed into thinking that there is virtually no difference between agents, then the industry is all but dead. It has become commoditized. Weak agents void of high-level skill and ability find their only competitive advantage is that they will almost work for free. They, knowing they bring nothing significant to the table, are reduced to the only tactic they can think of, that is, lowering their commission. And, just like in everything, you get what you pay for. I can't tell you how many times I have been called to take on clients after they have suffered with a low-skill commoditized discount agent. I have almost always been able to negotiate a higher price for the home that more than evens out the increased payment to me.

Thankfully, there is a huge difference between a smart and highly skilled agent and the rest. It's just that they are the minority and have to swim upstream to convince people they are better and different from the rest. For great agents it's hard to sometimes convince people because it sounds self-serving, but after a really bad experience with a weak agent, the axiom becomes more true than ever: you get what you pay for!

It's really odd. While low housing inventory in many metro areas is driving home prices up the glut of real estate agents running around every town in the United States drives commissions down. Low inventory creates high prices. Saturation creates low costs. Few houses, many agents. Everyone fighting for a smaller and smaller piece of the pie.

My buddy is an agent

If the market for real estate agents is saturated, and it is, then just about anyone walking around will know at least one agent and oftentimes several. If this is true, and it is, then just about everyone will have a friend, coworker, neighbor, or family member in the real estate business. If this is true, and it is, then two things emerge: people like deals, and people like to do favors for those they know. Who doesn't like a bargain? If I can get the same quality of product or service for a lower price, I will almost always do that. So will you. Nobody, regardless of income levels, likes to waste money. Such bargain shoppers are in luck because just about every real estate agent in the United States will drop their commission for you if you happen to be a friend, coworker, neighbor, or family member. I'm not necessarily saying it's wrong; it's just a reality of the industry and the high volume of agents running around. Anyone in business likes to do favors for those they know. The problem lies in the fact that there are so many agents out there that their "buddy" discount then has far-reaching impact.

Can you imagine if restaurant owners saturated their communities as much as real estate agents? Can you imagine if everyone had a neighbor, friend, coworker, or family member who owned a burger joint or a bar where they got discounted food and drinks on a regular basis? The whole restaurant industry would be impacted. If you decide to list and sell your home, you virtually have unlimited options of those you know who carry real estate licenses. If it is commoditized and there is a glut of agents, then you can indeed find a bargain. They will be happy to reduce their commission from 6 percent (3 percent for them and 3 percent for the other agent representing the buyer) to 4 percent as a "favor" to you because you guys are buddies and all. At 4 percent they still have to offer 2.5 to 3 percent to the buyer's agent, which means they are working for 1 to 1.5 percent. If the median home price in your area is $250,000, then this discounting buddy of yours will earn $2,500 to $3,750 income less fees, dues, and taxes. Not bad money but not the $7,500 they would have earned without the buddy discount.

Still $2,500 to $3,750 isn't chump change, so in their mind, less is better than nothing. Then he can walk around the office and brag how he sold eleven houses this year. Of course, the secret is that he heavily discounted his commission in order to conduct any business at all. He won't ever tell you how much money he made because that would reveal his weakness and inability to stand up for himself or the fact that he only sold homes to people in his friends and family circle of relationships.

This may seem great for the consumer; however, the long-term impact of this phenomenon is that commissions and, therefore agent income, is eroded due to saturation and commoditization. If income is eroded, then the quality of agents attracted to the business will continue to lessen. At less than 15 percent, the pool of quality agents is already fairly small. I can't imagine where things will be in the coming years. If real estate agents are continually diminished regarding the value they bring, they will eventually be regarded as order takers not dissimilar to workers at a fast-food restaurant. If this is so, then their income will be dramatically reduced to commensurate levels.

The Motivation

It's important to know what motivates the people you do business with. If I was to hire a real estate agent, I would want to know what really drives them. Why do they do what they do? What logic do they employ in their business model? Do they actually have a business model? Why do they get up in the morning and go to work? You must uncover their motivation because that is what will determine their work ethic and how the whole transaction will flow. Motivation directly impacts the quality of the process. If you discover that beyond the sweet talk of the listing appointment where promises are made and accolades are given, the agent indeed is lazy and really unmotivated to aggressively pursue your best interests, you will regret ever opening the door to them.

It is imperative that you understand what drives this person because after all this is your home we are talking about, and you don't want someone who is not properly motivated involved with dealing with what is most likely your most costly asset. There are as you can imagine a variety of motivators. Fear is a great motivator because going hungry is a bummer, but fear can also sabotage a deal because the fearful agent may be scared to negotiate or push back. Ego may get someone out of the bed in the morning believing they are God's gift to real estate, but that same ego if unchecked can get in the way of respectful communication with the other agent. Greed may push an agent to be aggressive, but if all they are looking at is the paycheck, the customer service levels may dissipate. The only way to know what drives a person is to ask questions and listen. Most discerning people can get a sense for what motivates someone just by being a good listener and being perceptive.

The why, the what, and the how

In my personal life, I use this formula to create lasting improvements and effective modes of behavior that allow me to achieve my goals. The why is the reason or motivation we do what we do. It drives us from an inner place deep in our soul. The what is the goal or end result, and the how is the strategy or action we employ to achieve our goals. The how is the map that shows us how to get there.

Most people in business jump right to the what and the how. With confidence they will be able to clearly say what the goal is and how they intend to achieve the goal. Very few start with the why though, which cause them to come across as overly driven, crass, impersonal, or robotic. Because they haven't connected with themselves on a deep level, how can they possibly connect with you? They are merely machines doing a job, performing a function. They act like pre-programmed robots because they have never considered the why.

Real estate agents are the same. The industry is indeed flooded by people who not only lack business, communication, and negotiation skills but also lack an understanding of why they are even in real estate to start with. Oh sure they will tell you their reasons, I have listed several below, but they really haven't processed their values and what motivates them. If you listen to most real estate agents, you'll hear some pretty sappy or poorly thought out reasons, which is why, of course, why most Realtors fail. They don't do enough business to be professional and just become more dead weight in an already overcrowded industry.

Here are some of the reasons I have heard over the years:

- Our Realtor was horrible, and I thought I could do a better job.
- I just got out of the military, and I thought being in real estate looked good to me.
- The kids were older, so I wanted to bring in some extra income.
- I was in insurance and was burned out, so I thought I'd try real estate.
- I'm a retired detective and needed something else to do.
- My husband kept yelling at me because I was spending too much money shopping, so I became a Realtor.
- I just did the math on some of these houses, and man do real estate agents make a lot of money!

None of these are compelling whys. They don't connect with inner passion, and they don't provide a vibrant engine to drive high production with professionalism and efficiency.

The why

The "why" has to do with the articulation of values. Motivation, drive, and commitment flow from solid inner values. Simply put if something is important to us, we will have an internal engine compelling us to achieve goals that are in alignment with those inner values. We won't need to be reminded. We won't need an external force nagging us to do something. We will be intrinsically motivated and have an inner push to achieve.

Many people go through life and don't even give a second thought as to why they do the things they do. They have never paused to discover what is important to them and why. They just drift through life and make decisions that oftentimes create tremendous conflict because they never consider their internal values. When we don't know what our values are, some of our decisions will invariably be opposed to our inner plumb line. When we make those types of uninformed decisions, we create an incongruent condition of heart, and it manifests as stress, conflict, anxiety, and sometimes anger.

For example, some people could say a core value is honesty, but when pressed they may fib a little bit just to get out of an awkward situation. Perhaps they're a little uncomfortable with confrontation or being put on the spot. They never seem to have the right words, so in a moment of emotional fluster, they take the easy way out and just lie. Of course this is against their core value, so then they endlessly brood and can find little else to think about besides their little white lie. Then fear enters because while they are obsessing they wonder if the other person will find out the truth. Later they become anxious and purposely avoid that person causing a negative impact on the relationship. Do you see how things can really spiral out of control when we aren't able to articulate and act upon our core values?

Like the example above, some real estate agents fib when they tell their prospective client that they will work tirelessly to get the best price for their home and that they will fiercely negotiate on their behalf. In reality they may actually be scared of confrontation. The conflict occurs for the agents when they make such promises but their core value may be peace and harmony. When pushed by another agent presenting an offer, their value of peace and harmony may manifest as avoidance or even surrender. Can you imagine the internal conflict of such agents? Can you see how poorly they invariably serve their client? Do you see how such an agent can really make a mess of things?

They have inadvertently overpromised beyond their ability and will certainly under deliver because the described actions are not in alignment with their core. They then may become angry when the client calls them and asks for the things they promised. They perceive the client's inquiry as a threat and become defensive even though they are in the wrong because they are not following through on what they promised. The client simply took them at their word and didn't know the agent actually needs therapy to discover what their core values really are! They avoid their clients and won't answer the phone. Then things don't get done, and the whole process turns into a mess. It's especially bad if such agents were referred by a third party, because then that relationship with the client can become messed up too. It's obvious they are in the wrong line of work because they do not possess that inner drive that brings out the best in them.

I know pastors who are strong introverts. That is out of alignment. This is a vocational choice that is not in harmony with core values or personality design. Think about that for a moment. Ministry is about people. Sure there's prayer, study, and message preparation, but really it's all about people. That's like being an elementary school teacher but finding that little kids and the noise they make drain you. Why would you ever do that to yourself? One pastor I am familiar with can't even get out of bed until Tuesday afternoon or evening. The weekend services wipe him out so completely that he finds himself exhausted and can't function for days. He told me he usually gets his wits about him around Wednesday afternoon. Think of the strain, the stress, and the wasted time. He literally loses half the workweek because what he does is incongruent with who he is at a core level. To me it is nuts to spend a lifetime in a career that is not in alignment with our inner values, but teachers, pastors, and real estate agents do it all the time.

It is the equivalent of continually driving a car that is out of alignment, which means the wheels are trying to go in two different directions. When this occurs tremendous pressure and strain are placed on the connecting points, and eventually the structure that supports the wheels will deteriorate from the vibration. In addition the tires will wear unevenly, and the car will shake when driven and eventually break down. If you want a smooth drive, you have to be in alignment. If you want a smooth real estate process, you have to have an agent who is internally aligned with his or her core values.

Why are people drawn to real estate?

In life you get paid according to skill, talent, and ability. In no other industry can people with such low talent, skill, or ability make the amount of money that real estate agents do. Some mediocre agent may stumble upon a buyer of a million-dollar property, and this person will make a $30,000 commission check. $30,000! That's the bigger chunk of what most Americans make in a whole year! Do you know how big of a deal you would have to close in a corporate job to earn that kind of commission check in one month? Please.

Many people generate a negative opinion about real estate agents after buying or selling a home. Since the vast majority of agents are mediocre at best, the experience is usually mediocre at best. Homeowners of at least average intelligence might feel insulted seeing an agent they consider a simpleton walk away with thousands of their hard earned dollars. Many people get into real estate exactly because of that reason. They see real estate agents with limited skills collecting significant commissions, so they say, "Heck if Johnny Nicklefritz can do it, I certainly can!" I've known more than one person who got into real estate solely because of the negative experience they had. They hated their agent and the whole frustrating process and figured they could do it better.

The real bummer here is that it's not the fault of the general public they have such a low opinion of real estate agents. They have perfectly valid reasons for feeling the way they do, and you know what? I share those opinions. My own experiences with other agents in countless deals are the same. I not only hear the stories, but I also have to fix the messes created by incompetent and poorly trained agents. I have to deal with agents on the other side of each transaction. Some are perfectly pleasant, while many are, well, you get the idea.

I look around the room at real estate training events that I attend. I see who my so-called competitors are. Overweight, slovenly dressed, hairstyles stuck in decades past, unprofessional, disorganized, and unaware of their appearance and how poorly they come across. If reality is perception, many real estate agents have no concept of how badly they are perceived. They don't know how to present themselves in a professional manner because many of them do not come from professional backgrounds. They are people who do not come from a business context, are not well read or educated in business, lack people and communication skills, don't know how to effectively negotiate, and are generally trapped in layers of incompetence.

So why are people drawn to real estate? They are drawn to it because of the money, plain and simple. The average person makes around $50,000 a year in America. This means that their pretax monthly income is around $4,000. The median American home price is around $250,000 and will generally yield a $7,500 pre-tax, pre-fees commission. So people get into real estate because they walk around doing the math all day and tell their sweetie pie, "Gee whiz golly, Marge. If I sell just one home a month, we can double our income!"

Well, yes and no. First of all is the painfully glaring national statistic of the average agent selling less than four homes a year. Not a month, a year. Now let me ask you a logical question: if you only did something four times a year, would you be proficient at it? Would you be considered a pro? Would you do it full time with absolute dedication, competency, and commitment?

Second, even though that $7,500 is real what is also real are commission broker splits, fees, and dues. It is not uncommon for new or low-production agents to pay a 40 percent split to the broker, which means $3,000 disappears right off the bat. So now we're down to $4,500. Fees and dues can easily choke off another $500, and that's not including monthly and annual fees and dues to the brokerage, the real estate franchise, local MLS, state ruling body, and national real estate organizations. So now we're down to $4,000 if we're lucky, and that is exactly the average monthly pre-tax income of most Americans. Taxes will whack off another say $1,000, so now we're down to $3,000. One average home sold and the average income for a new or low-producing agent will be $3,000. Not exactly a windfall.

You know who is making a fortune, though? The agent's brokerage. They are more than happy to load up on new, low-producing, and inexperienced agents because they can make the most money on such agents. Experienced, smart, or top-producing agents would never stay with a brokerage that took so much of their earnings because their production creates leverage. With high volume they are able to negotiate better deals elsewhere.

So if you do the math of four homes multiplied by $3,000, the average agent in America, who has flooded the market with his or her inexperience and incompetency, makes about $12,000 a year. Is that enough to feed a family and pay a mortgage? Is that enough to pay for ongoing education to improve their skills? Is that enough money to go to seminars to learn about all the new technology to better serve their clients? Is that enough money to do real estate full time? The answer is a resounding *no*, which is why most agents are part-timers or dabblers with another job, or drop out of real estate altogether. Their other job is their main source of income, while real estate is more like a hobby. These are facts, not opinions, and this is why the real estate industry has such a negative reputation.

My struggle in real estate

It's really strange. I've never really struggled with the actual work of real estate. I have launched and owned businesses before. I have held corporate sales jobs before. I have a lifestyle of continual personal and professional improvement. When I decided to get into real estate I figured things out, researched and studied, attended classes, and went to seminars. Equally enjoyable for me is to work with buyers or sellers, high end or entry level. I love everything about real estate—except working with other agents and dealing with the negative reputation of the real estate industry. It's challenging being part of an industry with such a negative reputation. However, I use it as one of my competitive advantages. When people meet me and we begin to have a conversation, they are usually shocked and then delighted that I'm in real estate. Their expectations are so low that they are pleasantly surprised that someone with my background and experience is an agent. While that makes me feel good, I am simultaneously conflicted to be part of an industry held in such low regard.

My mountain to climb is the fact that I am in an industry filled with such subpar individuals that my main function over the years has been in exerting effort to differentiate myself from lame agents. It's really hard to be in a field where you are lumped in with everyone else, 85% of which are failing. As I state elsewhere, there is an 85 percent turnover in real estate agents every five years. This means that at some level, the massive majority of agents you will encounter are failing. It's hard because in other professions you are surrounded by committed and competent professionals. Pilots, university professors, architects and doctors all enjoy a collegial fraternity of sorts. Not so in real estate. The only place where there is some camaraderie and mutual respect is with those of us at the top fifteen percent level. Among top producers there is a natural affinity because these people are the professionals who are thriving and succeeding. We inspire and learn from each other.

It's challenging to be in an industry with virtually no barrier to entry and no performance accountability. As you will discover, I too hate real estate agents. Well, maybe not hate, but I sure struggle with many aspects of this business. You will note in my style of writing that I spare no insult or jab at the underperforming agents or stupid and useless tactics the real estate industry is filled with. In this book I not only pick on lame agents and the real estate industry overall, but I will provide what I hope are helpful insights garnered from many years in the business. Interwoven through my sarcasm and cynical comments, you will learn many practical things you can put into practice the next time you approach real estate. You may think it's super weird for me to not care for the people in my chosen profession, but it's the truth. I imagine another place where that is true is in politics. Can you imagine being a hard-working, honest, and logical politician? You would definitely be in rare company. There are some really great agents out there, and I delight to work with them. However, like you, it's been my experience that the great ones are few and far between.

The future of real estate

Real estate in the United States is stagnant. Virtually nowhere, except maybe the airline industry has experienced such little innovation and still maintained a healthy market position. Airlines have literally not accomplished any major improvements since they switched from propellers to jet engines and what was that, sixty years ago? Oh sure they have made improvements in the actual inner workings of the industry such as increased fuel consumption, the use of composite materials, and better aerodynamics, but the customer has largely been ignored. As a matter of fact, customers are being treated worse!

I remember reading online about the new Boeing 787 Dreamliner. I read page after page of Boeing bragging about all the improvements of this new amazing plane. Sure, better fuel consumption increases corporate profits and may be better for the environment, but what about the customer? There was virtually not one thing that spoke to the two key desires of any traveler—speed and comfort. As a traveler I don't care about increased overhead bin capacity. I don't really care about carbon-fiber materials. And outside of slight environmental concerns, increased fuel efficiency literally doesn't impact me at all. As a traveler what I long for is to not take all day to cross the country and to not have my feet fall asleep in my tiny and, yes, shrinking seat. That's it. Get me there faster, and get me there more comfortably.

Our planes have been chugging along around 500 mph for decades, and the seats are getting more and more uncomfortable. Particularly hilarious is that while Americans are getting fatter, the airline industry continues to shrink the seats to a now average width of seventeen inches. My desk chair I am seated at right now as I write this chapter is twenty-four inches wide. It's perfectly cushy and comfortable, and I don't have some stranger next to me digging his elbows into my ribs. The airline industry has done little for its customers in regard to what consumers truly want. To the contrary they are doing everything else but paying attention to what consumers really desire. Real estate is no different. There have been lots of innovations that make it more efficient and profitable for the industry and the agents but little actual improvement for the end user, the customer. Like the airline customers who want comfort and speed, real estate customers also have two desires—value and service. Both of those are largely ignored by the real estate industry. The vast majority of agents have no concept of what real customer service means, and they are grossly overpaid in spite of their incompetence. They provide little if any actual value.

As a customer you are told that you can search for homes in real time on an agent's MLS-connected website. Great. You can sit at your kitchen table in your pajamas and search for that perfect house. Terrific. What the industry won't tell you is that this development is primarily for the exclusive benefit of the agent because now he or she doesn't have to work as hard finding you that perfect home. You do all the legwork and then contact them to play taxi. This isn't to say that there isn't any benefit to the buyer. There is. The fact that people can search online in the privacy and casual atmosphere of their own homes is a great improvement. People have more input and information regarding their home search. It can not only be empowering but also more efficient for all parties involved. The issue is that the agent is the one who benefits the most. Instead of physically looking at maybe fifteen to thirty houses, people search online and usually choose three that are within their parameters. It takes far less time and energy for an agent to show three houses than dozens. I'm not saying it's right or wrong; it just is. Similar to the airline industry, the so-called improvements usually benefit the real estate company or agent and not necessarily the customer.

There are slick and somewhat deceptive little technology plays in the real estate industry too. You can call a special phone number that is on a sign, enter a code, and get a recording that renders all the pertinent information on the property. It's convenient, and you don't have to talk to anyone, which, of course, most people prefer. Pysch! It's bait and switch time. You thought you were innocently just getting some info, but then your phone rings. Magically, it is the listing agent who kindly states, "Hey there! My name is Marcia Dingeldorf, and I am the listing agent on 123 Main Street. I just noticed you dialed into my info line. What other questions do you have about the property that I can answer?" Gotcha!

There are little fun features on agents' websites that ping them when you are poking around online. Then an automatic feature pops up on the website that states, "Hi. This is Howard Shawoonsizer, the listing agent on these properties. I happen to be online now. Do you have any questions about any of these properties?" Implying that this chat box coincidentally happened to pop up just as you were surfing the net looking at the exact same house! Wow! Impressive. This agent just sits around online, waiting for people to poke around his website, so he can answer their questions. Man! Little do they know Howard is in his recliner picking lint out of his belly button while watching the football game, but, hey, in real estate, it's all about perception! If you respond to his "chat" pop-up, he can sit there and text you from his recliner while with his free hand continue eating his jalapeño cheddar popcorn.

Now listen, I'm all for not having to work harder to get the same results if there is a more efficient path, but can we at least be honest here? I'm for technology, and I'm for increased efficiency. The problem is that many improvements are for the benefit of the agent and encourage laziness in an already lazy industry. I don't know. Maybe I'm old school, but I just think people ought to work hard for their money and really earn it.

Real estate stands alone in this category. When technology made it possible for people to trade stocks by themselves online, the power was taken from the broker, and the costs went down from forty dollars a trade to under ten dollars. The entire securities industry had to revamp and retool. The consumer won. The same thing happened when technology made it possible for people to book travel on their computers at home. The entire travel agency business model vanished almost over-night. Technology caused prices to come down and rendered old busi-ness models obsolete. Not in real estate, though. You still have to cough up 6 percent of the value of your home to get it sold. This model is already under assault nationwide by discount brokers and flat-rate models. While it's true you get what you pay for, I don't know anyone who feels real estate costs are reasonable. Like the airlines that ignore the two main customer desires of speed and comfort, the real estate industry ignores value and service.

I have a fairly pessimistic, but I think realistic, view of the future of real estate. I think between the low threshold of entry for new agents, greed of shortsighted brokerages and governing agencies, the exorbitant costs, and new emerging business models eventually the industry in its current form will unravel. To be clear there will always be a need for housing. There will also always be a need for deal makers, negotiators, and agents who are consummate professionals. I just can't see an industry continue on its current path, pretending to be a professional organization while virtually allowing anyone with a pulse to carry their license and have an industry wide failure rate of an 85 percent. It just can't continue. It's no wonder why people hate real estate agents.

Chapter Two

Cost and Commission

Real estate firms charge a lot of money to sell your home. No secret there. Check with your accountant, but in some cases, it is my understanding that some costs associated with selling your home and moving may provide you with a tax deduction. Unfortunately, that's about all the good news associated with that topic! It costs a lot, and there are reasons for that. There is a lot of misinformation out there, so I thought it was important to provide some insight on the costs involved with real estate transactions. There are two big chunks of money generally involved with real estate: one is commission, and the other is closing costs.

Commission is what is paid to the real estate brokerages who in turn pays the agents representing the transaction on both the buying and selling side. You are paying the broker, and then the broker pays the agent after taking their share. The closing costs are the fees generated by the lender as well as a third-party title or escrow company. This service oversees many aspects of every transaction including title search, financial reconciling, coordinating with lenders, and prorating taxes and HOA dues. In addition closing costs may include the resolution of delinquent taxes and HOA dues, or the resolution of any outstanding liens. The closing process is quite complicated and has many moving parts. Having a sharp title or escrow officer working on your transaction is very important.

Broker Costs

Every real estate company has an owner or owners and a broker. Sometimes they are one and the same person, and in other cases, they are not. Colorado is a little confusing because they call agents brokers instead of agents. Yea, it doesn't make any sense to me either. Technically they are called Broker Associates, but most people drop the Associates part, which makes it even more confusing. California is easier in that the broker is the usually the owner, and agents are, well, agents.

As you can imagine, there are intense legal and financial responsibilities laid upon the shoulders of the owner of a real estate brokerage. There is tremendous potential liability if the owner doesn't get it right, so a portion of costs goes to legal fees and counsel. A brokerage as well as agents will also have what is called E & O insurance, which stands for errors and omissions. In other words this kind of insurance covers mistakes. This kind of insurance is above and beyond standard liability insurance. The building or office the broker owns or occupies also of course engenders some costs. Rent or mortgage payments, mortgage insurance, taxes, commercial HOA dues, maintenance, and improvements are just some of the ongoing expenses. There are also utilities including Internet, phone, air conditioning and heat, electricity, and natural gas, for example. They will also have a general liability insurance or umbrella policy for the property that covers the office building and contents.

Some people think brokers are just awash in money. While it is true that anyone who runs a business of any kind has the potential benefit of a handsome income, but it's not like this stuff just falls out of the sky. There are many costs, considerations, and responsibilities involved. It's like a church. Some people kind of get after a pastor for bringing up money or giving too often. The flip side is those big buildings don't pay for themselves, the lights don't go on for free, the A/C and heat aren't imaginary, and all those staff members who take care of your kids, conduct your weddings and funerals, and do summer camps all have families to feed and sort of enjoy a paycheck from time to time, just like you!

In addition to other legal aspects of being a broker, there are also strict bookkeeping and accounting requirements mandated by law in addition to good business practice. So a portion of costs goes to pay for skilled bookkeepers, administrators, managers, and accountants. There is a saying: "The devil is in the details," and highly qualified people in this category keep the owner out of a lot of hot water. Then there are marketing efforts an owner will embark upon as part of his or her overall promotion strategy. If the broker is part of a large national chain, sometimes these costs are partially offset by the national company. Then, on the other hand, if they are a part of a large national company, they will operate basically as a franchise and pay dues and a percentage of sales to the parent company. On the other hand there are independent real estate brokerages. There are of course pros and cons to being an independent owner versus being connected to a regional or national company. Independent owners don't have to pay dues and costs up the food chain, but they don't benefit from huge national marketing campaigns and brand recognition either. Franchise owners may have to pay dues, but they also have significant referral business from brokers in other parts of the country that have clients moving into their local area.

The owner also has to pay other staff members. Somebody has to answer the phones, pay the bills, and manage the agents. Other people have to maintain the office or building, wash windows, clean bathrooms, and vacuum carpets. Sometimes there is an office manager who runs the office and is in charge of administrative duties. Some offices have transaction coordinators who oversee the paperwork on behalf of the agents. The transaction coordinator can be paid by the broker or the agent or both. On the other hand, I have seen where the agent pays the coordinator exclusively, and a portion of that income goes to the owner, providing the owner with a nice passive income stream.

In an attempt to offset costs and increase income, some brokers or owners are also agents. Usually the ones who do this are former agents and over the years have amassed a body of customers, so they continue to stay involved in sales as well as ownership and brokerage responsibilities. This of course can become a little sticky, because some agents-turned-owners/brokers may get caught up in the selling side and allow the company responsibilities and business matters to suffer. I have written about this elsewhere in the book, so I won't belabor the point here.

Broker commission

Commissions charged in real estate transactions are usually called agent commission; it is, however in all reality, the broker commission. The money is paid through title or escrow directly to the broker. The broker then takes out any related costs, fees and, dues after which the agent gets their commission check. As I said in my opening words in this chapter, no doubt about it, brokers charge a lot of money. There is also no doubt that there are some pressures and mounting competition coming from new business models that are threatening the traditional real estate structure. Let's take a look at various models of brokerages and their correlating costs.

Full-service brokerage

This is probably the type most people are familiar with. The brokerage can either be an independent office or a franchise of a large regional, national, or even global chain, but basically as the name would imply, the full-service brokerage handles pretty much everything. You just simply sign the contract and then wait for the closing date. The broker will take care of virtually every single detail. Full-service anything of course costs more, but that is the general model for real estate in the United States.

Standard commission is 6 percent of the sale price of the home. Generally speaking, 3 percent goes to the brokerage that provides the buyer, and 3 percent goes to the brokerage that lists the property for sale. So out of that 3 percent on each side, the brokers take their slice for operating costs, dues, and fees, and the agent receives the remaining portion as their income. As most agents are independent contractors, they are responsible for paying their own taxes, expenses, and individual marketing costs.

The financial arrangement between agent and broker is established upon the agent coming on board and can usually be renegotiated at every anniversary date. The financial arrangement is called the split and can be 95/5 all the way down to 50/50. Some brokerages focus on entry-level agents. They provide an office, materials, training, and a lot of handholding and therefore charge an aggressive split whereby they take a larger portion of the agent's commission. Other brokerages like RE/MAX focus on top producers and experienced agents and thus provide a very generous split in favor of the agent. Such brokerages often subsidize their low portion by charging transaction fees and rent for an office an agent might use. There are some costs that are fixed such as franchise fees, and there are some costs that are negotiable. Every brokerage is different.

The discount model

The discount model provides a limited service, which means they don't do everything for you. In return they discount the costs involved. There are endless variations on this theme, but the basic idea is that they do some things and you do some things. Some discount brokerages don't even have agents. You are responsible to be home and open the door. You make your own flyer using their templates. You're in charge of marketing your home. They handle the legal and transactional side of the process.

Flat-rate model

As the name suggests, it charges a flat rate and not a percentage of the sale price. Frankly, of all the non-traditional models, I think this model has the most merit. It always puzzled me why real estate commission was based on a percentage. Is more work required to sell a $400,000 house than a $150,000 house? Not really. Yet the percentage-based commission costs are very different.

On the upper end, as homes approach a million dollars, clearly there are additional costs. People at this level expect a high touch and professional marketing that is extensive and comprehensive. There may be costs associated with advertising in national or global publications, radio, or even TV. Sometimes a professional video production is created to market a home in the multimillion-dollar category. There may be extravagant invitation only events for brokers complete with entertainment, wine, and catered food. In addition professional photography, and drone video services are expensive. There are also 360 degree video tours that people can access from the agent's website. In the higher end of home prices, there are significant costs involved with getting such a home the necessary attention and exposure in order to attract the right buyer. However, for most homes in the median home price category, the costs involved are fairly fixed, so I can see why the flat-rate model has emerged. Having said that, due to the high costs of running a brokerage this model hasn't really caught on because of the economics.

FSBO hybrid

The FSBO or "for sale by owner" idea is when a homeowner tries to sell their home themselves. Full disclosure many years ago, long before I ever was involved in real estate on a professional level, my wife and I sold our first home ourselves. It was easy and successful. Now I say easy, but I was a business owner with substantial communication and marketing skills, which clearly gave me an advantage. Plus because I owned my own business, I could always be available for a showing. In addition I had professional legal counsel and accounting advice. There is tremendous potential liability and exposure in this model personally and legally and is not for the faint of heart or inexperienced. There are some companies that aid the do-it-yourselfer by providing some minimal assistance and guidance, but you will be required to do a lot of the heavy lifting yourself.

The impact of technology and access to information

There is a trend nationally if not globally that started with the invention of the printing press and has dramatically escalated in the last few decades. Once the printing press emerged and common people could read for themselves, provided they were literate to start with, the educated elites began to lose their power. Rulers in government and in the church could no longer take liberties with what their laws or books actually said because now this new technology made it possible for regular folks to find out for themselves what the words actually said. Any emergence of a technology is disruptive, and disruptions create a loss of power in the stakeholders. It was true of society with the onset of the printing press, and it was true of stock brokers and travel agents. When technology made it possible to buy and sell stocks online in the comfort of your home, on your couch, on your laptop, in your pajamas, for a fraction of the cost, things dramatically shifted for the high-cost, full-service stock broker. There was a day when stock brokers used to charge forty dollars a trade. Can you imagine anyone doing that now when you can do it online yourself for less than ten dollars? Technology and access to information changed the game forever.

What was true for the stock broker was also true for the travel agent. In the old days when you wanted to fly somewhere or take a vacation, you would have to go to a travel agent. This may seem ridiculous now with so many online options, but there was a time when such options were not available. Odds are if you're under thirty, you don't even know what a travel agent is! With so many online options to book travel directly, that industry has been flipped on its head. The only ones I know that are actually still in existence are corporate and group travel companies.

Technology is disruptive, and the real estate industry is not immune. There was a day when brokers and agents had all the power. The MLS sheets were printed weekly or monthly, and the real estate agents with yellow jackets escorted you all over town because they alone held the power because they alone had the information. You want a house? You had to go to them. For those of you who are on the younger side, there used to be a real estate company whose agents wore mustard yellow jackets. Yeah, I know.

With the advent of new technology, information became disseminated and readily available to the general public. Access to information is no longer the exclusive domain of agents. So brokers and agents have lost a lot of power over the years. Good brokers and agents adjust, and the agents who still wish it was 1973 miss out. Instead of fighting the trend, good agents work with it and provide their clients an opportunity like never before to be part of the process. Clients can now search for their homes online in the privacy of their own home. Over 65 percent of all home searches these days begin online, meaning people don't exclusively need an agent to do the searching for them. Smart agents harness this power and become more efficient and provide better customer service by partnering with their clients and give them the tools they need to search on their own.

Instead of the agent doing all the work, clients are now empowered to search on their own and then relay to the agent the homes they want to see. The agent's job is more streamlined, and the clients have a sense of personal participation. It's hard to say if real estate will go away as it is known today. I don't think it will go the way of the travel agent, but it certainly is feeling the winds of change blow, and new models are being developed all the time. I feel that because real estate is so cumbersome, so expensive, so complicated, and with such huge legal implications, professional agents and brokers will always be in need. I don't see the full-service brokerage going away anytime soon. Regarding other models, oftentimes as with anything, you get what you pay for.

The agent and commission
One of the little secrets that of course most agents aren't huge fans of people knowing is that commission is fully negotiable by law and is not set in stone. The brokerage sets the commission but may give the agent some leeway in making adjustments if he or she needs to. Some might think a perfectly acceptable time an agent might lower a commission is if an agent "double-ends the deal meaning they list the home and also provide the buyer. However the agent is still doing the full amount of work on both the buyer and seller sides and has equal costs on both sides. As they are doing double the work it is feasible they make double the commission. A more viable time an agent may reduce his or her fees is in the case of hardship. I have reduced my commission for a couple going through a divorce, a family with a sick child, and an elderly woman who was leaving her home of many years for an assisted care facility. Regardless of business model and financial goals, I think we still need to have empathy for people going through a hard time.

Sometimes there are sellers who just flat out insist on a lower commission for whatever reason. Such people demand a bargain but if you think about it, there's a reason Porsches never go on sale. I know some strong agents who, if they are unable to convince the prospect of their value, simply shake hands and walk away. They place a high value on themselves, their business, and their time, and they are not willing to work for less. And unfortunately, I know many weak agents who will melt like a snowman in the sun and take the lower rate, no questions asked. Remember 85 percent of agents are failing at some level and such agents are desperate for business and will easily surrender their income. As with most things in life, someone will always do it for cheaper, but you have to ask yourself, "Why?" Why would they do it for cheaper? I'm not talking about a merciful gesture to someone who is down on their luck. I'm just talking about day-to-day business. If someone could make more money but chooses to make less, what reasons would there be to do so?

There are two main reasons I have seen over the years. The first is that the agent is weak. Plain and simple. If the weak agent also has a fear of confrontation and is generally not in the habit of standing up for themselves and negotiating, they're even weaker. Now I'm not talking about them as a person. God, I'm sure, loves them. Their mother loves them too. I'm sure that they're swell in many different ways. I'm talking about being weak in business. A weak agent will fold like a poker player holding 7, 2 off-suit. If agents can't stand up for themselves regarding the money they earn, how well do you think they will stand up in negotiations with the other agent behind your back? If they fold with you regarding their own income, I'm fairly certain they will fold with others too. Strong agents will fight for their money, and they'll fight for yours. Weak agents will surrender their own income and sail you down the river as well.

Think about it. A weak agent who will work for let's say 2 percent on a $300,000 home will save you $3,000. That seems like a lot, but what if this weak agent who can't negotiate their way out of a wet paper bag, presents you an offer of $285,000 and convinces you it's a good deal. You lost $15,000 to save $3,000. Do you see it? So again, while commission is negotiable, you get what you pay for, and cheaper isn't always better. Sadly many people are shortsighted and only want a bargain, not thinking through the deeper implications of hiring a weak or inexperienced agent.

The other reason agents would reduce their commission is because they have a negative perspective on themselves. They may feel they don't add a lot of value to the process and thus don't feel they should be paid as much. Indeed there is an undercurrent of commoditization that has attempted to entrench itself in the ranks of agents over the last several years. As I've mentioned before, what I mean by commoditization is the idea that if all things are equal, the price should automatically go to the lowest agreeable level. In that regard the whole structure of the real estate industry would be disassembled in a race to the bottom. In other words whoever is cheapest wins. The problem is the cheapest is usually also the least experienced, the weakest and the least competent.

Commodities like corn, copper, sugar, or oil have volatile pricing because there is no way to differentiate or provide additional value. If all things are equal, why would someone pay a higher price for bushel of corn if another farmer is willing to sell it for 15 percent less? That's the challenge of commodities. However, all things are not equal in real estate. There are massive and long-lasting consequences from the actions of incompetent agents who can't strongly negotiate, effectively market, or conduct themselves professionally. There are massive legal and financial implications in the real estate process. There are endless details to pay attention to and time deadlines that are not yielding. The difference between a top producer with years of high-volume experience and a dabbler who does two transactions a year are as far apart as the east and west sides of the Grand Canyon! Remember, you get what you pay for. If you want a bargain, set your expectations accordingly.

Chapter Three

The Promotion

Everything that is and has ever been sold has first been promoted. Promotion basically is about the methodology used to get a product or service into the minds of potential buyers with hopes of engendering a sale. Marketing and advertising along with other methods are part of the promotion process. Some methods are very effective, some are counter-intuitive, some are super creative, and some, well, are just plain dumb and a waste of money.

In this chapter we'll go over the concept of promotion and how to leverage your budget and ideas to create the loudest megaphone to let the world know about this awesome house you have for sale! This section is primarily written to agents, but it is also important for others, especially sellers to read because you want to know the best forms of promotion out there. You also want to know so you can grade your agent. Do they promote your home in professional and effective ways, or do they do silly things that really don't do much? It's important to know because the ability to get your home sold largely depends on the skill of the agent and the methods they employ in promoting your home.

When considering promotion there are two fundamental categories: you can promote the house, or you can promote yourself. This is a little tricky because in reality they are combined to some degree. However, if you pay attention to ads that are out there, you can tell which agent is promoting a home and which agent is really just pretending he or she is running for mayor. I don't get it about the real estate profession, but some people actually act like and feel they are celebrities. It's the weirdest thing to me. I personally don't understand how selling a property can inflate an ego to that degree, but it's true in every town in America.

First let's cover some of the ineffective methods:
Credibility marketing

On the personal promotion side of life, there is credibility marketing. This game is played by spending a lot of money and consistently having your face show up in the same predictable place over and over again, for years. The idea here is to become a household fixture with name or facial recognition. People who believe and participate in credibility marketing spend money on park benches, bus stops, grocery carts, and sponsoring little league teams and worthy causes in the community with hopes that they will appear as stellar citizens and then, by proxy, stellar agents. Now I am not quite so cynical as to believe that everyone who sponsors teams of young athletes is doing it for ulterior motives. I'm just saying it happens.

All of the following are actual people whom I knew: A stay-at-home mom turned agent with the help of her husband, who had a high-paying job and financed her marketing program for her. A business man turned agent who sold his company for millions and then promoted himself all over town because he could afford to. An agent who was a poor performer but took out a loan to advertise everywhere in an attempt to change the perception of his skill level.

Some people call this buying your business, and it can get expensive by the time you pay your monthly bill for newspaper, local real estate magazines, park benches, bus stops, shopping carts, and billboards. I knew people who spent north of $10,000 a month to give the appearance that they were amazing agents. The kicker was that they were far below my sales level even though I never engaged with marketing myself that way. For that matter I achieved top 6 percent sales in the nation and never took out one ad or felt the need to plaster my face all over town.

Besides being expensive the problem with so-called credibility marketing is that how you start is how you have to keep going. If you are going to be the local sports sponsor for children's leagues, then you have to keep doing that, indefinitely. That can get really expensive. Once you start you have to do it for a very long time otherwise people will wonder what happened to you. You can't have your face plastered all over town for two years and then stop. If people start wondering where you've vanished to, your credibility, manufactured or otherwise, will certainly be in jeopardy. Visibility must be ongoing and again, that costs a lot of money.

Saturation marketing

Somewhat related to credibility marketing is saturation marketing. However, it's like credibility marketing on steroids. Proponents of saturation marketing are big fans of plastering their face, name, phone number, and website all over town. It's like the Bruce Lee of promotion. You couldn't make a move against him where he didn't beat you there.

It's the same with saturation marketing. No matter where you go, there's the smiling face of your favorite agent beaming at you. You go to the grocery store, he's there. You drive and look out your window at a bus enclosure, he's there. You walk your dog in the park and sit down on a bench to take a break, he's there. You open your mailbox, he's there. You open your front door, he's there as a flyer hanging on your doorknob. Similar to credibility marketing, it can get really expensive. Trying to maintain a large presence in the community through saturation marketing takes real commitment and real dollars!

Caravans

I write about this in the brokerage chapter, but basically a caravan is when, usually after a motivating pep talk or "team" meeting, all the agents line up their cars and go look at all the office listings. They drive from house to house and look at every home personally. They physically walk through the listings in an attempt to expose other agents in the office to the home.

The hope, of course, is that the brokerage will "double-end" the deal and scoop up both the buying and selling commission.

As I write in another section of my book, this is a leftover method from the old days when the MLS wasn't automated or online because the Internet hadn't even been invented yet! The more feet you got walking through your listing, the better odds you had to get it sold by someone in your office. This outdated and obsolete method is long overdue for a swift removal from real estate strategy. If someone told me that an agent caravan was part of their promotion strategy, it would be hard not to burst into laughter right in front of them.

Bus stops

I am always amazed at how many real estate agents spend money on bus-stop enclosures. If you just stop and logically think about it, people who ride the bus generally are not in a financial position to purchase a home. Except in some densely populated metro areas where public transportation is the preferred way of getting around, if people can't afford a car, they obviously can't afford a home.

Shopping carts

Has anyone ever been shopping at a grocery store and, after picking up a head of broccoli, looked down at their cart and said, "Gee whiz Mable. We oughta call this gal. Look, she's a pretty thing, and besides it says here she's ready to find us our dream home!" I can't imagine who falls for such things. Moreover I can't imagine what kind of non-thinking agent actually believes this is an effective marketing campaign. You know the phrase "there's a sucker born every minute"? It certainly applies here. The only agents I can imagine plastering their face on hundreds of shopping carts are rookies who don't yet know what they're doing, experienced agents who don't' really understand marketing, and ego agents who have enough money they don't really care if marketing is effective or not. They just want to see their handsome face everywhere in town. With shopping cart advertising, the promotion company splits the revenue with the grocery store that provides the carts. The promotional company wins. The grocery store wins. Nobody else really does.

Park benches

Has anyone ever gone for a walk in a park and been persuaded to call a real estate agent after seeing their smiling face on a bench? I doubt anyone has ever said, while walking their dog, "Wow! We need to call that guy and have him find us a house!" This is yet one more of those things where just because some agents do it, doesn't mean it's a good idea. Ego has a lot to do with it. Some agents are quite possessive of their benches and won't yield them for anything! They enjoy seeing their face on the same bench year in and year out. It must give them such satisfaction, and it must make their mother so proud when she drives by.

The agents feel quite content with their marketing strategy as long as you don't ask, "How many transactions a year do you conduct directly as a result of your park bench?" That's when you get the deer in the headlights look. In order to discover whether your marketing methods are sound, effective, and actually increase your sales, you need to have a mechanism in place that measures results. In other words you have to have data backed up by facts that economically justifies the amount spent. For example, if I spent $400 a month on a park bench and three people a month told me the reason they called me was because they saw my face on a bench, then it's measurable and profitable. In this case it's a good deal to invest in park benches because the income far exceeds the expense. However, because most agents have never run a business or understand effective marketing, they never know how to measure their efforts. Park benches are just one more of those buckshot approaches to personal promotion that in reality have very little to do with actually getting a house sold and more to do with the agent's ego. It is an aspect of that fuzzy and expensive world that is credibility and saturation marketing.

Phony magazines

These are popping up everywhere. You get a magazine in the mail that you haven't subscribed to or paid for. It's got a snazzy title like "Your Home, Your Life" or "Great homes America." You know, something that sounds official and real. There on the cover prominently plastered so it's unavoidable is the smiling face of a real estate agent along with her name, phone number, e-mail address, and website. Written in an equally unavoidable way are the words, "Complimentary magazine subscription from your neighborhood real estate agent." It is designed to impress you. "Say Gladis, come in the living room and take a look see at this magazine here. A real estate agent named Suzie Susquehanna is sending it to us for free! Isn't that nice of her. What a sweetheart. Sayz right here it's complimentary!"

She didn't produce the magazine. She didn't write a word. She didn't pay an editor or proofreader. She doesn't have a degree in graphic design. She doesn't have ten years of experience in the printing industry. She actually hasn't written a thing since high school English class. She pays a company to crank out these useless phony magazines and paste her face on the cover. What's better is the company drop-ships the magazines every month or every quarter, and she doesn't have to do anything except supply the company with names and addresses and of course send them a check. It's designed to make the agent look smart regardless if they are or aren't.

Fake e-mail newsletters

These have also gained popularity in recent years especially in real estate and insurance. You get an e-mail from your agent or someone fishing to become your agent. Their name, information, and picture are on the first page. The newsletter is professionally produced and is chock-full of information from how to plant gardenias to new trends in technology to how to eat healthier. Terrific! If you have time to waste and feel like reading stuff like that, go for it. It's just not real. The content is real I suppose, but the agent didn't stay up all night on his MacBook Pro and design this newsletter and create all this content. It's a subscription-based service where the agent pays for a pre-produced newsletter that somebody else writes and formats. The promotion company will e-mail them directly to the agent's mailing list , so the agent doesn't have to do any work at all.

The impression they hope to make is that they have produced it and are being so very helpful giving you all these keen tips on life. However, in reality, it's just a slick, pre-produced newsletter that gets e-mailed to everyone in their database. They had nothing to do with it besides paying for the subscription. Maybe people think I'm nitpicking. It's just the deceptive side to it that rubs me the wrong way. It is produced with the intention to make you think, "Gee, look at this dear. Our real estate agent Paul Dubinhour makes these helpful newsletters every month. Boy, is he sharp! I didn't even know he was a writer! Glad we're with him!" Just tell people the truth. There are enough straightforward marketing strategies out there that you don't have to be sneaky and try to convince people that you're Earnest Hemingway when you barely passed ninth-grade English class.

Business cards
While effectively designed business cards can help get the word out, it is for all intents and purposes just a way to give people your contact info. However, I have seen some creative uses for business cards. I was at Starbucks the other day and saw a guy from our local Keller Williams franchise place a business card on every empty chair. Keller Williams is a great company but maybe the local brokerage needs to ramp up their training on effective marketing! I have been at Barnes & Noble and opened a book to my surprise finding a real estate business card stuffed inside the pages. I have even been in a restaurant bathroom and seen a business card stuck into a piece of trim above the urinal. Boy that's classy! I have come out to my car after grocery shopping and had a real estate agent's business card placed under my wiper.

While at first glance, these ideas may seem like a good way to get the word out, it's just not how people find agents, and it's not how business is done. Nobody is going to hit the restroom at PF Changes, look up and see a business card stuck on top of the toilet paper holder, grab it, and run back to the table telling his wife, "Gee, good golly honey, our luck is getting better. Look what I found! Woohoo!" The real estate industry is so crowded and so overpopulated that it's not like finding an agent is hard. Finding a good agent is. Nobody is going to entrust a perfect stranger with the most expensive purchase of their lives just because they saw your card in a book or on a chair. It's just dumb and a waste of paper. Beyond that it really makes the agent look cheap and low class. You think it's a high-class thing to stick your business card in a public bathroom above a urinal?

Call-in scams

There are some marketing tools where you call a number from a sign, enter a code, and then listen to the information about the home. Pretty cool huh? Until you start getting calls back from the listing agent saying, "I noticed you called in for information on 123 Alphabet Lane. Let me tell you about the property! Oh gee, you'll love the home. It's so amazing. It's got four bedrooms and three bathrooms..." Then after they bloviate for ten minutes straight, they ask, "Do you have any questions I can answer?" I call it a scam because a scam is something that is deceptive or not forthright. They don't' say, "Call this number, enter the code, listen to the information, and we will capture your phone number, and then our agent will call you and bother you forever." If they did it would at least be honest. I'm sure "scam" is too strong a word. It actually is a decent method, but I am always just a little leery where a marketing mechanism is used to trap people. There are ulterior motives and a hidden agenda in the method that I am personally uncomfortable with. I don't think people appreciate being hoodwinked.

It's like those promotions in stores where they ask for you to fill out a three by five card for a chance to win a new Harley or something. What they don't tell you is that they make far more money selling your information to mailing list companies than the cost of the motorcycle. They are being truthful about the fact that you have a chance at winning but, of course, aren't really quick to point out the odds. You also have a chance at winning the lottery, having a meteor land in your backyard, and becoming best friends with Tom Cruise. Not likely on any account, but you have a chance!

Coupons in mail

This is one of my favorites. Yes, that was sarcastic. Some agents routinely send out postcards with a coupon or promotional code attached. "10 percent off Booseldorf Burgers! A coupon from Jane Wigglesmiler, your friendly real estate agent!" Of course, prominently displayed on the postcard is a picture of Jane's big smile with freshly bleached teeth along with her contact info. Yawn. If someone can afford to own a home or have the capacity to buy a home, they aren't really going to be impressed with saving two dollars on a medium-rare cheeseburger with a fried egg on top. It's just another attempt at buying the business instead of earning it.

Similar to the fake magazines and fake e-mail newsletters, these coupon postcards are made by promotion companies and real estate agents simply pay for it and provide names and addresses. Like other ridiculous attempts at marketing and self-promotion it costs money and you have to do it for a long time. Again, most agents don't think it through and realize that once you start your little coupon marketing program you can't exactly stop because some cheap people will get used to those things hitting their mailbox. Many agents do it monthly, and that gets expensive. There's the cost of creating the postcard, mailing it, and then paying the restaurant the discounted price. Beyond all this it does nothing to actually sell a home. It's just one more lame and fundamentally ineffective saturation marketing attempt.

Doorknob hangers

Pulling into my driveway the other day I noticed something hanging on the front door of my home. It proclaimed:

> Want to find your dream home? Looking to sell your current home? CALL A PROFESSIONAL YOU CAN TRUST! I'm your local neighborhood real estate agent who would like the opportunity to work with you for all real estate needs. Follow me on Facebook and send me your email address to be added to my monthly newsletter. I include local discounts that I can provide my clients and neighbors!

She had her picture, phone number, e-mail, website, and Facebook info listed after her name. There were two tear-off business cards at the bottom. "One for you and one for a friend." I think I may have thrown up in my mouth a little when I read that. OK, so let's look at this. First of all, nobody, and I mean nobody, buys or sells a home because some stranger hung a flyer on their doorknob. Period. I have more points about why this hanger was so horrible, but really I could stop here. If nobody buys or sells a home after reading your glorious doorknob hanger, why would anyone do it? Man, it's just one more of these stupid gimmicky things real estate agents do, and I have no idea why because they just don't work, and if they don't work, they are a waste of time and money and for that matter trees. Why would anyone want to waste time or money? Real estate agents are a naïve bunch with precious little, if any, real marketing or business experience.

I felt like calling her and asking her if she would trust someone to handle the largest financial investment of her life from a doorknob hanger. So this, like many things, can be easily judged as ineffective and ridiculous. Does it pass the "Would I do that?" test or the "Does that really work" test? The answer is a resounding *no!* That's a pretty easy way to determine whether an investment of time and money is worth it or not. And here's the thing: you kind of automatically know the good agents from the weak agents just by their marketing and promotion campaigns. You never ever see top producers wasting their time, energy, and money on ineffective marketing and foolish promotions that yield nothing. So it's pretty much a nonstarter. Thanks for trying! "A" for effort. "F" for effectiveness.

She stated she's a "PROFESSIONAL YOU CAN TRUST!" in all capital letters. It was also in red color by the way to really stand out. Do true professionals waste their time, energy, and money on ineffective marketing campaigns? Beyond that, think about how trust is established. Is it from a doorknob hanger? Or is it from a person proving their character and skill over time? If we don't know this person, how in the world can we trust her? Unless of course you are in the habit of trusting perfect strangers.

Then she states, "I'm your local neighborhood real estate agent." What does that even mean? Everybody is local who sells real estate. Do you think there are agents who live in Wisconsin and sell real estate in Alaska? So that's just silly. Neighborhood? I've lived in my neighborhood for years. I've never seen her. Then for giggles I looked up the address she had on the flyer. It's exactly 10.8 miles from my home. She apparently thinks half the city is her neighborhood! It's nothing more than an attempt to manipulate people by creating a false folksy relationship by projecting local proximity and presence. Then of course the kicker comes in: she wants you to follow her on Facebook and surrender your e-mail, so you can get a three dollars off coupon on your next plate of nachos. Really? Seriously? If people have enough wherewithal to own a home or are positioned to buy a home, do you actually think a coupon for Taco Bueno is going to make a difference? It's utter nonsense. Beyond that I don't know about you, but I get over eighty junk e-mails a day. I want to add to that list like I feel like dropping a brick on my toes. As a double whammy, she's one of those lame agents who's going to e-mail you a fake newsletter with her face plastered on it as if she wrote and designed the whole thing herself.

Finally, there are clearly marked signs that my neighborhood is a "No Solicitation" neighborhood with a strict HOA. That means that the people who live here enjoy their privacy and are fully capable of finding someone when they need a roofer, a plumber, or a real estate agent for that matter. Apparently my "neighborhood" agent didn't bother to notice that she was in violation of the neighborhood and HOA rules. But then again her office is almost eleven miles away!

Open house

These are so dumb I have dedicated a whole chapter on the topic, but let me share some points here as well. You must understand that there is always an angle or reason why people do the things they do. Open houses are an old and outdated technique that in my opinion is not only ridiculous for so many reasons; it's also potentially dangerous. Let me explain.

One reason agents and brokers push open houses is so they can double-end the deal. They want to scoop up the buyer commission in addition to their listing commission. They are hoping a random person may stumble into the home on some Saturday afternoon and want to buy the house. You might think that's OK; however, that's not how people buy houses. People buy houses by planning, working with an experienced and trusted agent, and then going out and looking at specific properties that fit their parameters. No one drives to the grocery store and then upon seeing an open house sign, does a huge U-turn in the street, goes to the open house and puts in an offer. It doesn't work that way.

The national statistics of a sale actually happening at an open house are less than 1 percent. What actually does happen and why most brokers and agents do them beyond the hopes of double-ending the deal is to fish for new customers. They in effect are using your home as bait to draw people in and then convince them that they are the best agent in the universe in hopes to gain a new client. That's it. Plain and simple. The agent wins. The broker wins. You know who doesn't' win? The poor homeowner who has strangers trampling through his or her home all day. Beyond that, the homeowner has to be away from the home for hours on end, and that's an inconvenience to anyone. Especially when it's most likely not going to get the owner's home sold.

I recall one homeowner in particular. No matter how logical my presentation, no matter how many facts and statistics I referenced, no matter how clear I was that open houses don't bring about a sale, the owner really wanted me to do one. Upon the owner's insistence, I conducted an open house. Sure enough, I scooped up a couple of leads and a new client from their open house, but the home didn't sell. It sold later in the normal way, with a buyer's agent who had crafted a list that fit their clients' needs and upon viewing the home presented an offer. Open houses are a nice opportunity to waste time and talk to a bunch of largely unqualified people, but they don't work to accomplish the objective, which is to sell the home. Some people just don't listen.

There are four types of people who go to open houses: bored people, neighbors, people looking for decorating tips, and criminals. Yes, you read correctly. When people insist on me conducting open houses, I ask them, "Are you usually in the habit of leaving your front door unlocked, advertise that you won't be home, and then let untold numbers of complete strangers go through every nook and cranny of your home?" I would usually get a blank stare and then a slow, "Um…no!" I respond with, "So why are you wanting to do it now?" I then share the statistics and the reality of open houses with them, and they usually change their mind.

A criminal looking at the weekend real estate section of the newspaper is getting a free shopping list. People with bad intentions could go from open house to open house if they wanted to. They could easily have an accomplice distract the agent while they pilfer your bedroom, home office, or kitchen. They could also steal your identity by gathering a few key pieces of information. Moreover, they could leave a couple of windows ajar and come back later. Am I writing this to scare people? You bet. I hope I can scare some sense into somebody. The concept of an open house is ridiculous and risky, and it doesn't even accomplish the objective, which is to sell the home. Don't' be naïve. Be informed and aware, and don't waste your time on risky things that don't work and that can even be dangerous. I wish more agents would be straightforward and honest about open houses instead of perpetuating outdated and ineffective techniques. There's literally no advantage or benefit to an open house except for the agent. Serious buyers who aren't in the habit of wasting time get pre-qualified and get connected to an agent. Then the agent can arrange for them to see all the houses they want to see.

Final thoughts on ineffective promotions

There is no shortage of promotional companies pitching products and service to agents across the country. Real estate agents are for whatever reason, a gullible bunch and just can't get enough of such promotions, which is why of course there are so many of them out there. Some are effective, but the vast majority are not and are simply a waste of effort and money. At the end of the day, everything maybe helps, but the issue here is focus and budget. As I mentioned before, I've known people who spent over $10,000 a month in promotion, and it was scattered, lacked focus, and was largely ineffective because it was not targeted or sustainable. So yes, some might argue, "Every little bit helps." While I agree that lots of approaches may be helpful, it also may cost a lot of money, lack a comprehensive and sustainable strategy, and be a huge waste of time.

Now let's take a look at some effective promotion:
Street-side flyers

There are few things as effective for the price as a box on a pole or sign containing flyers in front of a home for sale. I actually had an agent argue with me that he was sick of filling the box because the "only people taking the flyers were nosy neighbors." It was hardly worth responding to. First of all if that was true, the only way he would actually know that was if he staked out the home like a detective, hoping to catch someone in the act. Second, and more importantly, you *want* the neighbors to pick up flyers! Duh! My attitude was completely opposite his. I befriended the neighbors. I viewed them as partners. I talked to the neighbors. The more people who knew about the listing, the better. Someone might know a coworker, friend, or family member who would love that home or need a strong agent. The more people who knew about me and the home I listed, the better. I was always eager to discover more opportunities for new business.

The disgruntled agent also said another reason neighbors take flyers, besides being nosy, was to get a feel for what their home was worth. "And that's a problem?" I asked. I can't understand that kind of shortsighted and narrow-minded mentality. You *want* the neighbors to be interested in the price of their home because if they ascertain that the market is strong and they have enough equity in their home, they may consider moving. Hello? Maybe, just maybe, if the agent is positive and open-minded, he or she can befriend the local neighbors and drum up some more business!

Flyers have to be well done, though. I have seen black-and-white flyers that not only looked hokey and homemade but were printed crooked on the page. All that communicates is that the agent was an amateur, cheap, or incompetent. The idea here is to create an impressive and professional looking, descriptive flyer that has all the pertinent information on it. I never understood why some agents just don't take this seriously. It is a reflection on themselves and their brokerage. And just like in many professional athletic events, the difference between winning and losing is often measured in small increments. It's not that much more effort to have a quality piece that reflects an attitude of excellence than it is to put something out that's mediocre. Some agents are so cheap that they don't realize part of running any business is to promote it and spend money on effective marketing. Then again some agents just think all you have to do is stick a sign in the ground and wait for the money to pour in.

If you can do it yourself and it looks professional, then do it. Otherwise pay someone. I don't think I've ever paid more than $150 for professional, double-sided, multi-picture, color flyers on thick stock paper. Don't do it in black and white; it looks cheap. Don't do it on copy paper; it feels cheap. Beyond that copy paper usually curls down and flops in on itself in the box because it's not stiff enough to stand upright. Don't do it only on one side. Why let the back side of the paper go empty and waste all that valuable space? Make sure you use a high-quality, thick paper, even glossy if you can. I have always done mine in glossy card stock. The gloss makes the pictures pop, and the high-quality paper feels good in the hand. You always make an impression with a flyer. Either the impression will be "Gee, whiz this agent is lame!" or "Wow, honey, look at this flyer! This guy's a pro!" I'm not kidding. I have actually won listings in neighborhoods because my flyers proved to people that I was a professional agent who took my job seriously and had sound marketing sense.

I mentioned having all the pertinent info on it. I can't stress this enough. Square footage of home and lot, the amount of bedrooms and bathrooms, and of course price. Beyond that any extras, upgrades, or features should be mentioned and if possible pictured as well. If there is a home office on the main level with hardwood floors so office chairs roll around nicely, say so. If there is a huge game room or home theater, don't make it a secret. If there are amazing views off the back deck, let people know. If the HOA has a huge pool, club house, and tennis courts, I think most folks would like to know that. Also have any available incentives on the flyer like "$5,000 paint allowance" or "Seller to pay all closing costs." This will definitely make an impression and make people take note of your home.

Can I share one of my biggest pet peeves? I am continually amazed at how many agents play games with the general public by omitting the price. Isn't that kind of the most important piece of information? Man that drives me crazy. Do you really get how stupid that is? Go to Best Buy and see if anything they are selling doesn't have a price on it. It's just nuts. What they want people to do is call them for the price and then in some outdated, manipulative way capture them once they're on the phone and talk their ear off. "Thanks for calling sir. Before I give you the price would you please give me your name, phone number, e-mail, mailing address, blood type, mother's maiden name, and expected annual income, so I can mindlessly badger you and send you junk mail forever?" Let's be honest. People resent that kind of demeaning dance that withholds information for some kind of power play. That's a throwback to the day long before the Internet when agents held all the information and consequently all the power. The MLS used to be printed and distributed to brokers and agents. If you wanted to get any information on a property, you had to go to them. I don't know if some agents think it's still 1971 rolling around in their pea-soup-green Chevelle with vinyl seats, but, here's some breaking news—people can skip calling the agent and just go online for the price.

If you're an agent, stop trying to control everything, and stop wasting people's time. Give people what they want when they want it. The old days of withholding information, holding power, and manipulating people are way long gone. People are savvy. Get over yourself and just give consumers the information they need. If the information intrigues them, they will call you or have their agent call you. The reason people use these outdated, coercive techniques is so they can double-end the deal, scooping up both the listing and buyer commission. They also want to add you to their e-mail and mailing lists, so they can hammer you with junk mail, fake magazines, and newsletters along with a two-dollar coupon for the chicken parmesan at the Spaghetti House.

Make sure the flyer box always has at least twenty-five flyers in it. Drive by the house often to make sure the box is full. If you don't have time, have your assistant do it. If you don't have an assistant, then pay some neighbor kid ten dollars a week to fill it for you. Of course lazy agents could always have the homeowner take care of it, but it's not really their job, is it? How many times have you seen a for-sale sign with an empty flyer box? All the time? Every day? I see it virtually every time I go anywhere. It's ridiculous. What's the point of even having a box out front if you can't figure out a way to keep it full? It's not really that complicated. Also count how many flyers need to be replaced. Eventually if you keep good records, you will come up with a standard formula for how many flyers are taken before a home sells. All statistics are useful. Finally, make sure the box you buy has a lid to protect the flyers from the elements. No one is impressed by waterlogged, faded, soaked, and wrinkled flyers. If anything is worth doing, it's worth doing well.

Knock on doors

In one neighborhood I had seven homes for sale at one time on the same street. It was an awesome feeling. People couldn't look in any direction without seeing my signs. How did this happen? I knocked on doors. I know, I know, nobody likes to open the door to strangers. Knocking on doors generally doesn't work, a fact that has somehow escaped the Jehovah's Witness crew for decades! People pretty much resent an invasion of their privacy especially when it is an uninvited solicitation. However, I wasn't selling people anything. I was informing them of their neighbors' listing. See the difference? One is a nuisance, and one is providing helpful and interesting information about what's going on in their neighborhood. I have never had a negative experience. People are always interested in real estate activity in their immediate area.

I do it before the sign even goes up. That way they feel like they're on the inside. I simply introduce myself and tell them I'm an agent with RE/MAX. I then tell them, "I just listed the Johnson's home three doors down from your home. The price is $455,000. Here's my card if you know anyone like a coworker, friend, or extended family member who might like to move into your neighborhood. I would sure love to speak with them if they're interested! Thanks for your time." Short and sweet. Sometimes the neighbor thanks me, takes my card, and closes the door. More often than not, they ask me all kinds of questions about the listing. Sometimes the questions lead them to ask about what I thought their home might sell for. I also circle back once the home is sold to let all the neighbors know what the home sold for. Once a home is sold, it's real. At that point you have hard facts to discuss with neighbors and they are more eager to listen to you.

One time I had a really rough listing. It was a major fixer in a lower-middle-class neighborhood in Los Angeles. It had belonged to the grand-mother of a client of mine. My client had warned me it was in really bad shape. She also told me the horrible story about what had happened on the property. Not only did the house look dilapidated, there was a death in the home that involved foul play. Every state is different, but legally in California, any death in a home had to be disclosed to a buyer. The grandmother who was ill and struggling with dementia also had a young member of the extended family living with her, supposedly to help around the house. Sadly what he was actually doing was stealing money from her and cooking meth in a locked bedroom. Also in California any controlled substance on the property had to be disclosed to a buyer. My client had warned me. Fair enough. I didn't put a sign in the ground, and I didn't even sign a contract with my client. I told her to give me a few days to figure out a strategy. Wow! What was I going to say in my marketing? "Home is in horrible disrepair, very neglected, leaking roof, plumbing needs to be re-placed, death and drugs on the property...great neighborhood, though!"

As I sat in my car scratching my head, I decided to go knock on some doors. I started with the next door neighbor. I was just starting to share my hard luck listing story when the sweet lady interrupted me and said, "We know, we know. We know all about it!" Living right next door, they had plenty of stories about late-night drama in the neighborhood that focused around that house. Her sister happened to be visiting from Chicago and was actually interested in the property. We went over and looked at the home as it was empty. Within an hour I had a solid offer from the visiting sister of the neighbor next door. Her husband was a contractor, and the condition of the home didn't bother them one bit! They got a home for a good price due to the damage and condition. Sisters got to live next to each other, and I got the miracle sale of my life. All because I knocked on a door and talked to a neighbor.

One last note on knocking on doors. There was an agent in my office who made a habit every Saturday morning to knock on doors and pass out business cards. If anyone answered, he would say, "Hi. My name is James Bingleding, and I'm with ABC Brokerage. If you're ever thinking about buying or selling, I would love the opportunity to speak with you." Yawn. Seriously? Again with the "if you're ever thinking about selling your home" pitch? I wonder if some agents are ever thinking at all! No one, and I mean no one, who decides to sell his or her home uses some "nice guy" who just happened to be walking through the neighborhood. James was undeterred, though. In true hard-core sales fashion, he would often say, "Every rejection is one step closer to a sale." Yes…but really no. Not this way. Not in real estate. He didn't last long.

Signage

This should get the "No kidding, duh" award, but it's not quite as clear as some would think. The other day I was driving on a major road that has some undeveloped land to the east of it. Beyond the raw land is a neighborhood of homes on acreage. Many of the homes have barns or outbuildings, and it's common to see horses or other animals roaming around on the properties. Some of these homes back up to the undeveloped land.

There is a real estate sign near the road I was traveling on. On the sign was a picture of the agent (I've never understood why that was important!) and her phone number. That's all. No flyer, no sign rider, nothing. It's impossible to tell if the undeveloped land is for sale, and if so, how many acres or if the home behind the land is for sale. So once again I am amazed at the fact that someone did 85 percent of the work but omitted the remaining 15 percent, which is the most critical part. At a minimum she should have had a box with flyers connected to the sign, so potential buyers could get some information to see if they are even interested.

In addition, sign riders would be very helpful. Riders are those extra placards that can mount above or below the sign and communicate additional information. They are not designed to give you all the information, just the key points. Riders clarify what may or may not be obvious. For example, if you drove by a home that clearly looked distressed, it would make people raise their eyebrows and drive past. However, if a rider stated "fixer-upper" or "foreclosure" or "bank owned," then the obvious is clarified. Without the clarification people are left wondering, and if people are left wondering, people generally don't pursue further. Everyone is busy, so make it easy for them to understand what is actually for sale and what is included. For this sale, her clients would be far better served if there was a rider that stated Five Acres of Raw Land or Horse Property with Barn or Home with Acreage. That way people get the clarification and information they need. People hate calling just to get the pitch. It's lame, and it's tired. Give people the information you know they are looking for and then leave it to them to contact you if it fits their needs. It's not 1971 anymore. Buyers are savvy.

Other sign riders that are important are Sale Pending and Sold. A sign in a yard always creates interest and energy. Neighbors take notice as do others driving by. One of my strategies that gains me lots of additional business around my listings is that I add a Sale Pending rider as soon as the offer is signed. It's the second thing I do after doing the necessary administrative work. Many agents don't do that. They just leave the sign as it is in hopes to get more calls. Then when the home closes the sign is removed. The problem with this is that while they are hoping for some random call, the neighbors don't know what's going on and the sign, because it sits there for so long makes people think the home is stale or the agent is lame. Then suddenly the sign vanishes and nobody has any information which adds to the confusion.

A Sale Pending rider is important because a for-sale sign leaves everyone in the neighborhood wondering how things are going. They are curious as to how many people have looked at the home and the time frame it is taking to get it sold. They are also ultimately interested in the price the home fetched. It's an itch in the neighborhood, and a Sale Pending rider scratches the itch. It always creates a buzz because it is the culmination of the process. It is the objective. It brings closure, and the neighbors have a sigh of relief and increased curiosity. Beyond all that it tells everyone in the neighborhood and driving by that you are a sharp agent, especially if it sells quickly. After the home is closed I will replace the pending rider with a SOLD rider in big red capital letters. This lets everyone know the home is sold and it gives me an opportunity to advertise another successful sale. If it's a particularly active neighborhood I may even ask the new homeowners if I can leave the sign up for a week. The SOLD rider reinforces my efforts when I come back and knock on doors to update everyone. I often hear, "Yea, we noticed the sold sign! Congratulations!" It's a great opportunity to have an informative conversation.

Make sure sign riders are mounted correctly. They generally take two screws and two nuts to affix them to the sign frame. Make sure they are tightened down firmly. I was on my morning walk the other day and saw a real estate sign in someone's front yard. The rider that was placed on top of the sign was hanging by one screw. There it was dangling down toward the grass, covering up a portion of the sign. Not only is this bush league and unacceptable but also a bad reflection on the agent and brokerage. If people can't read your sign and get the information they need, what is the point of the sign? Also, don't make your sign too busy. It confuses people, and when people are confused, they get frustrated and drive by. Have you ever been at someone's house that has young children and their refrigerator is plastered with magnets, school assignments, achieve-ments, awards, and artwork? It's fine when there are little kids around, but it looks really unprofessional when your real estate sign has that look.

I saw a sign the other day that had two phone numbers on it and then a rider with a third phone number. Seriously? How many numbers do you need? One! Better yet there was one website on the sign and another website on yet another rider. The sign had a picture of the agent. I think you know by now how I feel about this, but stop wasting space on your sign with your face. Nobody cares, and nobody will remember you. You're not a celebrity. You're not the mayor. You're a Realtor. Do your job, and get the home sold. They also had another rider that said in red block let-ters FOR SALE, even though the sign clearly said the same. Then there was a flyer box, which of course was empty, and another rider of some gizmo that if you take a picture of it with your smartphone, apparently something magical happens. The uninitiated think that the more stuff you slam on your sign, the better. Sophisticated marketers know that less is more and simple is better. Avoid clutter at all costs. Keep your sign and riders direct and to the point, so they clearly and easily communicate the necessary information to those passing by. Signage is the primary way of identifying a property is for sale. You should take full advantage of the options a good sign yields. Name, phone number, website maybe, definitely riders. Skip the picture of your smiling face. Nobody cares but your mother.

Postcards

There are companies that specialize in mass mailing. Once I list a home, I go online to a website where I upload a picture of the home, enter some information, and then format the postcard. Then there is a link to a map. I simply enter the zip code or address and determine the distance from the home I want to send postcards to. It gives me options by street, by radius, or by zip code. It's brilliant, and it never costs me more than $300. Good marketing is targeted marketing. I have never wasted my time with silly things like bus-stop enclosures or shopping carts. It is far more effective to market something you are actually doing and not how awesome of an agent you are. That's played out, and people are super over it. Homeowners should receive a detailed marketing plan that explains line by line what you are doing to get their specific home sold. They don't want to hear how you have a billboard on the freeway that shows your smiling face with new dental work and chin tuck.

The postcards I send are informative, not some cheesy attempt at generating more business. They don't say dumb things like "Thinking about selling your home? I can help!" I simply show a picture of the house, the pertinent information, and what the price is. I include my contact information, and if people want to contact me or view my website, they can, but I don't come across as some desperate agent fishing for more business. I send out the postcards in concert with my door-knocking campaign. Remember I only knock on neighbors' doors in the immediate vicinity of the listing. After I list a home, I probably knock on twenty to fifty homes depending on the layout of the neighborhood. Then three days later, I have the postcards arrive in their mailbox while our conversation is fresh in their minds. In addition I also send a postcard and knock on doors after the home sells as well. This brings closure to the conversation, and people have all the information they need. Instead of plastering my face all over town with saturation marketing, I specifically saturate the neighborhood with a strategic marketing campaign. Postcards are an intelligent, targeted promotional aspect of any thoughtful marketing strategy. I'm clearly not against building more business. I just do it strategically and in a relational way that doesn't come across as forced, coercive, or manipulative.

Professional home magazines

There are publications that are entirely professional and sharp with wide distribution. You will see them in hotels, convention centers, restaurants, grocery stores, and broker offices. There are many different ones out there, and they go by various names. These are very good options to advertise new listings. However, in all but the slowest of housing markets, the home may be sold before the magazine is even published. Regardless, potential buyers may call on your ad, and a good agent may be able to drum up some additional business.

Multiple Listing Service

Commonly known as the MLS, this online electronic database is the primary information resource for all active, pending, and sold properties. You may think it's odd that I include the MLS in a chapter on promotion, but it is one of the key attributes to getting a house sold. The MLS is where agents go to find a home for their buyers. It is the first line of offense. If a home is listed for sale, usually another agent will bring the buyer. The listing agent and the buying agent splits the commission and the effort. It takes two. It's astounding, but many listing agents will spend fortunes on slick marketing campaigns, but overlook the most basic and fundamental aspect of selling a home which is a fully filled out MLS page complete with the maximum amount of pictures. As a listing agent, it is incumbent upon you to make sure the MLS is filled out completely and accurately. I can't tell you how many times I have gone to a home with buyers in tow only to discover that the information on the MLS was not even close to accurate and missing a lot of details. This is not only frustrating and a complete waste of time for everyone; it reveals the lack of competency of the listing agent. Some local real estate boards fine agents for incorrect information, but usually the punishment for such stupidity is other agents simply won't show that agent's homes anymore. I'm not saying it's right or that it's even ethical or legal for that matter, but it happens.

Some agents will fudge a little with their description if there is something unsightly about the home. They may say the home is a four bedroom when in fact it is three with a loft. They may intentionally omit information that might be deemed as negative. Another trick is having preferred angles of the pictures to not show the power lines or shopping mall directly behind the house. No one wants to do business with a deceptive agent who is intentionally trying to hide things or exaggerate aspects of the home.

A good agent will not only be careful to be accurate but in addition will maximize the available space the MLS allows. I am continually perplexed by some agents who don't give any description, or if they do, they just put down a few words. A friend of mine recently told me that their agent back in Virginia simply put, "This house is awesome" in the MLS. There is an entire section where agents can give tremendous insights into the home. The more information, the better. Also, this is where incentives should be placed. "$4,000 slate pool table to remain in game room" is something people should know about. In addition if the home is a little rough, you can state "$5,000 paint allowance and $2,500 toward closing costs." Believe me, those phrases make a big impression and can be the difference between having a home looked at instead of ignored.

Now before I continue, let me say a few things about descriptions. Some agents apparently think they are paperback romance novel authors. Their descriptions are so corny and so forced that they border on ridiculous. "Upon entry after passing through the enhanced courtyard, you will marvel at the soaring cathedral ceilings. A short saunter toward the back of the home reveals a generous family room, which flows effortlessly into the open gourmet kitchen fit for a five star chef. The dining room boasts vaulted ceiling and chandelier designed to magnify the dining experience. From the ample and spacious deck, you can enjoy breathtaking sunsets and unobstructed vistas while the cares of the day slowly ebb away." Gag me. It's honestly ridiculous. It's another one of those cheesy things real estate agents do that I just don't get. I mean where do they learn these things? Is there no way to articulate in an honest and unpretentious tone the features of the home without superfluous and flowery verbiage? Maybe I'm a little too pragmatic, but I think people are sick of such stupidity and see right through the fluff. Simply reference the aspects of the home, and give all the pertinent information. Save the flowery adjectives for date night.

Agent reputation

I touched on it earlier, but, yes, the reputation of the agent is a part of their promotion package. Agents are people. People like to deal with kind, friendly, smart, competent people no matter what they're doing. Real estate is no different. If you line up three listing agents and one is terrific but the other two are total monkeys, who would you rather do business with? Furthermore agents talk, and they ask around. I do. When I am dealing with an unknown agent, I ask around my office to see if anyone has done a deal with them. I remember one time I asked about a particular agent who brought a buyer for a listing I had. The response from my broker was "Fasten your seatbelt, and prepare for the drama." The broker had dealt with her before, and she was a nightmare to work with. I know agents who won't even show some listings because the listing agent is such a pain to work with. Again, I'm not saying it's right; I'm just saying it happens. Life is hard, and business is tough. Nobody wants to work with someone who just makes things harder. Though real estate is grossly overpopulated and saturated in virtually every community in America, people still get to know who the knuckleheads are and who the aces are. People want to work with aces.

Buyers commission

Remember the buyer's commission has to be right. You have to give an incentive for agents to show your home. It's not right and may be illegal or at least unethical, but some agents simply look at the commission on the MLS when deciding which home to show their buyers. Again, agents are people, and they have to pay their bills just like anyone. When a weak listing agent in concert with a cheap client mindlessly put 2.5 percent commission or less on the MLS when everything else is 3 percent, does that make agents want to show their home or not? Do you enjoy working for less money? I don't think agents do either.

Beyond that a buyer's agent bonus or higher commission can also be used as an effective incentive. On a hard home to sell or in a tough market with lots of competition, it might be a good idea to increase the agent's commission to 3.5 or 4 percent. It's about incentives. Which home do you think an agent might be more excited to show, one with standard or lower commission or one with a higher commission? You can also incentivize the listing by giving, for example, a $1,000 bonus to the buyer's agent or tickets to Disneyland or whatever. There's no limit to how creative you can be!

Pictures

Whether in a magazine, website, flyer, or on the MLS, the pictures must be high quality. Again, as with so many things, I am continually amazed how horrible some pictures are. I look on the MLS and see pictures that are dark, dim, or out of focus or the wrong size. I wish I was kidding. I've even seen pictures that were installed sideways or upside down. The level of incompetency out there is endless. Also, you want to make sure you use all the space for pictures. If you are allowed twenty pictures in the MLS, then take twenty. If thirty, then take thirty. There is no excuse for not filling out those spaces. If the pictures allow for text, make sure you fill out all the text lines for each picture. "Main level master" on the bottom of a picture reinforces the location of the home's biggest bedroom. "View off the back deck" lets people know what to expect.

Beyond that you want to make sure you are taking pictures of important aspects of the home or property. I can't tell you how many times I have gone to homes with views or that back up to beautiful forests or green belts without there being one single picture of the private backyard or terrific views. Why would you not include that? It boggles the mind. Moreover I'm super tired of lame agents taking pictures of a nearby park or community pool with no text. With no words there is no context to know what we're looking at. Is this the backyard? Is this next to the home? It happens more often than I care to recall. I remember one agent took a picture of the HOA pool but took it at such an angle that it looked like it could be in a backyard. My clients were excited to see the home, but I knew better. I called the agent to confirm, and sure enough there was no pool on the property of the home. I don't know if agents do it to be deceptive or because they're dumb, but it gets really old when all you're trying to do is find the right house for your buyers.

It should go without saying but I've seen it so often that I must say something here. A big motto of mine is, "Anything worth doing is worth doing well." So make sure what you are taking pictures of is appealing; I see online pictures of bathrooms with toilet seats up. I'm not kidding. Seriously? How hard is to use a little brainpower and just walk over and drop the seat? I've seen pictures of unmade or messy beds. I've seen pictures of kitchens, home offices, and living rooms that were so cluttered that it would have been better to never take a picture. Making sure the items in the picture are pleasing to the eye are important. Having said all this make sure the pictures are done with a high-quality camera or hire a professional to do it. Remember pictures are worth a thousand words, and those pictures are the first thing potential buyers see. The vast majority of searches begin online, and high-quality pictures are one of the first and best ways to impress a potential buyer.

Final thoughts on promotion

The litmus test for me and how I spend my money is simply in this question: Is this promoting me or a home I am needing to sell? While it is true that sometimes the line between those two is a bit blurred, promoting yourself is not targeted or intentional, whereas promoting a home is. To sell a home, you're better off spending money on targeted, efficient, and focused marketing that brings measurable and tangible results. Again, nobody ever drove down the street and after seeing a billboard with some agent's face plastered on it said to her husband, "Gee, Wilbur. We oughta call that nice fella. He seems like a nice guy, and he's handsome too!" It seems to me that most of the expensive and ineffective promotion ideas focus on agent promotion but may not directly market the home. With agent ego being what it is, there is no shortage of real estate agents willing to fork over big bucks to see their toothy grin on a local billboard or park bench. There's agent promotion, and there's home promotion. One of these strokes egos, and one of these sells houses.

Chapter Four

Why Open Houses Are A Bad Idea

"Open houses." Just the phrase conjures up the sense that you're welcome to pop over anytime you like. It's kind of like swinging by your best friend's house uninvited. You almost don't need to ring the doorbell. You can just walk on in, and your friend is always happy to see you. But that's just the issue isn't it? Anyone can just pop right in. Think about it. When in your life do you leave your home and allow strangers to traipse through your home unattended? "Oh, but the agent is there, and she'll keep an eye on things." Really? Did you hire a security guard or a real estate agent to sell your home? Trust me, she is focused on selling the home, and anyone showing the least bit of interest in your home she is going to be on them like white on rice. She won't be keeping track of everyone. She won't be counting the number of people in your home. She will be trying to make money.

Oftentimes more than one person or a group arrives at an open house at the same time. It's not like the agent is going to lock the door and ask people to wait on the porch while she personally escorts people through the home one by one. Hence the term "open" house. It's wide open. Now let's not be naïve here. We're all adults. Think like a criminal for just a moment. I know it might be hard for you because you're so dog gone nice and you have never been in trouble with the law, but just think for a moment. Think like a criminal. Is it possible that a criminal could wake up Saturday or Sunday morning, open the newspaper or go online, and look at the open houses scheduled for that day and view it as a strategic shopping list? Of course it's possible. Then could it also be possible for that criminal to find out whether the agent of the open house is a male or female? Sure they could. Then couldn't the criminal bring an accomplice, a member of the opposite gender, maybe good looking and charming, to distract the agent while they case the home? Of course they could.

Couldn't the criminal steal pretty much anything he or she could stuff in their pockets? Yes. Couldn't the criminal unlock strategic windows for a break-in later on? Sure. Couldn't the crook look around for vulnerabilities or the absence of motion sensors, alarms, or video surveillance? Absolutely! Listen, the bottom line is we are not in Leave it to Beaver America anymore, and anyone who wants to have an open house needs to think it through a little bit. You might say I'm being dramatic or fearful. No, I'm just being realistic—it's not 1950. Beyond the criminal element, think it through some more. Why would you want nosy neighbors and total strangers walking through your home in the first place? Nobody buys a home that way. Well, I guess some people do, but the actual national statistic of selling your home at an open house is less than 1 percent. Did you catch that? Less than 1 percent. So think it through and really process if are willing to risk your personal belongings, your privacy, and quite possibly your safety for a 1 percent chance of selling your home. Those odds are the worst ever! Even Vegas gives you better odds than that!

So why do agents do open houses?

It goes back to many years ago when the MLS was not available to the general public. This is before the computer and Internet. The MLS was printed weekly in a paper booklet or stapled sheets of paper. It was quite a process. Then it was delivered to every brokerage. In order to look at homes, you had to wait for the publication to come out, make an appointment with an agent who had the new printout and then go look at homes.

It was a lengthy and cumbersome process, where the real estate agent had all the information and consequently all the power. The open house concept emerged as an efficient alternative. It gave people power to go and look at homes without the agent controlling everything. It was a treat. The public didn't have to go through the formalities. They could just see a sign and pop in. No waiting for the MLS printout or for the agent to make an appointment. Buyers would actually be really excited Saturday morning to see what open houses were advertised in the paper. As a seller of a home, open houses were a great way to drive traffic to your home and increase the amount of people who could see it. With no technology or automated MLS, this was a strategic option to give your home some exposure.

If that's how it was, then why do agents do open houses now?

Well, it's certainly not to sell the house. "What?" you might ask. "Did I read that right?" Yes, you read it right. In the age of Internet and access to real time MLS, well over 65 percent of people start their home search online, in their pajamas, in their kitchen, with a hot cup of coffee! The open house is a ridiculous, outdated, and obsolete method that needs to die. It's also deceptive. Weak agents will state that they will do an open house for their sellers, and the sellers might be impressed that the agent is willing to do that for them. The agent includes the open house into their overall marketing strategy and explains with great conviction and enthusiasm that she will do an open house every weekend until it sells.

The reality is the agent won't tell them the truth, though. She won't tell them that the real and actual national statistic for selling a home through an open house is less than 1 percent. She'll tell her clients that it will bring "potential" buyers. She'll talk about "foot traffic." She'll talk about how she'll put signs out at all the major intersections with red arrows pointing to your home. She'll make it sound like open houses are an absolute necessity. After all other weak agents will validate her claim, because Mr. and Mrs. Seller will leave their home Saturday morning to be inconvenienced for the entire day in order for their agent to conduct an open house. While they are driving around, they will notice many open house signs, some with balloons and streamers tied to them. "My, my," they will say to each other, "I'm glad our agent is doing an open house too! She sure is a hard worker!"

Peer pressure, inexperience, unquestioned assumptions, and absence of factual information make all weak agents participate in herd mentality. It's like peer pressure of the ill informed in junior high school. Like so many things in life, just because "everyone is doing it" doesn't mean it's right. For that matter it doesn't mean it's strategic either. The reality is a lot of weak agents have nothing else to do, so they will be happy to sit in house all day long and pray one in a hundred wanders in and actually expresses real interest in the home. I've said it elsewhere in this book that there is an 85 percent turnover in agents every five years. You always have to remember then that in real estate, 85 percent of agents are at some level of failure, so it takes considerable effort to find strong agents with solid business and marketing skills. The strong ones don't waste time doing open houses.

As the sellers are driving about, they will look around and see the other open house signs and interpret that as validation for their agent's marketing strategy. Except it's all nonsense. That's not how homes are sold. Think about it. Who in the name of all things logical is on their way to get bagels Saturday morning but sees an open house sign and swings off the road thinking suddenly, "Whoa, I think I'm in the mood to buy a home…right now! I'll just skip the bagels and cruise on over to that open house in my sweat pants and ball cap. I'm sure the agent will be perfectly delightful and maybe she'll even have coffee and muffins!"

Nobody, and I mean nobody, buys a home that way. Purchasing a home for most people is the single largest investment and expense of their lives. Do you actually think it's a spontaneous decision, or do you think there is some planning, time, and calculation involved? We're not talking about spontaneously picking up a pack of gum at the checkout counter after shopping for groceries. We're talking about spending hundreds of thousands of dollars.

So a third time you might ask, "Why do agents do open houses?"
There are several reasons and they all have to do with the fact that the agent is not being straightforward with the sellers.

1. Weak agents are scared to educate their clients for fear of offending them.
They won't speak of the dangers of open houses nor will they speak of the inconvenience to you. They just include it in their proposal as part of their overall marketing plan. They don't want to come across too strong or too direct. They certainly don't want to tell you open houses are a waste of time, and they, for sure, don't want to draw attention to the fact that you will be inconvenienced for many hours every weekend while total strangers roam through your house. Beyond that they want you to think they're working hard for their commission.

2. Weak agents certainly will never reveal the fact that less than 1 percent of homes are ever sold this way.
They want to appear eager and willing to work for you. They are happy to sit in a house all day being totally unproductive while they wait for some random stranger to appear at the front door. Yet who would logically do such a mindless activity? Who would rationally attempt anything with a 1% chance of success? You have to question the mentality of a person who would embark on something with such a ridiculously low success rate. Would you climb Mount Everest with a 1% chance of summiting? If you were a military leader would you ever send your troops into combat with a 1% chance of survival? Would any businessperson or stockbroker ever invest in anything with a 1 percent ROI (return on investment)? The answer for all would be a resounding "no."

Weak and non-thinking agents will certainly never put it together that this method is horribly ineffective and obsolete. They won't bother researching the history or origin of open houses in the real estate industry. They won't come up with intelligent questions that challenge the efficacy of open houses. For that matter weak agents have never really thought about it at all. They just do open houses because "Isn't that what you're supposed to do?" It's just thoughtless herd mentality.

3. Weak agents will sell you on the imperatives of conducting a weekly open house.

They will dazzle you with how many signs they plan on sticking in the ground all over the neighborhood and at intersections. They will inform you that they are buying balloons to connect to all the signs in a display of absolute *Fortune 500* marketing genius! They will even tell you that they plan to advertise that they will have fresh baked cookies, milk, and coffee available. Boy, that will bring in the crowds for sure! Of course, they will need to use your oven to bake them, but this way when people walk in, they will smell fresh baked cookies and, after all, who doesn't like the smell of fresh baked cookies? Yes sir, I can see people whipping out their checkbook the moment those melted chocolate chips hit their eyeballs. What the agent won't tell you is that all those signs out there give her more exposure to people driving around, and the more her name is plastered all over town, the more potential business she can capture.

4. In some cases the seller may insist on the agent having an open house.

Because they are not informed, they may be determined and convinced of its utter necessity. Maybe the sellers are older and remember a time when having open houses was an important aspect of selling a home. Weak agents will cave to their client's demands, regardless of success rate, strategy, logic, or even safety. They wouldn't dare challenge the client with the truth. They'll just go along with it because, after all, that's what the client wants.

5. Weak agents are not good business people.

What smart businessperson would waste his or her time on an ineffective marketing technique that rendered less than a 1 percent return on their investment of time and effort? In a corporate job, a *real* job, the supervisor would banish such foolishness as a total waste of time and effort. Something with such a miserable return on investment would never in a thousand years be green lighted. In real jobs every minute and every penny counts and you are accountable to deliver measured and tangible results. You are never permitted to embark on useless activities that render nothing. The vast majority of real estate agents have never held down a high-level corporate sales job. They don't understand effective marketing. They can't tell the difference between a sharp, professionally executed strategy, and doing something just because everyone else is doing it. Such agents are mentally lazy, uninformed, or naïve and apparently live their lives based on unexamined assumptions or outdated information.

6. Beyond all that the main reason agents conduct open houses is, wait for it...they use your home as bait to catch other clients.

Ding, ding, ding! Yes you read that correctly. Your beautifully cleaned and appointed home is bait, plain and simple. An open house is a great way to generate more business for the agent. The whole idea here is that the agent will extract information from everyone walking in the front door. If it's a neighbor, the agent will be delighted to discover that they are actually thinking about selling. The agent will perk up and wax eloquent about her marketing plan including, you guessed it, open houses. The agent hopes she can scoop up a listing in the neighborhood. It always looks strong for an agent to have a couple of signs on one street.

Maybe after talking to a person for a few minutes, the agent will discover the person is indeed interested in buying a home. "Are you working with anyone?" she will ask, hoping to hear the answer "no," in which case she will spring into action, offering her services to go look at homes. You see? Your home is merely bait for the agent to generate more business for herself. The open house has absolutely nothing to do with actually selling your home. It's a bunch of busy nonsense that produces no results. So while you're mindlessly driving around or going to the mall trying to kill time thinking your agent is working hard trying to sell your home, you are actually a sucker who has allowed the agent to use your home as bait to attract more business for herself.

When you get back to your home several hours later, the agent will be enthusiastic while she's washing the baking trays. "Oh, hello, Mr. and Mrs. Seller. Welcome back!"

You will ask, "Oh, how was the open house?"

She will provide you with a list of contacts and with great energy declare, "It was fantastic. We had seventeen people come through in five hours. Yes sir, I talked to many people today. There was one person who said she was going to think about it. She looked around, ate one of my amazing cookies, asked me some questions, took a brochure, and left. I think I'll hear from her soon!" The whole while the agent will be thinking about following up on her leads from the open house to see if she can drum up some more business. And "wow" you will say. "We sure do have a hard working real estate agent, don't we sweetie?" All the while you are being inconvenienced for no reason and don't realize you have been duped into working with a weak and dishonest agent.

"Come on! Are there that many dishonest agents out there?" you might ask. Well, maybe every agent who does an open house isn't dishonest. Maybe they're just bad at business. Maybe they're inexperienced. Maybe they're just bored and have nothing to do. Maybe they're just weak. Maybe they are stuck in the "that's how we've always done it" mentality and never question the effectiveness of an open house. Maybe they're totally ignorant of how real estate actually works. Regardless of the reason, there aren't any good ones why you should ever do an open house.

So who goes to open houses?

I drove by an open house sign last Saturday. The sign said Huge Gifts! Are you kidding me? Now let's think about this. If something was awesome, would you have to bribe people to come? That's why mediocre and failing restaurants are always cranking out coupons. What they are offering is so forgettable that they have to create an incentive for people to even show up. Beyond that think about who would be really enticed by a free gift, huge or not? Would successful, well-qualified buyers suddenly be attracted by a gift? I think you know the answer.

When you go to an open house, you notice other people walking around, so clearly people like to go to open houses. Sure they do, but what kinds of people?

People who like to be treated like royalty. Agents at open houses fawn over everyone who walks in the door, and frankly some people like to have their ego stroked.

Criminals love to go to open houses. It's a dream come true for any thief. No lock picking necessary!

Nosy neighbors go to open houses. They've always wondered what color carpet you have.

People who like free stuff. For some people the lure of free donuts, cookies, bagels, coffee, or yes, even huge gifts are enough to get them to turn into the driveway.

Researching people go to open houses. People looking for interior decorating or design ideas often go to open houses. I wish I was kidding, but it's true.

Bored people go to open houses. People who have nothing better to do with their time always love to go to open houses on Saturday morning, especially if there's bagels and coffee!

Curious people go to open houses. We call these people "lookie-loos" because all they like to do is look. God knows why. They just love to look around in different neighborhoods.

Notice how none of the kinds of people who go to open houses are actually financially qualified, ready to shop, buyers. It just doesn't work that way. As a seller you must be aware of how real estate works and how homes are bought and sold. You must receive truthful answers from an agent you are interviewing, and you must understand what methods are effective and which ones are a waste of time. As an agent how about you be truthful with your clients? How about informing them as to how homes are correctly marketed and actually sold and stop using their home as bait to bring you more business?

Chapter Five

The Brokerage

In this section I will write about three aspects of the brokerage. I will address the importance of an agent selecting the correct brokerage. I will point out the pros and cons for a consumer in working with a particular brokerage, and I will speak directly to the owners of the brokerage.

As any broker in any industry, a real estate brokerage is the middle entity, the go-between. Their primary purpose is to represent the interests of another through their proxies, the agents. The agent always works for and remains submitted to the rules and authority of the brokerage. Agents come and go, but the brokerage remains. All listings and all business belong to the brokerage. The agent owns nothing but is merely the representative of the brokerage. The brokerage will operate under the rules of the local, state, and national guidelines and laws of various governing bodies. They are bound not only to sound business practice and the highest possible levels of ethical ideals; they are also responsible to conduct their business according to the dictates of the bodies that have authority over them. Various real estate commissions and committees are generally established in every region of the country for this purpose. They provide oversight, guidance, information, enforcement, as well as correction and discipline if needed. In addition such groups will often provide mediation services when disagreements arise.

Two models of brokerages
There are two basic models of brokerages: ones with lower percentage agent commission splits with free offices and those with higher

percentage agent commission splits that rent offices. The reality is that every brokerage is a for-profit business and has to generate income somehow. Basically they will do it one of these two ways. Oftentimes beyond the split, there are also transaction fees connected to every deal as well as monthly or annual dues.

The traditional model that many, especially small locally owned brokerages, employ is a low split/free office model. Typically a new agent will join the office and be able to enjoy a "free" cubical. In exchange the agent will be charged a relatively inferior commission split such as 60/40. In other words, the agent will keep 60 percent of their earned commission, and the brokerage will take 40 percent. When agents become proficient or even top producers, the brokerage will invariably have to offer a better split due to competitive pressures from other brokerages. The split, for example, may rise to 85/15. They will most often also upgrade the agent to a free office as well as some other perks.

Retention in any kind of sales organization is challenging because, for obvious reasons, people are always on the lookout for higher income and better benefits. Brokerages must remain competitive or risk losing their best agents. RE/MAX International became the largest real estate brokerage in the world by intentional design and strategy. RE/MAX is located in southern Denver, Colorado, and was cofounded by Dave and Gail Liniger. They strategically focused on attracting top producers in every geographic location. With more beneficial terms and better splits along with superior technology, they easily recruited top producers from other brokerages. This happened with me when we lived in Los Angeles County. I was a top producer and nationally ranked Realtor with another firm when I was approached by John and Alice O'Hare, owners of RE/MAX of Santa Clarita.

In order to discover new top-producing agents, they kept track of listings and closings and which agents were involved. They also noticed signs in front of people's houses. My production attracted their attention, and after sitting down and offering me a vastly superior package, I left my old brokerage and joined RE/MAX. Companies like RE/MAX might do like a 95/5 split and charge several hundred dollars rent for an office along with a transaction fee and monthly dues. That's why they are structured to attract top producers, and indeed in most metro areas, RE/MAX offices and agents dominate the market. Sadly, some RE/MAX brokers are straying from this proven model and falling into the "warm body" trap. Instead of bringing in only top shelf agents, they are just trying to fill their ranks with warm bodies. This dilutes the brand and potentially ruins the image and reputation of the local brokerage.

Regardless, in the original RE/MAX model, a brand new agent, even if he or she were invited, would most likely not want to work with RE/MAX because the costs would be too high in the short run. New agents typically don't generate a lot of business, so even though the commission split would be superior, they would spend a lot in rent and fees before they ever got their first commission check. When I started in real estate I enjoyed a "free" cubicle and was OK with a 60/40 split, because I really didn't know what I was doing. I was just starting out and learning every day. However, once I got the hang of it and started producing, seeing 40 percent of my income vanish grew to be quite painful. The brokers offered me a nice window office and a better split that worked for a time, but eventually the RE/MAX model was a better fit for me. Clearly there are many quality real estate companies and brokerages out there. Some are local franchises of huge national or international companies, and some are smaller, regional companies. One thing is clear though; it is hyper competitive and everyone wants to be the market leader.

Choosing a brokerage as an agent

This topic is a bit subjective as a large part of this depends on feel. As people sometimes don't use logic in making decisions, emotion is oftentimes the primary driving force in selecting a brokerage. Most agents want to feel appreciated. They enjoy receiving awards and accolades. Not unlike anyone in the workforce, they want to be comfortable, and they want to feel like they belong. People use emotional and illogical words in describing their work environment. "It just feels like home." Or "They're my family." To which I respond, after recovering from my nausea, "You only have one home, and you only have one family."

Although I am a fan of making a work environment as pleasant as possible, I personally don't subscribe to the gushy side of things. I chafe when people describe their workplace in glowing terms like "It feels like home" or "My coworkers are family." Does your real family kick you out for underperformance? Would your real family look at you funny if you started failing? Will your real family dismiss you if you don't pay the bills? Yet that is exactly what will happen if you started floundering and didn't pay your real estate fees and dues.

Therein is the logical rub for me. Work is a conditional environment. You produce, and you keep your job. You don't, and you won't. It's quite simple really. This is in stark contrast to the unconditional love you should feel in your real family in your real home. Your real home should be a place that is rooted in acceptance, grace, and abiding affection. I encourage people to place realistic expectations on their work environment. Maybe I'm a little too pragmatic, but I've seen so many people emotionally devastated when this so-called family never communicated with them after they left the brokerage. These are transactional relationships that are connected to a vocation and location. I'm not saying you can't or won't ever develop lasting friendships in your workplace. I'm simply saying emotion shouldn't really play into your decision regarding the selection of a brokerage.

The main thing for agents to keep in mind when selecting a brokerage is to understand where they are in their real-estate journey and what they need. A new agent needs a brokerage that moves a little slower, has ample training, and has abundant support staff. In exchange for such provisions, the brokerage will take a larger cut of the commission. That is usually fine for a new agent who is just learning the game but is highly intolerable to an established, successful agent. Such agents will look for a brokerage that has less handholding and more of an emphasis on personal income.

If a successful agent ends up in a slow moving, beginner-focused brokerage, he or she will make less money and probably have low morale.

Conversely, if a rookie agent ends up in a fast paced, top-producing brokerage, they will quickly become overwhelmed. He or she will quickly feel disenchanted and isolated. It's important for each agent to carefully select the brokerage that best matches his or her needs and desires. There is no right or wrong here. Agents just need to be in a place that will best facilitate their needs in their particular stage of growth. Most agents don't think this through, and it is to their own detriment. The brokerage an agent connects to can either be a major asset in creating a successful future in real estate or be a total drain on energy, morale and income.

Choosing a brokerage as a consumer

There are pros and cons to every brokerage and every business model. Just as the agent has to select which brokerage is the best fit for him or her, so too does the consumer. The consumer has needs and desires as well as expectations. The consumer often gets connected to the agent but never considers the brokerage he or she works for. You can have a great person working for a lame brokerage with gross limitations in marketing, horrible signage, inept processes, and incompetent owners. No matter how amazing the agent is, their success will, to some degree, be directly connected to the brokerage's ability to support that agent. If the brokerage is owned by sharp people who thrive to excel and dominate the marketplace through cutting-edge technology, brilliant marketing, top-shelf training, and world-class customer service, then odds are their agents will thrive. The opposite is also true.

There are large, nationally known franchise brokerages, and there are small, local brokerages. To a consumer this can be a little subjective. The reason it's subjective is that for some people certain things are not important, whereas for others those items may be critical. Regarding geography, I have found that large, national brands tend to dominate in large metro areas but that in small towns and rural areas, private, local, smaller brokerages have the larger share of business. This may have more to the relational aspect of smaller towns than with anything else. So part of this depends on what your needs are, what your perceptions are, and your location. Some things like an aggressive national marketing campaign may be important to some people who own a huge cattle ranch near Fort Collins or a luxury home in Aspen but to others such marketing exposure really adds no value. Furthermore, some things that you might think are key are really irrelevant, and other things that don't feel like a priority should be.

There is no doubt that perception is reality for many people, and it's hard to compete with the size and stability or professionalism that a large national brand offers. In the minds of some, brand recognition creates a familiar confidence that perhaps a smaller local brokerage sign can't generate. Some local brokerages tout themselves as being the local experts who really know their community, but that's kind of silly because even large national chains have agents who live and work locally and are every bit as adept. Large national chains do have an advantage with a larger budget for marketing, training, and technology. They may be more up to speed on the latest trends and techniques. Because they're national or even global, they also have referral and relocation programs that may benefit some people. For example, RE/MAX, being the largest real estate company in the world, has created an online portal for their agents to access. In this portal they can look up high quality agents in other cities. If their client is relocating, they can be of great service in recommending a seasoned RE/MAX agent who will be waiting for them at their new location.

In the final analysis, however, the quality of the agent is really what makes the difference. The agent is the one you will interact with, not the brokerage. There are horrible agents at large well-known brokerages, and there are horrible agents at small local offices. And to the contrary, there are amazing agents at national brokerages, and there are amazing agents at small local brokerages. The key is to find an agent who is the best fit for you and your needs.

Some thoughts for brokerage owners and managers:
Over many years I have observe amazing brokerage owners and I have witnessed some pretty pathetic ones. I have seen some owners who operate like a total pro and I have seen some who frankly have no idea what

they're doing. Running a brokerage is running a business. The two cannot be separated. If you own or manage a brokerage, either a branded, nationally recognized one or a small, private, local brokerage, there are some things worth pointing out from the perspective of both the agent and the customer. Keeping the following thoughts in mind and implementing them into your brokerage will ensure a high level of efficiency and effectiveness.

Brand protection

Every business has a brand and reputation in their realm of business. Every hire, every agent, every listing, every advertisement, and every transaction are a reflection on your brand. It will either create a positive or negative perception in the eyes of the community. It is vital that you as the owner or manager protect your brand with vigilance. Your reputation and correlating business is at stake.

Review and approve all listings

The other day on my morning walk, I saw a for-sale sign in front of a home. The brokerage was a huge national brand. The problem was the home looked abandoned. The paint was faded and peeling, the window screens were damaged, the lawn was shot, there were dead trees and shrubs in the yard, and weeds in the driveway cracks. It was such a bad look to have this sharp, professional sign from an easily recognizable national brand in front of such a shoddy house. Now, I know a sale is a sale, and you make money from sales. I get it. However, some sales are not worth the damage to your brand.

An easy way to remedy the situation is take the listing but have a rider on top or below the sign that states "As is" or "fixer-upper," which everyone knows is code for "this place is rough!" Also, it has to be priced right for a quick sale. If a property is in poor condition, it must be priced accordingly, or it will never sell. Weak agents who are desperate will take just about any listing out there. Weak agents also will get bullied by unrealistic homeowners regarding price and terms. You shouldn't have any weak agents, but if you do, make sure they understand your brand is more important than their ambitions.

Review and approve all advertisements

Advertisements should be part of your overall promotion or marketing program. Your brand must be consistent across all venues including websites, flyers, magazine and newspaper ads, radio, TV, business cards, and signage. Few things confuse the general public more than mixed messages from an inconsistent marketing program. I don't care how witty or creative your agents think they are, it is your responsibility to protect your brand and review and approve all marketing that's out there in your community.

Hiring agents

Real estate is a little odd because agents don't really get hired so to say because they're not employees, they're independent contractors. Regardless, technically brokerages hire agents. The reality is there are desperate agents, and there are desperate brokerages. Some weak agents will do anything for a transaction, and some weak brokerages will do anything to have warm bodies in their office. Again, everything reflects on your brand. If you have a weak agent who is slovenly dressed, inarticulate, unprofessional, and poorly skilled out there with your logo on their shirt, it will make people think, "Gee whiz! What's the matter with ABC Brokerage that they hire guys like this?" You want sharp people who are appropriately trained, confident, know what they are doing, and strong at negotiating. You want people with solid business skills, personal awareness, and effective communication abilities. You want professional agents who know how to present themselves. I would rather have a small office with six really sharp agents than an office of a hundred mediocre ones.

The temptation is to pack your office with as many warm bodies as possible because you make money on fees and dues. I unfortunately see it all too often. Many brokerages not only make the money on each agent but also like to brag how many agents they have, so they will virtually hire anyone with a pulse. My advice would be to resist this shortsighted temptation and focus on attracting and retaining the best of the best. Anything less dilutes your brand and increases the odds of your brokerage having a negative reputation in the community.

Training

Initial training for new agents and ongoing training for existing ones is very important to have a consistent level of quality among your people. In the last paragraph, I mentioned the phrase "appropriately trained." This means not only training in real estate competency but also in the culture and standards of your brand. Again, for the sake of continuity and consistency, training is vital. There are some brokerages that are entry level and some that will only take experienced agents. Both types of brokerages need training. The rookie agent will need to learn not only real estate competency but also your methodology and culture, whereas the experienced agent perhaps may only need a primer on office culture and the unique aspects of your brand. You might have a rookie agent come in with great posture and body language, strong sales skills, and great people skills, but they will still need to enhance what they already possess by learning the way you do things.

Invest time in your agents

Few things express how important people are than time spent together. It means a lot when a business owner or manager takes an agent or employee to breakfast, lunch, coffee, or drinks at a local happy hour. As everything can always be better, these are opportunities to listen and learn what needs improvement. Not only does this increase morale and engender trust and loyalty, but it also gives you as the owner or manager clues to where the weak spots are in your operation. I think when people feel valued and that their opinion or experiences matter, you dramatically increase your chances of retaining your agents. You want to not only serve your agents by creating the best office possible; you want your agents to feel connected. Being an agent is being an independent contractor, and it can feel like you're out there in the water floating alone. It's good to know that a broker, owner, or manager is being intentional about touching base with their agents.

The broker, owner, or manager should develop relationships with the agents. One by one they should be met with outside the office in a casual, relaxed setting. You could even do small groups if meeting everyone individually is impractical. People should understand that they are appreciated. Most brokers make a big deal at the monthly or annual meeting when they hand out plaques and awards, but the reality is people need encouragement, support, and connection all year long. Also, there are many agents who will never receive an award, so the monthly and annual hurrah show fails to touch them.

An appreciated agent is a loyal agent. Most brokers, owners, and managers are too busy doing the stuff of business that they forget we are dealing with human beings here. People have choices, and other brokerages are always on the lookout for new talent. Their recruiting efforts will succeed and steal away your agents unless you have empowered your people through your human touch and personal interaction. Changing brokerages is a major hassle, and agents generally won't want to disrupt their routine unless there is a compelling reason. As the owner, broker, or manager, it is your job to create such an awesome environment that your agents won't be able to think of a compelling reason to leave.

You don't have to be best buddies. You don't have to golf together every week. You just have to show you care and are interested in what's going on with your agents. You want to understand what their joys are as well as their challenges and frustrations. You should want to know how they are feeling about working for your brokerage and if there is anything you could do to better serve them. Get your ego out of the way, stop being so mechanical, and connect with your people on a heartfelt level. If you do so from an authentic place, they will reward you with high morale, strong production, and ongoing loyalty.

Create an agent round-table or think-tank
Unfortunately many business owners are more interested in hearing praise than they are in hearing criticism. This is the number one way I can tell if an owner, manager, or leader is weak: if he or she is more interested

in having their ego stroked than with improving. When leaders live in a type of echo chamber where they only hear their voice and those who agree with them, their effectiveness radically diminishes. I think a broker, owner, or manager needs to have their finger on the pulse of their business, and the best way to do that is to have regular meetings with specific people who don't blow smoke. This should be true of every business and organization under the sun. If you hide in your corner office you will never know what is actually going on in your company. Worse, if you avoid coming into the office at all, things will spiral out of control even faster. If you surround yourself with kiss-ups and yes-men, you'll never hear the truth. If people around you have something to gain from their relationship with you, they will never tell you the way things really are. They'll just tell you what you want to hear and smile all the way to the bank.

Every leader needs to have a certain kind of person around them. Such a person is confident, clear at observation and analysis, able to articulate challenges, and see weak spots. They must also be able to possess a mentality that is able to logically see how things are operating with a critical and truthful eye. They must also be a person who can generate creative solutions and present viable problem solving options. I believe having an inner circle of such people make for a superior brokerage or business.

Be present

Many people think an MBA is a great degree, but equally important is an MBWA, which means Management by Walking Around. As the owner, broker, or manager, you need to be present, approachable, and available. Ghost Brokers are ridiculous. You know, the kind of leader who claims to be a leader but is never around? Don't be a Ghost Broker. How can you possibly have your finger on the pulse of your organization let alone run your business effectively if you're not around? Yea sure, I know, the answer would be that they delegate responsibilities to competent people. While this is clearly good management, better management is being around. You can delegate tasks but you can't delegate leadership. That was worth mentioning twice. You can delegate tasks but you can't delegate leadership.

This is one of the major challenges with owners or brokers who are also agents. Oftentimes a successful agent will buy or open a new brokerage. The problem is that the agent is motivated and skilled at selling, not necessarily at running a business. Though linked they are two completely different skill sets. There is not only an inherent conflict of interests in an owner being an agent, but their attention and commitment is split as well. If the owner/agent is making more money selling homes than running the business, his or her loyalty and time will obviously be slanted toward selling, and in so doing, the office systems will suffer. It's kind of like being an absentee landlord and not checking on the condition of your rental. Moreover, some brokers are actually slumlords who truly don't care about the success of their business. They just want to collect the checks. They will deny this to the ends of the earth but the proof is in the pudding. Some brokers need to look deep into their heart and admit they don't have what it takes to run a business and just plain get out. There is no shame in just being a successful agent. Don't let ego or opportunity push you into an area your skill set can't sustain you in.

Ghost Brokers who are pursuing their own ambitions, leisure, goals, and agendas at the expense of their brokerage really need to conduct a gut check. Without caring, competent and present leadership, things will eventually slip through the cracks. Over time the cracks in your business will grow bigger. When cracks grow big enough buildings fall. Such is the nature of every organization and business without effective leadership. Sooner or later things will fall apart. It's not if but when.

Provide an in-office transaction coordinator
Once agents have learned the basics of the transaction, there is really little value in staying involved in the paperwork. Real estate coaches will tell you that the only way an agent makes money is by going out in the community and drumming up new business. Doing paperwork is of course very important, but like in many areas of our lives, it can be delegated in order to increase productivity. One brokerage I worked for in California provided an amazing transaction coordinator. Her name was Helen, and

she was highly efficient. I informed my clients that Helen was an indispensible part of my team, and they should expect to hear from her. After my clients entered into an agreement, I simply put the file in her inbox, and she did the rest. That freed me up to go and generate more business, which created more income for me, for Helen, and for the brokerage.

Any logical broker, owner, or manager should provide an in-house transaction coordinator. Free up your agents to go out and capture a larger market share for the brokerage instead of having them sit in their office or cubicle doing paperwork. An agent using a transaction coordinator can pay anywhere from $350 to $500 per deal, and a portion of that goes to the brokerage. So not only does it make agents more efficient and productive, but it also generates a passive income stream for the brokerage. The agents are more efficient, which means they sell more and the brokerage makes more money in the end. The transaction coordinator earns a living, and the brokerage receives a passive income stream. It's literally a no-brainer.

Be a resource for your agents

Real estate can be complicated. There are many moving pieces. Be a resource for your agents. Provide them with the latest training, technology, and techniques out there. Have contacts at the ready for home repair, inspection, escrow, title services as well as financing options. I was with one brokerage where there would be ten to fifteen broadcast e-mails a week from agents asking for referrals on everything from sprinkler repair to real estate attorneys to painters. This was not only obnoxious and a waste of my time; it was totally unnecessary. Instead of having all your agents reinvent the wheel and go find people on their own or waste everyone's time with annoying e-mails, have the contacts available. An office I worked with in the past had representatives come in frequently and give presentations, so they were familiar to all the agents. Believe me, if you ask inspection professionals if they would enjoy dedicated and exclusive referrals from fifty or one hundred agents, they will be more than happy to go above and beyond to ensure everyone is well taken care of.

Exclusivity breeds loyalty and efficiency. When a service provider gets a large portion of business from you, they will return the favor by bending over backward to take care of you and your agents. They may even provide discounted pricing in exchange for the volume. You should gladly enter into such arrangements. It's good for your agents. It's good for your business, and it's good for service levels. When you are in a pinch and you really need to get something done, those contacts will go the extra mile for you if strong relationships are in place. There is no reason why a good, business-minded owner, broker, or manager wouldn't have a list of contacts printed out and given to every agent. Or of course you could ignore my sound advice and let the agents fend for themselves.

Seven thoughts on office morale:

Few things erode a great corporate culture than declining morale. There are many reasons people begin to detach emotionally from their workplace and become sour or even worse, toxic. Here are some reasons things go sideways:

1. Protecting weak agents

If you protect weak agents just because they are your personal friend or have stayed with you the longest, or belong to some prominent family, you will eventually undermine your business. Let everyone stand on the merits of their own production.

2. Hiring lame agents

I have dedicated an entire chapter on this topic. Top producers and high-quality people like to be around other top producers and high-quality people. When you begin to flood your office with warm bodies in order to capture fees and dues regardless of any business sense or skill, you risk creating an office culture of mediocrity. Eventually you may lose your top producers because they won't want to be associated with such incompetent agents. They will go to a brokerage that is well run and only brings on the best agents.

3. Having favorites

I suppose we all have people we prefer over and against those we do not. However, in business, especially in a competitive office setting, it can quickly become toxic. If there is preferential treatment toward some in the office, it will create friction with the other agents. You want harmony in the office. If you give leads, better floor time, or call rotation only to certain agents, you will erode trust with the other agents. Believe me word gets around even if you think you're doing everything on the down low.

4. Nepotism

This is close to having favorites, but it has a special bite to it because as the saying goes, blood is thicker than water. It's OK to have family members work for you. Nobody begrudges that. What people despise is the protection and promotion some get just because they share a last name with the owner. This infuriates people and ruins morale. Family members will earn the respect of others in the office if they are not artificially propped up but stand on their own production. If it is a level playing field, then it is a fair field.

5. Lack of training or resources

Few things are as maddening as joining a new firm and not having the tools, training, support, or resources to do your job. If an agent has to beg to find out the basics, you are already blowing it. Give your people what they need in order to succeed. If they win, you win. Plain and simple.

6. Not connecting with agents

I touched on this before, so I won't repeat myself. The dynamics of not having a nine-to-five job and being an independent contractor can get kind of isolated and lonely at times. If you connect with agents on a personal level, they will feel more a part of your brokerage.

7. Understand the effects of a selling owner/broker

I also mentioned this earlier. Some brokers want to own the brokerage but also want to sell. I have never seen this work smoothly. Running any business but especially a real estate brokerage is complicated and very time intensive with endless details, responsibilities, and obligations. Regardless of how good a broker thinks they are at delegating, sooner or later, the strain of both running a business and selling homes will create pressure and stress. Those unresolved and ignored pressures will eventually cause cracks as I said before, every building that has ever collapsed starts with cracks. Usually it is the business that will suffer along with those delegated administrators left to carry the load of the incompetent and absent broker. Selling and running a business are two fundamentally different skill sets. An owner may be attracted to the hunt or the thrill of the chase of working with a buyer or seller, but the business will become unstable in their absence. The owner may appreciate the additional income, but it may come at the peril of the core business.

If the broker really enjoys selling but sees management as drudgery, their energy and attention will be divided and they will favor selling. This of course means that the management of the brokerage will suffer. And believe me it's a quick spiral downward if your lack of focus and unprofessional management means that agents get their commission checks late or don't get the support they need. In some offices where the owner/broker is also selling, many agents and staff feel they could fall off the edge of the earth, and the broker wouldn't ever notice because they are too busy blindly pursuing their own personal interests, goals, and sales. There are some offices like this where the broker/owner is actually never even around. I don't know a single business that can thrive long term with an absentee owner. If the owner/broker really enjoys selling but not managing, it calls into question his or her motive for owning a franchise in the first place. It comes off as disingenuous, and they should probably just admit the truth and get out of pretending to be a business owner.

Some agents may resent the broker if they run the business and work as an agent. Think about that. The very person you are working for is also your competition. I was with a brokerage in Valencia, California, for several years. The brokerage was owned by a married couple. The man ran the business, but the wife, in addition to being the de facto office manager, acted as an agent. She was consistently ranked as a national award-winning agent. She was a good agent; I won't take anything away from her in that regard, but the reality was she scooped up a lot of business through her status as co-owner of the brokerage. Clearly her husband would recommend her over any other agent. All the "relo" (corporate relocation) business was given to her. Relo business is usually high net worth corporate executives purchasing or selling significantly expensive homes. Such homes pay very well as the corporation not only covers all costs but usually guarantees the sale of the home regardless of market conditions. As those correspondences came into the franchise, she was very happy to scoop up all the relo business.

I'm not saying they did anything unethical. They didn't. I just know it created a lot of resentment among the agents. It felt a bit self-serving when at the awards banquets the wife would walk up giggling and smiling to collect her national award for production that she really didn't have to work too hard for. It also created suspicion. Agents started wondering if the owner's wife also scooped up the more lucrative leads that came into the office. When the system seems rigged, morale will tank, and agents will begin to defect.

My point is this: either be an owner/broker or be an agent and avoid conflict of interests. It's just cleaner that way. To sell versus running a business is two entirely different skill sets that need two entirely different temperaments. It's almost impossible to do both well. As a matter of fact, I've never seen it done well. When I worked with RE/MAX of Santa Clarita in northern Los Angeles County, the owners, John and Alice O'Hare, ran the business. They didn't work as agents. They ran a highly profitable and professionally managed brokerage that had the trust of their agents.

Don't waste your agent's time

One brokerage I worked for insisted that all agents join in on a weekly caravan. For those of you who weren't born sixty years ago, you may not know what this is. It is an old and outdated way of exposing properties to office agents. I mentioned it elsewhere in this book but basically it hearkens back to the day when the MLS was printed out monthly or weekly. This was way before computers and the Internet. Usually after an office meeting where all the new listings were pitched, everyone would get excited and drive out and see the new listings. By exposing agents to the properties, it was a way for brokerages to drum up additional business. If an in-house agent had a buyer for a home on a caravan, the brokerage would "double-end" the deal, meaning they would make money on the selling and on the buying side. Great. No problem. I never begrudge anyone for wanting to increase revenue.

The problem is nowadays only weak agents with nothing to do will be happy to go on your corny caravan. Odds are they don't have any buyers because they're busy doing dumb things like going on caravans to make their broker happy. With everything available at our fingertips online, real time access to the MLS and sophisticated websites, there is absolutely no need for caravans. Yes, it worked at one time. So did wearing mustard-yellow blazers.

Don't mandate that everyone, especially top producers who are out dominating the world, stop and come to your cheesy mixer or cocktail party. It's a waste of time for them. They aren't impressed by free drinks and finger food. They are impressed by reaching and smashing their sales goals. And if you're going to have weekly or monthly mandatory sales meetings, make sure it's worth their time. Such meetings are usually a horrific waste of time and the only reason most agents go is for the free breakfast. Productive agents aren't impressed with free food nor do they like to waste time.

Brokerages are no doubt kind of weird in that they don't really hire people but have a pool of independent contractors. At times it can feel like you're trying to herd cats. It's hard to establish protocol, loyalty, or corporate culture in such a context, but it can be done. Through thoughtful, intentional, and engaged leadership, any brokerage can be a thriving real estate machine with high production and happy agents.

Chapter Six

The Seller

Deciding to sell your home is a big decision. It's a lot of hard work, it's expensive, it's disruptive, and it can be overwhelming. In some situations moving is exciting. A new job or promotion may lead you off to a distant city. For some, a new baby means you are now completely out of space, and it's the season to expand into a larger home. Perhaps retirement has brought you to a place where the empty nest is too much to take care of, and a low-maintenance condo that will enable you to travel is a wonderful next step.

Then there are difficult reasons some people have to move. A business failure or being laid off from a stable job makes it so your current home is unaffordable. An ailing parent in another city may mean it's time to move to be closer and help out. For some the end of a marriage means it's also time to separate from the shared home. For some a loss of mobility means their two-story home is no longer functional. There are literally endless reasons people sell their homes. Some of the reasons are joyful, and some are difficult, but the common denominator is that selling and moving can be stressful and is hard work even in the best situations. Leaving something familiar for something unknown is challenging. Familiar home, familiar neighborhood, familiar neighbors and friends, familiar school, and familiar roads are just some of the things that are involved in transitioning out of your current home. Though there may be a measure of excitement to discovering all new things, there are many unknowns that cause some additional stress to emerge.

Stress creates pressure, and too much pressure for any of us is not healthy. There are so many critical decisions to be made that you must be empowered with as much accurate information as possible to ensure a smooth transition. Packing, saying good-bye, and moving are stressful enough. Don't add more stress by not being fully informed. Part of the information you need to know is what the financial implications of selling your home will be. You may owe capital gains tax if your home has dramatically appreciated. Your home may have a lien from an unresolved issue. You will need to consult with a qualified CPA and title or escrow professional to get a handle on things. You will need the guidance of an experienced real estate agent to guide you through the dynamics of your local market and how you can best position your home for the upcoming sale. It's still hard work and it's still expensive and it can be emotional, but with accurate information you will be empowered to take the appropriate steps with confidence and clarity.

Time to move
Once the decision has been reached that a home sale and move is the correct path for you, then the next step is to decide on how to sell the home. Selling a home is similar to buying and selling stocks or investing your money. You can either do it yourself or hire someone to do it for you. And just like stocks and other investments, some people have the ability to do it themselves while the vast majority of people are better served by having a trained and experience professional help with the process. Like anything else if you do it yourself, you will obviously save money. If you have to hire someone, it will cost you more. Pretty simple. However, cost should not be the only consideration. Selling a home has a many legal and financial implications, and the law doesn't show mercy due to ignorance or lack of experience. You have to know what you're doing and abide within the constraints of legal, financial, and ethical requirements. Beyond that there is a significant amount of paperwork that must be filled out correctly with fixed deadlines.

It's expensive to sell a home, no doubt. That's why people don't do it every couple years, and that's why nobody should enter into a contract lightly. There may be some aspects of the real estate transaction that are deductible which is a small benefit, but again, you would have to speak with a CPA for the specifics of your personal situation. If you decide to use a real estate professional, then it's time to look for a good one, hopefully even a great one. Most people like to get a referral from a trusted co-worker, friend, or family member. While that is fine, you still must do your own homework. The quality of the agent will have a direct correlation with the quality of the entire experience. As I've said before, because every community in America is flooded with real estate agents, finding one isn't hard; finding a great one is.

Hiring the agent

Remember, you are hiring someone to handle what for most people is the most expensive financial decision of their lives. You want to make sure you have the right person with a high level of experience and competency as well as significant skills in marketing, communication, business, and negotiation. You want to be confident in their track record. For the amount of money they charge, you absolutely deserve the best. You have to act like a business owner hiring somebody to work for you because indeed that is what is happening. You are hiring someone to do something very important for you, and it is imperative that the person is highly qualified. I know I say this a lot, but I am continually amazed at some people and how they make reckless and unwise decisions. Always remember you're the boss, and as such you should use facts, experience, and logic to make your decision. Emotion has no place in a transaction of this magnitude.

I remember one prospect I was talking to about selling their home. The husband was on board, but I felt a little resistance from the wife. I asked her what was holding her back. She said, "Well, Joanie my neighbor just got her license, since the kids are school age and she wants to contribute to the family budget. I just feel like I have to use her to sell our home. It would be awkward if I didn't use her. We've been friends for years." There were so many things wrong with what she said in those few sentences; I barely knew where to begin. I was a top producer with national awards and came highly recommended by a very close friend of theirs who had used me on several transactions. Yet here she was balking at the last minute because of illogical and emotional reasons.

The neighbor just got her license, so clearly she had no experience. She got into real estate because she wants to chip in financially. Noble, but not really the reason you get involved with something on this level. You engage with a new career because you have a passion for it, and that passion fuels your desire to become excellent at it. In return if you are excellent, the dollars will follow. She said she just "feels" like she has to use her neighbor. Numbers are not emotional; they are logical and factual. Although there is emotion in buying or selling a home, it is best for emotions not to override common sense, business logic, or sound thinking. Then she finished with the thought that it might be awkward if she didn't use her. So would it be awkward if her rookie neighbor made a mess of things because of her inexperience? Would it be awkward if she because of her inexperience and lack of negotiation skills cost them thousands of dollars? Would it be awkward if she forgot to respond in time and missed a critical deadline?

I was pretty frustrated with it all. They used the neighbor because the wife insisted, and, yes, it was a disaster. The husband called me after and shared how deeply he regretted not using me for the sale of their home. Is it too late to say, "I told you so?" I'm not minimizing relationships. A big part of this problem is that there are just *so* many real-estate agents. Virtually everyone knows several, and they may include family members, coworkers, or neighbors. I write about my frustration with the flood of agents in other parts of this book, so I won't spend too much time on it here, but the bottom line is the governing powers as well as brokerages make money off each agent; thus the more agents, the more profit. Combine this with the next to no barrier to entry, or minimum production standards, and shazam! You end up with a glut of real estate agents.

There is virtually no other industry with such dynamics. Most people don't know seven carpenters or five chiropractors or four private math tutors, but just about everyone knows several agents. This flood creates relational tensions everywhere and for all involved. If your kid sister got her license, she would be highly offended if you didn't use her or recommend her. As would your coworker who is dabbling in real estate as a side hustle, as would your neighbor whom you've known for years, as would the four agents at your church. Because there is a flood of agents in virtually every community in America, many agents then claim relational rights as if relationships are linear, exclusive and isolated. Many think, "Well, I've known Bob for eight years, so of course he's going to use me as his agent." The problem is that this agent is thinking in a linear fashion. He doesn't realize that good 'ole Bob may know ten different agents.

It's a conundrum, and there are no easy solutions to this relational puzzle. Somebody will invariably get their knickers in a twist because you didn't use them. It's just how it goes. The ones who are your true friends will remain so even after you sell your home. There are many agents who are a bit disingenuous and feign friendship for the sole purpose of getting your business. They smile a lot, invite you to parties, and are always glad-handing at events. They are the consummate networkers and use every angle to promote themselves. While on its face there is nothing wrong with self promotion, I chafe, as do most thinking people, at the idea of having phony relationships just for personal gain.

The interview

Yes, I said the word "interview." Who interviews people? Those in charge do. Bosses do. HR directors do. Employers do. Remember, you are the boss, and you are the one making the final decision. And yes, you are hiring someone just as if you were a manager of a local store looking to add staff to your company. You wouldn't hire the first person who walked through your door. You wouldn't hire someone whose name you saw on a park bench. You wouldn't hire the niece of a buddy of yours just because he said she was sweet. You would want to hire the best candidate only *after* interviewing several people. You would want to interview several people, so you could prove to yourself which one was the best. It is essential that you interview at least three agents when preparing to sell your home. This will not only give you an opportunity to have a selection to choose from, but it will also give you an idea of what's out there in the world of innovative marketing and novel usage of technology. Unless you have a go-to person whom you trust and has exhibited competency in the past, you will most likely be dealing with people you don't know really well, if at all.

Even if you know someone personally, you may not know them in the context of real estate or business. That's where the "neighbor" or "friend" issue develops. People assume that just because someone lives two doors down that they must be competent. People assume because their kids go to school together, the agent must be incredible. People assume because they're in the same book-reading club, they must be terrific in real estate. Those assumptions are the foundation of much heartache. I have heard people say they will never do business with a friend or family member again because of a bad experience. I think such processing and conclusions are narrow in scope. There is nothing inherently wrong with using friends or family. As a matter of fact, I am of the opinion that is exactly the first place you should look. Who would you want working for you? Someone you love, trust, and know well or a complete stranger?

The issue arises when we assume because Joe is our cousin and he's a great guy that it translates into Joe being a great real estate agent. That is not a logical formula or equation. Joe may be a great guy in some areas, but Joe might be a complete disaster in real estate because he has no business skills, doesn't understand marketing, he barely knows how to use a computer, and he is horrible at remembering details. Does that sound like someone you want to hire to handle the most expensive investment of your life? Friends and family are fine with one huge exception: they must have exhibited a high level of professionalism, success, and competency in their craft regardless of what it is. I don't care if you're hiring your nephew to hang cabinets, watch your cat, or sell your home. Make sure they are on the ball!

Interview questions

Have you ever interviewed for a job? They ask a lot of questions, don't they? The same is true when you are looking for a real estate agent. For some people you can tell if they're sharp just by looking at them. For others you have to ask a lot of questions to determine whether that person is the right agent for you. When the agent arrives at your home, pay attention to promptness, professionalism, appearance, and communication. Try to get a sense for their attitude and aptitude. Try to get a feel for the kind of person they are. Some of this is objective observation, but some may be intuitive and subjective. Listen to your gut. If something feels off, don't ignore it. Also pay attention to your BS meter if the accolades and flattery gets out of hand. Plenty of agents think they can hook sellers simply by worshiping your home and your amazing decorating ability. There are many sales techniques out there that teach an agent to complement you in order to build rapport. By doing so they falsely believe they can earn your business. I'm not saying agents can't give you a compliment. Just pay attention if they are offering a sincere compliment or if they are lavishing you with accolades. You'll know the difference. You'll feel the difference.

At some point, usually after the introduction and home tour, you will sit and get down to business. This is the perfect time to bust out your yellow pad and ask your predetermined questions. Have your questions written down ahead of time, and write down their responses. Remember, this is an interview. Take notes. Don't rely on your memory. Don't let it feel weird. This is a huge decision you are about to make, and you need all the information you can get. When you interview for a potential hire of a real estate agent, there are many questions that need to be asked. These wisely selected questions will reveal things about the agent and give you a feeling for how they conduct their business and whether that lines up with your goals and expectations. No one question will give you the complete picture, but when you combine powerful questions together in one interview, the picture becomes quite clear. The answers to these kinds of questions along with your personal observation should give you clear direction. Below is a list of twelve important questions to ask any agent before getting involved with them:

1. How long have you been a real estate agent?
You want to determine their longevity in the business. If they are a rookie, you may want to pass. Longevity isn't everything. Sometimes people who have been in the same industry for a long time are stale and crusty.

Sometimes they do things the old way and haven't updated themselves, their technology, or their techniques in decades. Beyond that some people do manage to hang around for years and then brag about how "I've been doing this for twenty-seven years" as if that means everything. Maybe they've been perfectly mediocre for twenty-seven years. Longevity isn't everything, but you do want to get a feel for the length of time the agent has practiced.

2. Why did you get into real estate?

This is a great question to ask. When motives are uncovered you really get a strong feel for the kind of person you are dealing with. "I got out of the Army and was bored" is different from "I grew up in a construction family and have loved being around houses since I was a child. I loved building them, and for the last eight years, I love selling them."

"I needed a little extra side money" is a far cry from "I love to negotiate and get the best deal for my clients. It energizes me."

"My neighbor was an agent and made a lot of money" is not near as powerful as, "When I was a child, my father left us and we were homeless for a while. I remember being in shelters, and I hated how that felt. I wanted to make sure I could be part of putting a roof over as many heads as possible."

You want to know why people do what they do. You want to understand what drives them.

3. Do you have another job or is real estate your full-time profession?

Again, it's not the end of the world if they have another job or do real estate part-time, but eventually it does come down to commitment. You want to determine whether the agent is "all in" or not. Are they a hobbyist or a dabbler or is this their main bread and butter? Do they do this on the side or are they transitioning to full-time? Beyond commitment there is the practical side to it. You want to know what expectations you should have. For example, if they have another job as their main gig, they may not be able to answer questions, negotiate, or respond to an offer from 9:00 a.m. to 5:00 p.m. You may lose a great offer if your agent doesn't communicate quickly.

4. How many transactions do you do a year, and how many have you done this year?

This is when things really get down to the nitty-gritty. This separates the con artist, the faker, the pretender, the dabbler, the wanna-be, and the poser from the pros. If they hesitate consider that the next words coming out of their mouth will be a lie. Every football player knows exactly how many touchdowns they've scored, and every real estate agent knows exactly how many deals they've done. If they pause and utter some nonsense like, "Well, I focus on quality over quantity," show them the door. Successful people are busy and productive people. They are getting things done. Successful, experienced, and highly sought after agents are busy and do a high volume of transactions. You don't have to get the agent with the most transactions in town, but you do want someone with significant volume. The average real estate agent in the United States does four deals a year. Ideally you want someone who does at least three or four times that, if not more. Follow up with their broker to confirm their volume.

5. What awards have you won or designations have you achieved?

When you see "Hall of Fame" or "Chairman's Club" or "Diamond Agent," ask about what that means. Achievements and the corresponding recognition for those achievements are important in life. It says a lot about the agent. It makes a big difference if the person you are dealing with is a top producer or a low quality agent who has never made an impact. Awards and designations are the objective proof that they are standing out in the crowd. This is not to be confused with designations of academic achievement. In real estate there are endless amounts of initials that can go after the agent's last name. All they mean is that they have successfully taken and completed a class or course on a certain topic. While commendable this is not the same as receiving a local, regional, or national award. Don't let some agent get you excited because they took a class. You want to know if they've actually sold something.

6. Do you have a team that supports you?

Like other questions this isn't a really big deal, but it does help paint the picture. Top producers and high volume agents often have a team that works with them. Having said that, there are plenty of really great agents who work alone. If they have a team, oftentimes the agents delegate various tasks to the other team players, and you may or may not deal all the time with the actual agent. If they don't offer, ask for clarification of roles so that you can have realistic expectations and know who to talk to when the time comes. No one likes to feel like they've been handed off to somebody else after they've bonded with the agent. However, if the agent tells you ahead of time, you can calibrate your understanding and know that you are dealing with a high-level outfit. If there is a team around the agent, this is usually a general indication they have high volume and solid business sense. I am not talking about a lazy agent who has a team so they don't have to work hard while others do the heavy lifting. There is a firm difference.

7. What is your marketing plan?

This is a big one. When you are interviewing agents, ask them for their marketing plan. Good agents will be prepared with a written plan that is current, efficient, effective, targeted, proven, and doable. Weak agents will hem and haw and tell you they're going to put a sign out front and do an open house. And don't let someone tell you they're amazing at marketing just because they have a park bench with their smiling face on it. Make sure you are dealing with a professional who knows how to specifically market your property to ensure the maximum amount of potential buyers have opportunity to encounter your home.

8. What is your process for taking pictures and making a flyer?

I have said it in other places in this book, but it is important to have professional flyers on high quality paper out at the street. The flyers must be two-sided, in color and have all the pertinent information including price, as well as important pictures. I say important because some people take a picture of a regular bathroom and think that's marketing. No offense to anyone but I think we all know modern homes have bathrooms. No one is going to jump out of their socks because you have a toilet, a sink and a mirror. Now, if your bathroom is amazingly upgraded, then it might be picture worthy, otherwise use the space on the flyer to feature areas in your house that are really noteworthy. Pictures should highlight things like upgraded kitchen, swimming pool, views, game room, fitness area, large deck, home theater and any other area that really stands out. The pictures will not only go on the flyer, but they will go on the MLS as well. The pictures on the MLS are the primary way potential buyers on the Internet gain an impression of your home. They must be high quality pictures of important aspects of your home. Many cell phones have great cameras, and for some situations, a cell phone picture may suffice, but in other situations, it may be totally inappropriate. It's best that the agent provides a professional photographer.

As you have probably gathered by now, I am a huge fan of being up front and honest. I don't believe anyone is served by being lied to or by being snookered. No one likes to deal with exaggerated claims. No one likes to feel like a victim of a bait and switch scheme. Unscrupulous agents will take the best pictures while omitting potential negative aspects of a home. This is understandable to a degree. While you want to present your home in the best light possible, you don't want to hide things or appear deceptive. That's just never a good policy. I have seen pictures of backyards taken at a low angle so as not to reveal the power lines directly behind the home. I have seen this same technique used to conceal a shopping mall or neighbor's house on a flag lot. Why in the world people do this is beyond me. It's like gee whiz let's think about this a minute. Do they honestly think being duped into coming out to look at a house will work? Do they think people will submit an offer when they become infuriated by viewing what was hidden in the pictures? You think that makes any sense at all? Why intentionally frustrate potential buyers, mislead them, and waste their time? I just don't get it. Take honest pictures and have accurate marketing. Though pictures are the responsibility of the agent, you as the seller have final say on what pictures are used. Make sure the agent understands that all pictures need to be approved by you. Remember, you're the boss.

9. What is inventory like? What is the average DOM? What trends are you seeing?

These questions are designed to gain insight as to the agent's general understanding of the local markets. If you know the industry jargon, they are less likely to fib. Inventory has to do with how many homes are currently on the market. Currently in our area the inventory is about forty-five days. This means that if no more homes come on the market, it would take about forty-five days for everything available to be sold. Normally our inventory is four to five months. If inventory is low, that signals that it's probably a seller's market. Basic economic indicators of supply and demand enter into this equation. If supply is low but demand is high, prices will be higher and thus to the benefit of the seller. In such markets a home will generally sell quicker and for more money.

DOM is days on market. If the average DOM is one week, clearly you have a smoking-hot market. It's important to ask how long the average home stays on the market in your area, so you can have a rough gauge on when you need to move out and plan accordingly. Remember you're always in control. Don't let a desperate agent or a demanding buyer push you into a time frame you are uncomfortable with. The agent may say, "You can always put your stuff in storage and live in a hotel until you find your new home." Really? And are they going to help you put your "stuff" in storage and pay for the storage and hotel costs? Doubt it.

You also want to be aware of DOM because if your home remains listed for significantly longer than the average, that may signal there's a problem. Your price may be too high, or there may be something about your home or neighborhood that potential buyers are finding unattractive or even repellent. A good agent will be on top of this for you and be fully aware of DOM as well as feedback from other agents.

10. Will you be at our home during showings?

This is my favorite question. Prepare to hear gasps and see mouths hanging wide open. Real estate is the only business I know of where the one selling the product isn't present. It's kind of weird when you think of it. I mean really try to get your head wrapped around that idea. It's so odd to me.

If you sell cars, you are present.

If you sell software to corporations, you are present.

If you sell apples from an orchard, you are present.

If you are a kid selling lemonade in front of your house, you are present.

Imagine you are the selling agent. You have listed a home for sale on the local MLS, done all the marketing, placed a sign in the front yard, and are ready for buyers to see the home, but you are not there to communicate with prospective buyers and their agents. It's sort of nuts. One of the things that people love about the high level of service I provide is that I commit to being present at all showings if at all possible. Some sellers insist that it's not necessary, and I honor their request, but for the most part, I am present. I find that it is a competitive advantage for me and reveals that I really am working hard to get the home sold. In contrast to the abundance of lazy agents out there, the fact that I am willing to be present at showings really speaks loudly.

In Colorado most listing agents have buyer's agents call their office or a centralized call center to schedule a showing. They call the office or call center, then those people call the homeowner, and then they call the buyer's agent back and tell them if it's OK to show or not. It can be a bit cumbersome to show multiple properties. Some call centers have a list of available openings which is a bit better but I still find the process inconvenient. Let's say you have ten houses to look at. You, as the buyer's agent, have to call several different offices or call centers and then wait to hear back from some of them. That could take a long time. Meanwhile your buyers are waiting. In Southern California most agents state in the MLS to call the homeowner directly, which is more efficient than Colorado. Sometimes there will be a note like "Give at least an hour notice." Every area is different.

I simply write in the MLS, "Contact listing agent for showing." I am in frequent communication with my clients and know their work schedule. With their blessing I tell prospects to just go direct and that I'll meet them there. Otherwise I contact my clients and let them know. Some might say, "Gee, that's a lot of work." Well, yes, for those who think real estate is just sticking a sign in the ground and waiting for a paycheck, it might appear like a lot of work, but that's how you serve people at a high level.

Another weird thing most agents do is keep sellers and buyers apart. I have no idea who thought this was a good idea. It's just another weird thing agents do just because it's always been done that way. If you were to look at a used car that was for sale, the owner would be there to answer any questions you might have. When people bring a buyer to my listings, I ask my sellers to stay home if at all possible, so they can meet the prospective buyers and answer any questions that pop up. What are we so scared of? If you're selling your home, you may have several showings during the week. Can you imagine having to round up the kids and tear out of your house every time the phone rings? Then what do you do go drive around in circles for a couple of hours? The whole things just seems nuts to me.

11. What is your communication method to inform us of progress or problems?

You may receive blank stares on this one, but it's important. If there are no clear words that flow out from their mouth after this question, you should know you can expect to be in the dark once you sign the paperwork. Many agents have a disease, which I call "sign and split." In other words, the minute you sign the contract they disappear. I write about this in the chapter titled Lame Agents. This kind is called the Vanishing Agent! As a seller it is very frustrating to not know what's going on. Really there's no excuse for it. We all have cell phones and can FaceTime, call, e-mail, or text. There is absolutely no excuse for not being in regular communication with clients. A great agent will give regular updates in addition to responding promptly to your questions. Even if there has only been one showing that day, I communicate with my sellers. I also give them any feedback from the prospective buyers. People want to know what's going on. They also want to know if there are any issues or problems developing. They don't want to be blindsided or left out of the loop.

When selling your home, you want your agent to give you a progress report. Good agents communicate with their clients and inform them as to how things are progressing. Weak agents disappear until there's an offer. Be sure to have an agent who is a strong communicator, one who lets you know when timelines and benchmarks are approaching, lets you know how many showings there have been, tells you about buyer feedback, and keeps you informed. It's no fun being in the dark and wondering what's going on. Regarding method, personally I prefer to speak in person or over the phone. Texting and e-mail may be appropriate for small details but there is always room for misunderstanding. I want to make sure all communication is clearly understood, timely, and informative.

12. What else can you tell us about yourself that makes you stand out from the crowd?

Here's where you want to become more conversational and perhaps let them share not only certain aspects about their business methodology but also some personal information. You want to be comfortable with this person as they will be a significant part of your life for the next stretch of time. What you are wanting to determine is a high level of competency and chemistry. In every industry there are people who are highly competent, but you might have low if any chemistry. You would never want to get to know them on a personal level, and you certainly would never invite them to dinner. The lack of chemistry may even become a point of tension. On the other hand, there are people with whom you have great chemistry, but you couldn't trust them to take out your trash or feed your dog. The goal here is to find someone who exhibits a high level of excellence and competency with whom you also have great affinity and respect for.

Presentation and the listing price

At some point in your time together the agent will give a formal presentation. I would recommend you allow them to do this after your questions.
They may give you a presentation on a laptop or just verbally with printed
items. This is when they will cover statistics, marketing, and any other
pertinent information. They will present the contract and terms. The price
they recommend will be a key part of their proposal. The price of your
home will be an important aspect towards selecting an agent. If you understand economics and the real estate industry, you will come to learn
that the price an agent recommends will tell you almost everything you
need to know about that agent.

Price is largely established through viewing comparables or what
is casually called comps. The agent will have this as part of their presentation. This is when you view homes that have recently sold that are
similar in size and amenities. Accurate comps only use homes that have
sold. The reason for this is because we don't care about what homes
are currently active on the market because that means nothing. People
could ask pie in the sky for a home and have to lower their price several
times before it sells so current and active listing prices are not accurate indicators. Only a dishonest, inexperienced, or poorly trained agent
would ever use active listings in their comps. You should be aware of
what current listings are out there in your area, because it's important
to know what you're competing against, but it cannot be included in the
comps. You can't use pending sales because you have no idea what the
final price is, if any concessions were given, or what the terms are. The
only accurate measurement is homes that have recently sold. I usually
go back no more than six months. You can use broader parameters
but because of market fluctuations you generally won't get an accurate
snapshot for current use.

There are three levels you can price your home at: below market, at
market, and above market. This is so simple it's easy to miss, and frankly
is the cause of much wasted time and frustration. If the property is in
disrepair or rough shape, it will need to be priced below market, which

means it will be offered at a discount. Greedy or delusional sellers will want top dollar for their home even if the quality of the home is poor. I don't know why people become irrational on this topic. No one would pay top dollar for an old used clunker of a car with dents and peeling paint but for some reason when it comes to their home some sellers just want the moon. It's irrational and it's ridiculous. Oh, sure, in some crazy hot market you can get all the money for an old tired house but I don't establish policy on such anomalies.

Second, you can price the home at market which means you are right on the bubble. In other words, when you use a carpenters level to determine if something is perfectly flat the air bubble will rest in-between the lines. This is the fair price that is validated by other homes that have recently sold. If similar three bedroom homes in the neighborhood have sold for $300,000 then a fair price for your home would be around $300,000. If your home has significant and verifiable improvements or upgrades, then you could ask for more. For example, if your home has an in-ground pool and amazing views, that would drive the price up if the other similar homes had neither. Conversely, if your home has never been updated but the other homes have all been remodeled and have kitchens with granite counters, new cabinets, recessed lighting and stainless steel appliances, you might have to offer your home for less.

Third, you can offer your home for above market. This is the other arena for irrational sellers. I shake my head in disbelief when sellers say, "Well, let's just put it at $390,000 and see what happens." Um, I'll tell you what's going to happen. Your home will sit on the market forever and get stale because no agent will show your home because your price is unfounded and ridiculous. This isn't a mystery. To such sellers, I ask if they are in the habit of overpaying for things they buy. In other words, if a pair of jeans costs $50.00, do they go out of their way to pay $75? If a burger costs $8.00, do they enjoy paying $13.00 for the exact same burger? The logical answer is clearly "no" yet when it comes to people's homes they kind of lose their minds a little and become totally illogical. Buyers don't overpay for anything, especially high ticket items like houses.

So the bottom line is if your home is weary or you're in a hurry to move, then price it below market. If you want to sit around forever and waste lots of time then price it above market. If your intention is to sell your home and get on with your life, then price it at market, taking into consideration any existing or lacking upgrades or amenities. It's not really that complicated. Beyond knowing all that, the reason you must understand pricing is because it will tell you a lot about the agent you are speaking with. If your home is perfectly nice and should be priced at market, you should be suspicious if the agent wants to price it below market. The only reason they would recommend this is because they are desperate and want a quick sale so they can get paid. If the agent wants to list your home above market you are dealing with an unscrupulous person. The reason I say that is because no thinking agent worth their salt would do that. So then why would an agent go along with that game plan? The reason is that once they get you under contract and the home sits for weeks with no offer, they know they can come back and browbeat you into a price reduction. They know full well your home will never sell for $390,000 when every other similar home sold for around $300,000, but they don't care, because they know eventually you will have to lower your price into a realistic realm and out of fairy-land. This is the oldest trick in the book and frankly it disgusts me. Such agents are sneaky and deceptive. They also lack spine in that they don't tell their sellers the truth about how homes are priced and sold. So, if you are the kind of irrational seller that will hire the agent that proposes the highest list price for your home, you both deserve each other. If on the other hand you are a realistic and sane seller who wants a truthful agent that doesn't play games you may want to talk to a guy like me.

Finishing the interview

After your questions are answered, you may ask the agent if they have any questions. Keep in mind although you may be done asking questions, the interview is still going on. This is also a great way to test their level of professionalism, awareness, and engagement. A good agent will always have questions. The kind of questions they ask will give you a glimpse into their thought processes. Be aware of closing techniques and concessions towards the end of your time together. If they feel unsure or insecure, the freebies may start flowing. Don't fall for it. If that is the level of their negotiation skill, they will do the same behind your back with the buyer's agent when an offer comes. While commission is negotiable, if they are the first ones to surrender their income in order to gain your signature, you can rest assured they will most likely sell you down the river when it comes time for negotiating. You want a strong agent that respects themselves and respects their clients.

I've seen it over and over. It's almost like a bribe. Weak agents who can't stand up for their own income don't suddenly become strong agents when the offers come in. If an agent can't fight for his or her own bread and butter, don't expect the agent to fight for yours. On the other hand, avoid the hard closers. Old-school manipulative and pushy sales techniques are off-putting. Such techniques are rooted in the Great Depression when sales people had to push people into a sale or the desperate guy didn't eat that day! Many agents are trained to "close" the deal on the spot instead of earning that privilege. If the agent becomes pushy toward the end of the appointment, and tries to "handle" you, kiss them good-bye. You don't need that kind of drama. People are smart and don't need to be handled, forced, pushed, or manipulated. Beyond that you never want to work with a desperate person.

General condition and preparing for listing

Once you have selected a strong agent you feel comfortable with, it's time to focus on your home. There are two fundamental things to consider when preparing your home for sale: First is the general condition of your home. Second is fixing things before the inspection. It should be a given, but your home must be in great condition in order to have great appeal and receive a great offer. It is delusional or illogically greedy to believe that you can get a first class offer with a coach class home. Having said that, I am continually surprised by the shortsightedness, greed, and illogical mind-set of some people where they feel they are entitled to receive top dollar for a tired looking home.

The exterior—curb appeal

This is the single most important aspect of the whole selling process. If you can't entice people to pull into your driveway, you have already lost. The home should sparkle. Windows should be cleaned inside and out, exterior paint or stain should be crisp, and your lawn and landscaping should make a botanist jealous. I can't emphasize this enough. It amazes me how many people, good people, smart people put their home on the market with a yard that looks subpar. Lawn and landscaping is one of the only places where it's proven you get more bang for your buck. Forty dollars in fertilizer and a watered lawn that's cut, trimmed, and edged could be the difference between getting a full price offer or being ignored.

Lots of people will see the sign in the front yard. Your home will already be getting significant attention. New things and new events draw interest. Why not capitalize on that emotional momentum with a curb appeal that screams perfection and pride of ownership? Little things stand out and communicate whether you are a slacker of a homeowner or one who is alert and capable. Pay attention to weeds in the cracks of your driveway and sidewalk. Some might think I'm obsessive, but I walk around with a weed-killer spray every weekend at my home. It's part of my routine. The lawn gets cut, and then I walk around on a search and destroy mission. I not only spray the weeds in the cracks of my driveway and sidewalk, but I spray the weeds in the street in front of my house. "But that's not even your property," some may retort. Correct, but it is in front of my property, and I don't want anything in front of my property to cast shade on the quality and appearance of my home. And here's the thing: How much effort does it really take? How much time? Less time than it takes to drink a cup of coffee, and yet I see endless homes with forests of weeds growing in their driveway, sidewalks and in the street. It just doesn't take that much effort or awareness to tidy things up.

The interior—expectations

Once people go through your front door, their initial impression will be a lasting one. This in turn will calibrate their expectations. If upon entrance potential buyers shrug their shoulders, roll their eyes, or smirk and shake their head, you're probably dead in the water. That meant that regardless of how well the outside looked, the initial impression upon entering was bad, and their expectations were crushed. When buyers see an amazing yard, they assume the inside will match. When it doesn't, their enthusiasm wanes. Curb appeal just gets them in the door. Then you have to deliver a quality experience on the inside.

Many companies don't look at their business through the eyes of the end user or customer. Many sellers don't look at their home through the eyes of a potential buyer. I am amazed, and I know I say that a lot, at the garbage out there that some sellers call home. They are so proud when they frankly should be embarrassed. Some people have this weird moral sense of self-righteousness and have delusional opinions about their home. Then when the issues are brought up, they respond with some awkward indignation as if you insulted their grandmother. We recently put an offer on a home that the agent as well as the sellers just glowed about. The home was partially updated, and they had hideous and outdated popcorn ceilings throughout the house that screamed decades of avoidance. Listen, nobody likes to deal with messes, and few things create more of a mess than removing popcorn ceilings, or acoustic ceilings as they are officially called. You have to cover everything in plastic, and the ceiling has to be moistened and scraped. A coat of drywall mud usually has to be applied, especially in places where damage occurred during scraping. Then the ceiling has to be sanded and perhaps have additional coats and more sanding, after which it has to be textured, primed and painted. It's an incredibly laborious, time consuming, and messy job. While you're scraping, the stuff falls on your head and all over the floor, and the dust from sanding also gets everywhere. So yes, I understand why people would want to kick that can down the road. Just don't manufacture emotional outrage when it's brought to your attention by a potential buyer, like my clients did on this deal I'm writing about.

You can't get top dollar for an outdated home unless the market is mercilessly slanted in the sellers favor. I remember sixty-year old homes in Burbank that had never been updated fetching ridiculous amounts during the real estate boom in the early 2000s. That's not normal, and yes, that balloon popped. Even if this particular home had everything upgraded but they skipped the ceilings, it's going to be an issue. So here's the straight fact: either a home is upgraded or it's not. Plain and simple. The sellers partially remodeled the master bath and made some upgrades in the kitchen. That is not an upgraded home. That is a partially upgraded home. Some sellers feel that because they painted their kitchen cabinets it entitles them to become millionaires. I will just never understand it. My clients still wanted the house, because it is a great home, with a great floor plan, in a great location, and inventory was very low. As a matter of fact, it was the only one on the market that had the requirements my buyers needed.

Agents and sellers alike fall into the trap of being defensive and protectionist and frankly delusional about such matters. They want to tell you all about the new tile in the master bathroom and the new quartz counters in the kitchen but avoid telling you how they screwed up and did a poor job painting the kitchen cabinets, the fact that the backyard is a disaster, and that there are four different kinds of carpet in the home. I looked at a million-dollar property the other day. It was a small two bedroom home on twelve acres close to town. The kitchen was recently remodeled but not done well. The layout was tortured at best, and the quality was lacking. Regardless, they were very proud of this renovation. As a former contractor, I can spot not only poor or high quality but also if the people had any experience in renovating properties. People who are skilled upgrade a home with current trends in mind. They also upgrade the whole home, not just a part of the kitchen. Sellers who are fumbling through the renovation process, just so they can charge more for their home are easy to spot. They're easy to spot because literally nothing else in the home is upgraded. Such sellers watch a TV show or get schmoozed by some agent or contractor who informs them that an upgraded kitchen will bring in more dollars. While that may be true, it has to be done right, and the correlating asking price has to be fair and realistic.

The problem is when they spend $15,000 on a partial kitchen remodel but think they can get an extra $150,000 for the property, which was pretty much the case on this house. Moreover if you renovate the kitchen, then the rest of the home should be upgraded as well, so everything is congruent. Otherwise it's just putting lipstick on a pig. No offense to pigs. It's like putting new rims and tires on a rusty old clunker and trying to sell it for an absurd price. Some people are either naïve or delusional. That home shouldn't have been on the market for anything over $700,000. While I appreciate horse property close to town, the home just did not support the asking price. They also advertised the home as multifamily and that there were two homes on the property. Well, there was the small outdated two bedroom home with the weird kitchen, and the other "home" was a two-car garage with stairs that went up to a converted open loft. Not exactly a second home. I get so tired of weak agents and irrational sellers trying to make something sound as if it is one thing when in reality it doesn't even come close.

I think it's human nature to magnify the positives and avoid the negatives. It's just that it comes across as disingenuous, even deceptive. Just be truthful and straightforward. I know I am repeating myself, but honestly there's so much nonsense out there I don't know what else to say but to say the same thing over and over again until people get it. Is your home updated? If you haven't done a dog-gone thing to the home since you bought it in 1967, it's not going to go for top dollar. The problem is people hear stories how twelve hundred square foot shoebox pieces of garbage built in the early 1960s are selling for half a million dollars in some parts of the country, and then they kind of get nutty. Well, yes, in some crazy hot markets and in some highly desirable cities, even old, outdated, beatdown houses will fetch crazy numbers. Oftentimes the dirt is actually more valuable than the old house. It's not uncommon to drive by a couple of weeks after closing and see that the entire home has been bulldozed to make room for a new larger home. It's not uncommon in some unregulated places with large lots to see those old homes get plowed and see apartment buildings or condos built in their place. That's not normal and that's not Everytown USA! For most people in most places, older homes need to have been remodeled and well maintained in order to garner a solid offer. Newer homes should look even better.

A lot of sellers confuse updated with upgraded. One just means you decided to live in the current decade, while the other is installation of high-end or luxury items. You get "upgraded" to first class on a flight. In other words an upgrade is usually the best or highest level of quality or luxury. A total kitchen remodel with granite counters, trendy pecan cabinets, recessed lighting, top of the line stainless steel appliances, and a farm sink with gooseneck faucet along with new travertine flooring can clearly be advertised as "upgraded kitchen." Just because you pulled the rectangular fluorescent light out of your 1972 kitchen and had recessed canned lighting installed doesn't mean you can market your kitchen as upgraded. It's partially updated. It means you have joined the current decade at least in your kitchen lighting, but it doesn't mean you have a first class kitchen. I could write a book on just this topic with all the nonsense I've seen out there!

As a seller prepare to give realistic concessions if your home is not updated or is in poor condition. As I've said before, in all but the hottest markets where the sellers can bully buyers into buying just about anything, most sellers need to be realistic. Again, as I've said over and over again, just be up front with people. They will appreciate it. "This home has never been updated since it was built in 1967. Therefore, the price is at $260,000, which is $40,000 below comps." Wouldn't that be laughably refreshing to read? Truth and honesty always feels good. Nobody likes to be hustled, and nobody likes to feel like they are victims of a bait and switch game. For sure nobody likes to be lied to. I know some agents who will say stupid things like, "You will love this quant home in a historic neighborhood. Upon entrance to this home, you will notice the cozy living room with original wood floors..." Garbage! It's all fluff. You have to un-derstand agents speak in code. "Historic" is often code for old as dirt. "Cozy" means it's cramped and small. "Original" means nothing has been done to the house since the day it was built. Just be honest with people.

Décor, furniture, and interior design

Some people, God bless them, have absolutely no sense of style. I've seen people try to sell their home for top dollar when even a cursory overview of the home would make anyone pause and clear their throat. I've taken buyers into homes painted all white, no pictures on the walls, and poorly laid-out furniture with some rooms like the formal living room completely empty! The weird thing is that the home itself might be fine, but most people can't look past random empty spaces, poor décor, and a home that looks like a dental office. It just feels weird, and people don't like to buy homes when they feel weird. A vacant home is better than a sparse home. On the other hand, sometimes it's necessary to pay for staging, which can really give a home more appeal especially if you're not good at creating a pleasant ambiance. Other homes that don't show well are cheap ones. I'm not talking about less expensive homes; I'm talking about cheap homes owned by cheap people. Houses that have zero up-grades. My favorite trick is when cheap people buy new home construc-tion with absolutely the bottom of the barrel, builder-basic materials but then want the upgraded top of the line price.

In new developments many of the homes get moved into around the same time. Generally speaking, in most new neighborhoods, there are several models with varying price points. Even when they are the exact same floor plan, they may have different prices based on a lot premi-um, location, and upgrades. We spent almost $100,000 in upgrades on one new home we purchased. There were other people in that neighbor-hood who bought the same model but didn't pay for a single upgrade. Everything was white, the floors were cheap tile, thin carpet and linoleum, the fixtures and doorknobs were all chrome, and the appliances were entry level. Yet I remember several years later, those same people looking at the comps and demanding they get a similar price as one that sold that was their same model but with significant upgrades and on the view side of the development. Again, delusional. Well, with a splash of ignorance and greed maybe but delusional nonetheless! You can't get top price for a home that has all the bottom amenities. White paint, cheap doors, and trim, linoleum, cheap carpet with even cheaper padding, ugly fixtures, and builder grade tile or plastic tub inserts in the bathrooms along with Formica kitchen counters with the world's cheapest kitchen cabinets will never fetch top dollar.

"Yea, but the same house down the street got top dollar." Well, yea, the same model but not the same house. While you're the cheap-o seller who hasn't invested a dime in your home, that other house has over $100,000 in tangible upgrades. It's not the same. It's just not reality. It has to be "apples to apples" in order to have a similar price. A nice idea is to create card stock placards that you can fold and place throughout the home. I provide this service for my clients. It doesn't take that much effort, but it sure makes a big impact. You have to understand buyers see many homes, and after a while, it all blurs together. Anything you can do to make your home stand out is to your benefit. They will remember the house with all the little signs inside. You can use the placards to point out upgrades or nice improvements that may not be readily visible. For example, maybe you have upgraded your cabinets to have pull out shelving. Buyers wouldn't notice that unless you put one on your pantry cabinet stating "Look inside! Pull out shelving!" If you had a large painting that fit perfectly on a wall, you could put a note on it stating "Magnificent painting stays with home." The more information you give potential buyers, the better. Just make sure you make it out of card stock and not regular copy paper. That way the little signs will stand up straight once you fold them over.

Clutter and organization

I don't understand some people. They hoard as if they're expecting a global shortage of some kind. These types of people just have too much of everything. It's just stuff. Stuff everywhere. Mail, newspapers, books, and magazines piled up on the counters, too much furniture, and general clutter everywhere. Homes don't show well when it looks like you're trying to cram 11,000 square feet of junk into a 2,300 square foot home. Before your home goes on the market, make sure your house is thinned out. Again, this is hard because most people who are disorganized or have a hoarding problem don't really see the issue or think they have a problem. Objective people from the outside may need to come in and help.

Even if you're not a hoarder, look at your home with a critical eye. Look at things through the eyes of a potential buyer. Do the things that are out on the counters need to be out? Does your living room need to have the video game consoles out on the floor? Could your home office be tightened up a bit? I can tell you my home office is usually a disaster. I have piles of books and paper on my desk and shelves. There are file boxes on the floor next to my desk, and there are Post-it Notes every-where. There's a difference between a working office and one that's just for show. If my home was to be on the market however, I would stash all that stuff and tidy up my space. If you leave your food processor, blender, coffee maker, toaster, and Ginsu knives all out on the kitchen counter, you may want to put half if not all of that stuff in the cabinets. If your cabinets are full, maybe the garage then. If your garage is full, then maybe think about renting a space at a storage facility until your home is sold. I'm to-tally not kidding here. It is worth it for some people to rent a garage, room, or closet at a storage facility than it is to show an overcrowded home. Sure it might cost you a couple of hundred bucks, but you'll probably make up for that in a quicker sale and for a better price.

You have to understand that when you list your home for sale, you are wanting it to be as attractive as possible. That should go without saying. That means that your home should not look the way it does when you are actively living there. Think about how most people act when they are expecting company. Things are put away, beds are made, stuff is hidden. That's kind of the vibe you want to be in while selling your home. My kid sister, whom I love dearly, has three coffee makers on her kitchen counter. She has an espresso machine, a Keurig, and a standard coffee maker with a pot. At first I was concerned but after explaining it to me it actually made sense. The espresso machine is for, well, espresso. The Keurig is for when they want a quick cup of coffee and the pot is for when they have company over. Makes perfect sense. However, if my sister was to sell her home, I would probably have her stash two of the three coffee makers while her home is on the market. Less is more. It's a fine line, though. It can't be so sparse that it doesn't look right, and it can't be so cluttered that it looks jammed. I like to advise people to consider a hotel room. That should be a good guide. Hotel rooms are tastefully appointed with just the right amount of furniture and art, with plenty of space to move around.

Then there is the garage. Garages for most people are notorious for being clutter magnets, and frankly most people aren't good at organizing their garage. That space just kind of turns into a catch-all. Some people's cars have never even seen the inside of a garage for that matter! Part of the problem is that modern garages are not designed for real life. Garages are notoriously too small and I think are generally designed for two Toyota Corollas! The other part of the problem is that people don't think of their garage in efficient terms. With proper shelving and various kinds of hooks and holders, the space can be very wisely utilized. Regardless, get all the junk out. Get rid of it, burn it, sell it, store it, give it away, or push it off a cliff. I don't care what you do with it, but clear the garage out.

Sometimes it takes an objective eye to help particularly if you're not good at this type of thing. A strong agent will give helpful direction and advice. However, weak agents are timid and scared to possibly offend their clients so they won't say a thing. They are more concerned with feelings than with getting the home sold. If you have the sad misfortune of having a lame agent who isn't much help on this topic, then enlist a trusted friend or family member who has a sharp home. Ask them how your house looks from their perspective. Better yet fire your weak agent, and get a pro in there to sell your home! Keep your feelings out of it, don't be defensive and don't make excuses. If your home is a cluttered mess, then get over it, be pragmatic, and go through every room and again especially the garage. There's no judgment here; just get it done! Beyond that obviously the home should be thoroughly cleaned and freshened up.

While we're talking about stuff, why do we tote around a refrigerator? Think about it. Are we really in love with our fridge? Technically, anything that isn't bolted down goes in the moving van, but if you really process it, does it make any sense to haul around a fridge? It's weird to me. Some parts of the country this is usually the case, and I never understood it. Usually appliances match. Same color and same brand. If you have stainless steel kitchen appliances by Whirlpool, why would you take the fridge and then have someone else bring in their almond color GE Fridge? There is no value in following that technical requirement so strictly. All that has to be done to remedy the situation is to state in the MLS and in the contract that the fridge stays with the home. For that matter are you really in love with your washer and dryer. It's such a pain to disconnect things and then cart them around. Just leave the stuff. It's just stuff after all.

Goodwill, garage sales, and Craigslist are all good options to get rid of stuff while you prepare to list your home for sale. For that matter you can sell anything you want with the house as well. Maybe I'm just a little too pragmatic, but my wife and I just don't get attached to stuff. We get attached to people, and, yes, our Persian cats and Golden-Doodle, but not stuff. "Oh, you like that desk? Two hundred dollars," and it's one less thing I have to move! "Oh, you love the Ginsu steak knives and the lava lamp in the living room, and the couches? And the TV? Perfect! One thousand dollars for everything!" I mean just get thin. Americans are so obsessed with their stuff and so many people are pack rats that they are literally drowning in stuff. Many people can't even fit two cars in their garage because they have so much junk. Purge! Moving is a great time to lighten your load. Remember, anything that isn't nailed down or connected to the house is considered personal property and goes with you. As such it is excluded from the purchase agreement unless otherwise noted. If you want it to stay, then say so in the MLS and in all marketing. "Salt-water aquarium, leather couches in great room, wall-mounted flat screen TV in living room, black light velvet posters in bedroom, and groovy bean-bag chair in great room—all for sale separate to contract for eighteen hundred dollars." Stuff can be sold separately as personal property through a bill of sale.

In addition stuff can be included in the sale price as an incentive. Stuff can be sold with the house at a higher price if the appraisal and financing will bear it, or in a slower market, things can be included in the regular price of the home as an incentive. I have bought and sold many homes this way. I had a newly divorced man who had a self-admitted horrible sense of taste for decoration and décor. We walked into a home, and he loved the furniture and decoration so much that he bought the home fully furnished right down to the artwork, silverware, pots and pans, patio set, and lawn mower. He literally just wanted to walk into his new home, hang up his clothes, and live. Another time I sold a home with a low-mileage Harley Davidson in the garage. You should have seen the flurry of activity around that property! It was like a parade of people coming and going. To date it was one of the most effective marketing campaigns I ever did. People just went crazy about the idea that they could get a home and a Harley in one fell swoop!

You're going to think I'm pulling your leg, but I sold a home with a Bichon Frise named Jojo. You know the ones, cute little white puff balls! A single man had it for years but was moving overseas and couldn't bring the dog with him. Instead of selling the dog or taking it to the pound, he thought the most gentle and humane thing to do was to have the dog remain in familiar surroundings. I listed the home with the dog included and found a family with a young daughter who was a perfect fit for the home and the dog! I sold a home where the owner said he would let the buyer drive his Lamborghini for a week after close. You think that might create some excitement? You bet! I sold a home with a one-year family pass to Disneyland. There is literally no limit to the creativity that can be used to promote a home. We are only limited by our imagination!

Odors

In preparation for selling your home, you must be aware of any peculiar, pungent, or significant odors. Your goal here is for your home to smell perfectly neutral or fresh, like open windows on a spring day. Beyond fresh, even a mild pleasant scent is good. A word of caution here: I say mild even though you might think vanilla, citrus, or cinnamon is a perfect scent for a home and have candles and air fresheners churning that stuff out. However, if people don't care for those scents, it may be a turn-off. Fresh and neutral is better. Babies and toddlers come with diapers and nurseries, all of which can carry, shall we say, a scent. Dogs can sometimes smell badly especially if the owners are not up to speed on washing their pet. Some people's cooking habits and preferences cause a strong food-based odor to linger in the home. I had great neighbors in Los Angles who cooked fish all the time. It was a main stay in their culture. They were awesome people, and their food was amazing, but it sure left a strong smell in their home.

I actually once took buyers to a home who, upon opening the door, turned and walked away because the smell of fish was so strong. You have to be aware of such things. In full disclosure we cook a lot of Mediterranean meals, which means garlic and onions are part of the deal. While sure adding flavor to any dish, the downside is that those two vegetables sure have a significant odor to them. In Bahrain most homes have a standard kitchen in the home and a "dirty kitchen" outside that is for cooking fish and other potentially smelly things. That's usually not an option here so be aware of your cooking preferences, and maybe make some adjustments during the selling period.

The vacant home
I always get the question on whether a vacant home should be shown as is or if it should be staged. Some people really have strong opinions on this matter. I do not. I have never staged an empty home, and they have all sold just fine. Other good agents I know swear by it and will easily spend $2,500 in staging vacant homes. Some people think appointed homes show better than empty ones. There's merit to that theory I suppose, but I happen to think people are able to walk through an empty home without any negative judgment. I personally find no problem viewing an empty home as I can imagine my own furniture going in without any distractions.

To counter some would say that not all people have a good imagination or are good at visualizing. I suppose that is true. Bottom line is it's kind of like what Henry Ford said, "If you think you can or you think you can't, you're right." In other words, if you think it's important, then it is, and if you don't think it's important then it isn't.

One thing for sure, though, is that if a home is vacant, it is incumbent upon the seller's agent to keep an eye on the property. It's just standard service a quality agent will provide. Some lazy agents love empty houses because they feel they don't have to do anything. Nothing could be farther from the truth. Strong agents will make sure there are no papers piling up in the driveway or flyers hanging on the front door. They will go there a couple of times a week and open up the windows for a while to freshen things up a bit. They will make sure the lawn and yard is maintained and if in a winter climate that the driveway and sidewalks are cleared. For my vacant listings, I like to visit the home every couple of days. Even then I had one listing that had a sprinkler malfunction and water was pouring out of the broken valve and into the yard. Thankfully an alert neighbor contacted me, and we fixed the problem. This brings up a valid point; communicate with neighbors and let them know that the home will be empty. I always knock on neighbors doors and give them my card. I ask them to contact me if they see anything odd or concerning.

I heard of one lazy agent who never checked in on his vacant listing. He received a shocking phone call from a buyer's agent who went to show the home only to see someone run out the back slider. Someone had broken in and set up shop in the home, complete with sleeping bag, food, and rubbish. Another vacant home I heard about had someone growing marijuana in the basement. Free electricity and water were abundant to this entrepreneur! Yes, in my opinion, all this is the agent's responsibility. It's part of the quality service a strong agent will provide for his or her clients that have moved out of their home.

Preparing for the eventual inspection
Once your home is on the market and you receive an offer, there will be a physical inspection. This is not a chance event but something you

can absolutely plan on. Why not get ahead of things and fix everything even before your home is listed? This is not some mysterious event linked to the Mayan calendar or a lunar eclipse out in the future sometime. The inspection will take place. The purpose of the inspection is to give the home a top to bottom look-over and make sure everything is operational and pleasing to the eye. Obviously the inferred purpose of the inspection is that if something is discovered, then it must be addressed. As the seller you're either going to have to get it fixed or give money to the buyers to address the issue. Of course you could tell the buyers to pound sand, but then you risk losing them along with their offer.

Any time something negative is discovered on your property during inspection, it weakens your hand. You lose your place of strength as a seller. You are placed in a weaker position to negotiate. Why do that to yourself? Why intentionally make yourself weaker and why add drama to the process? The only time this doesn't matter is in an "as is" or distressed home that is being sold below market value due to its poor condition. Another time it may not matter is in an extremely hot market where people will take your home, warts and all. In every other circumstance, any negative discovery will need to be addressed.

Listen, everybody who owns a home knows what's wrong with their house. Let's not play games here. You know which screens have tears in them. You know which faucet leaks. You know that the AC doesn't work all the time. Granted, some things may pop up during the inspection that you had no knowledge of but that is the exception. I had buyers who put in an offer on a home, and things were discovered during the inspection. Not huge things but annoying little things that the seller should have fixed if the seller was properly coached by a strong agent. The pedestal sink on the main level powder room wobbled two inches right to left. Clearly it wasn't anchored properly. It was glaringly obvious. So was the fact that the ceiling fan in the children's bedroom was so out of balance and so violently jerked around when turned on that we thought it would flop off the ceiling. So was the fact that the ceiling fan and light in the master bedroom didn't even work at all.

There is a thing called a property disclosure that every seller has to fill out. The wobbly sink wasn't on the list. Neither was the wobbly ceiling fan or the master bedroom ceiling fan that didn't even work. Are you telling me that the seller didn't know about these things? Are you telling me the owners never laid in bed, in the dark, and wondered why the light didn't work? See how it makes you look weak, lazy, even deceptive if you don't address these issues ahead of time? Now we're not talking about major things. I get that. I know this isn't toxic mold or a broken dishwasher or a flooding basement, but even in such minor things, you either prove you are a solid seller who is serious about the attraction, appearance, and functionality of your home or you're not. Remember you are selling something here. Would you sell a car with a huge scratch down the middle of the hood? Would you sell a car with bald tires and a crack in the windshield? You might, but if you did, you certainly couldn't expect a top offer. You would have to discount the price.

So besides looking weak and losing your negotiation power, what happens when such stupid and minor things are discovered? We all have to waste time and play this dumb back and forth game. The buyer has to issue a form that requests resolution of the items. That means you as the seller either have to fix things or throw money at the buyer. Those are your options. Of course, as I said, you could refuse and then the buyer can walk but that wouldn't make much sense would it? After all the idea here is to get your home sold. So again, if you know this is coming, why play games and waste time. Just fix things ahead of time, so you can avoid the whole silly circus. The other option is just to be honest and up front in the actual listing on the MLS. Every listing on the MLS has a section for comments. It's OK if you aren't Martha Stewart or Bob Vila. Just be up front with people. It would be perfectly fine in the listing comment section to say, "Pedestal sink on main level wobbles, children's bedroom ceiling fan out of balance and master bedroom ceiling fan not working. Seller to give buyer three hundred dollars for these items." Do you see how much better that is? Just be up front with things. People don't like surprises. Why look like you're being sneaky or deceptive, like you're playing dumb, or trying to hide something? Just get stuff handled ahead of time, and the inspection will be a breeze.

It's go time!

Once you have selected a strong agent with a brilliant marketing plan and your home is prepared, it's go time! Things are pretty much on cruise control at this point until you get an offer. Your main role as sellers is to keep your home looking crisp and clean while it's being shown. I know that's kind of hard because basically you need to have your entire home look like things do when you walk into a hotel room, but it just has to be done. It's especially hard with little ones, but you have to do your best to keep things looking sharp. Depending on where you live, either an appointment service, broker administrator, or agent will contact you to make appointments to show your home. This is the other challenging part to the process. While you certainly can say no if it doesn't work for your schedule or lifestyle, keep in mind the more you say no, the fewer buyers see your home. The fewer buyers see your home, the less chance you have to sell it, so you kind of just have to chalk up the listing period as a season of inconvenience. It's just how it goes.

Yes, you will be bothered and perhaps even annoyed. Yes, agents will say they're coming and not show up or show up late. Yes, you may have total strangers knock on your door because they saw the sign at the street. It's all part of the program. Do your best to keep your sense of humor about you and stay flexible. This phase doesn't usually last too long! A strong agent will give you updates as to how many showings there have been as well as any helpful feedback. He or she will give you a general feel for how things are going and what other agents and their buyers are saying.

The offer

Eventually, if all goes to plan, you will get an offer. The offer may be below, above, or right at asking price. You must remember you are always in control. If the offer, terms, or conditions are unsatisfactory, you can always reject the offer. You are under no obligation to move forward with a ridiculous low-ball offer for example. If the offer isn't favorable, you can also wait until a better buyer comes along. It all depends on your circumstance and time frame. Sometimes a bird in the hand is indeed worth two in the bush, and other times it's well worth waiting for something better. If you need to start a new job in another city, it may not be worth your time to dither over a couple of thousand dollars.

You, as the seller, must be assured that the buyer is not only serious but able to proceed financially. Included with the offer must be a copy of a pre-qualification or pre-approval letter from a reputable bank or lending institution. Smart and serious buyers with strong agents will already have their financing in order before even looking at homes. I always state in the MLS listing, "All offers must be accompanied by a pre-qualification or pre-approval letter." That ensures we end up with strong buyers. Having said that, due diligence is still necessary, and strong agents will follow up periodically with the bank to make sure everything is still on track. Lots of weird things can emerge while the home is under contract. The buyer can have their bank account seized by the IRS or State for back taxes. The buyer's spouse can split and run up his or her credit cards on the way out. The buyer may innocently forget to make their car payment, and the buyer's credit score may drop below the threshold necessary for a mortgage. You just never know. Again, strong agents will check in frequently with the lending institution and make sure there are no hiccups.

In addition there must also be a deposit or earnest money check along with the offer. This is held and then deposited by the brokerage, title, or escrow company depending on what part of the country you live in. Like the bank letter, the deposit communicates both the commitment and the financial ability of the buyer. Generally speaking, and it depends on your situation and where you live, the amount is usually between 1 and 3 percent of the listing price. So if the home is listed at $400,000, then the earnest money could be around $12,000 on the high end. Should things go poorly and let's say the inspection reveals something really negative like termites or toxic mold, the buyer can usually get out of the contract and get their deposit back. If, however, the buyer just flakes out and decides they don't want to buy a home after all, but want to live in a tent on a Mexican beach and surf for the rest of their life, the buyer's deposit is usually forfeited. The deposit is then either kept by the seller or split with the listing agent's brokerage. Of course this depends on what part of the country you live in and your arrangement with your agent.

Multiple offers

In a hot market, your home might be so sought after that you get multiple offers. You just never know what's going to happen. No matter what you are in control and must be fully satisfied with the offers. In that event a strong agent will know how to respond. Obviously if there are multiple offers, you are in a position of strength. Let's say one offer out of three is perfect. You can just accept it and call it done. My favorite technique in order to get the most money for my clients is to respond to all offers and state, "We are in a multiple offer situation. I need you to submit your best and final offer. We will make a decision within twenty-four hours."

What I love about making that statement is that all buyers and their agents now know they aren't the only girl at the dance. Also, by having a deadline, it creates kind of an auction fever dynamic. It forces buyers to make a decision. By stating they need to submit their best and final offer means we aren't going to be wasting time with counteroffers or going back and forth. Beyond that this is an opportunity for the most serious buyer to increase their offer. In this manner my sellers make more money, and we end up with the buyer who has the strongest commitment to the home.

Contingent offers

You may get a decent offer, but it is contingent upon the buyer selling their home. At first glance this seems fair enough; however, except in all but the slowest markets, you need to exercise caution here. The problem is that once you agree to the offer, you are now at the mercy of the buyers listing agent, their home, and local market conditions. What if the buyer is from out of town, has a rundown home, and a weak agent? What if the buyer's local real estate market is slow? What if it takes months to sell? What if the home never sells? Do you see how you lose power? Do you see how you're locked up and everything gets put on hold? Furthermore a train can be started without your knowledge. That's where every deal is connected to the next deal like railroad cars. If your buyer is contingent and they accept a contingent offer on their home, things get can get pretty complicated. Problem is if one falls off the track, the whole train flips over. Beyond that, now the time frame is really expanded, while you're frozen in place. Your buyers may take three months to sell their home, and their buyers may take four months to sell their home. Everybody has to wait.

It is usually my advice to pass on contingent offers. However, if you feel you need to accept the offer, I always recommend countering with a hard time frame such as this: "Buyer must remove contingency within forty-five days or contract will be cancelled and sellers home will be placed back on market." This way you're not locked up forever. It's still risky, but at least you have a back door to get out of the deal. Usually with contingent offers, I also recommend that the home continue to be shown and that back up offers are entertained. Clearly many buyers would not be interested to view a home that already has an offer on it, but it just gives you more options as the seller.

Besides the buyer needing to sell their home, there are other contingencies as well. An offer can be contingent on the acceptance of a new position. Sometimes a buyer will be in town interviewing for a new job. They may feel good about it and put an offer on your home. However, let's say the buyer doesn't get the job for whatever reason. The buyer clearly would not be interested in purchasing a home in Phoenix if he or she lives in Cleveland. Waiting for the school year to finish may be another contingency. No one likes to pull their kids out of school unless absolutely necessary. Most prefer to move during the summer or at least during a long break. Maybe the buyers are elderly and have put in an offer on your condo. What if they have been in their home for forty years, and they ask for a ninety-day period in order to clear out their home of four decades?

There are many buyer contingencies. Some you need to exercise extreme caution on because of potential negative implications, and others are merely issues of timing and convenience. Keep in mind that you as the seller may have some contingencies of your own. If school is out June 15 and you're hoping to move out shortly thereafter, you might put your home on the market at the end of March. However, what if you get an offer right out of the gate with a close date of May 1? Then you might have to put all your stuff in storage and live in a hotel until school is out. Then you have to move all your stuff out of storage and move it into your new home. Such a transaction can be overwhelming, costly, and unnecessarily draining. Moving twice isn't any fun. I'm not saying there aren't situations where this may be your best option, but unless you really have to, I think it's just better to state in the paperwork, "Seller needs close date after June 15." In this way you can relax, finish out the school year, and move when it's convenient.

Inspection resolution

Once you accept an offer, the clock starts ticking. Usually in most places, the first deadline is for the physical inspection. After the inspection is complete, the results need to be addressed. If nothing significant was discovered, the buyer signs off and the transaction continues. If you didn't follow my instructions and take care of everything ahead of time or if something unknown was discovered, then the items will need to be resolved. Some hard nose sellers will become combative over certain items. Every state is different, but in the states I have practiced, buyers can walk at this point so it behooves you to play nice. Most reasonable sellers will fix the items or give money to the buyer so that they can deal with it themselves. Both parties have to agree in order to move forward. It's not complicated, but you would be amazed at the ego some sellers have. It's like you insulted their grandmother by bringing up any issue with the house. Again, as you have previously read, my advice to sellers is to take care of everything before you even list the house. That way the inspection period will be smooth sailing.

Financing

The next major hurdle will be to clear the financing stage. This is usually toward the end of the process. While you have nothing to do and have no responsibilities, it is a period to kind of hold your breath. Anything can happen. Loss of a job, change in loan terms, or inability to get approved are all opportunities for your buyer to possibly walk. Again, it's different in every state, but where I have practiced, this has been the case. Two things have to happen before the financing deadline: loan approval and home appraisal. The loan has to be fully approved and ready to fund. As I've stated before, a strong agent will have been in touch with the lender throughout the process to make sure things are still moving forward. In addition your home must appraise for the offered price. If it comes in at the price, you are fine. If the appraisal is higher than the price, the buyer already has some equity. However, if the appraisal is lower, there is a problem, because the bank won't lend on a home that's not worth the price on the contract.

If the home doesn't appraise for the offer price, the buyer usually can cancel the contract. Another option is for the seller to lower the price to match the appraisal number, or the buyer can bring cash to closing to make up the difference. There is one more thing regarding finances. You as the seller may have some encumbrances. Hopefully not, but it does happen. You may have some unpaid HOA dues that need to be taken care of. There may be a lien on your home from an unpaid plumber or back taxes. Any lingering issues will need to be addressed. Usually the title company will handle this for you and just pay any outstanding bills directly with money from your proceeds. If, however, you are upside down on your home and owe more than you are selling it for, you will most likely need to pay these entities yourself. You may also need to bring cash to closing.

Moving out

Toward the end of the process, you will begin packing and preparing to move out of your home. There of course is a lot of hard work, some stress, and long days with endless details to remember. However, in the midst of all this, please keep in mind this is going to be someone's new home, and they are excited to start their new life. The home should be cleaned, and any wall or corner dings from moving furniture repaired. Speaking of walls, can you do the world a huge favor here? When you take down pictures and fill in the nail holes, don't use a pound of spackle and don't use a putty knife. Just take a tiny little bit on the tip of your finger and press it into the hole. You're not troweling on a new coat of texture. You're just filling a tiny hole. Man that one annoys me! I can't tell you how many times I have seen globs of spackle on walls just to cover a tiny pinprick of a hole. The carpets should be vacuumed and, if agreed upon during the negotiation phase, professionally shampooed and cleaned. Beyond this don't leave junk behind. Nobody wants to come to their new home and discover leftover lumber, cans of paint, and trash. Here is really where you show your class and thoughtfulness as a seller. Remember that whole "Do unto others as you would have them do unto you" thing you learned about in Sunday School? It's a good time to practice it here.

I recently walked into one home where my buyer was coming from out of state and the seller had already left for another state. It's a great home in a great neighborhood, but the sellers left a significant amount of random pieces of lumber and trim in the garage along with trash, bug repellent, cleaners, and basically junk that needed to be thrown away. The cherry on the cake was discovering an old used dishwasher under the stairs in the basement. Really? Thanks! Don't assume you are doing the buyers a favor by leaving stuff behind. You may think it's handy to have random pieces of lumber lying in the garage, but other people may have absolutely no use for it. You may think it's helpful to leave bug spray, cleaners, and fertilizer behind, but people generally have their own preferences.

Sometimes it's just that you're moving out on Monday, but trash pick-up is on Thursday. That's no excuse. Nobody wants to come into their new home with rubbish in the garage. Make arrangements to put your trash in your neighbors bin or take it to the local dump. If I was the sellers' agent, I would never have allowed them to leave that stuff behind and would have appropriately coached or helped them to leave a clean and clear home. As my buyers were driving from out of state I didn't want them to walk into a garage filled with junk so I made arrangements to clear it out. I also had the wood floors cleaned as there were footprints all over from the movers. That's what good agents do for their clients. They want to ensure their buyers have a warm and happy entrance into their new home. I also leave a large bouquet of flowers on the kitchen counter. That always brings a smile to my buyer's faces.

So that's it! Once all the hoops are jumped through and your home is clean and the property closes, you are on to your next adventure. If you had equity in your home and there was money left over after closing costs, you can usually pick up your check at the escrow or title company. That's always a nice way to finish things out!

Chapter Seven

The Buyer

Buying a home is an exciting event in your life. It is a major accomplishment to have a place to call your own. Whether this is your first home or you have done this many times, there are endless things to consider. This is most likely the largest purchase and investment of your life, so it is imperative that you do things correctly.

Find a great agent

The first thing you do is find a highly qualified agent. The market is flooded with agents as I point out elsewhere in this book, so finding an agent won't be hard as seemingly everybody and their cousin, sister, and mother has a license. The challenge is finding a great agent with a solid and proven track record. This business is like no other in its relational dynamics. Because there are so many agents out there many of whom share the same friendships, all the agents will likely assume you want to work with them. This is perfectly logical.

If I was an orthodontist and your kid needed braces and we talked about juniors crooked teeth, it would be rational for me to think you were going to use me to give your kid a great smile. If I was a drywaller and you wanted to drywall your garage, after talking about it, I would assume you would use me to finish out your garage. If I was a dog breeder and we talked about your love of Golden-Doodles, I would assume you would want one of my puppies. The same is true in real estate. Every agent assumes their friends and colleagues will use them as their agent, especially if they have had lengthy conversations about it. What the agent doesn't consider is that this friend may know half a dozen agents, so it can really make things weird. The other thing agents don't consider is their competency and experience and if they even deserve additional business.

While I usually recommend starting with people you know, keep in mind that just because you know somebody doesn't mean they are amazing real estate agents. I cover many qualifications as well as disqualifiers in other parts of this book so I won't repeat myself here. Just do your homework and make sure you are with a professional with deep experience that will know how to guide you through the process. As I say, you are looking for both chemistry and competency. In other words somebody you enjoy being with, but more importantly, someone who is really good at what they do. You may have a close friend who just got in the business. Maybe you have fun together but really, you have no idea if they are competent at real estate. You're also not just looking for someone who is "nice." You need someone who possesses significant business, communication and negotiation skills. Anyone can be friendly. Not everyone has the correct skills to succeed in real estate and make sure their clients have a great experience.

The couple in my office

Once you have a great agent you will eventually sit down and discuss the whole process. It amazes me how people, bright people, well financed, and capable people don't really think things through. One day a couple had set an appointment to meet with me to begin their home buying experience. They were referred to me by a satisfied and happy client. So here we were in the conference room around a big table with lots of papers, my laptop, and bank approval letters. This brings up a point worth pausing for here. Before you shop, before you dream, before you waste your or the agent's time, get pre-qualified with a lender. Every financial institution is different, but basically they will ask you for certain information like your financials, bank statements, paystubs, and work history. In addition they will run your credit and check your score. You will fill out an application of sorts, and then they will issue you a statement or letter that tells you the amount you are pre-qualified for. This is commonly known as a "pre-qual" letter.

It doesn't matter if the pre-qual letter comes from a bank, a credit union, a local branch, or online, just make sure you get one. A pre-qualification letter gives you parameters, so you know what to look for. Sadly there are many weak agents who jump at the chance to drive around and show people houses with no verification of financial ability. Some agents lunge at anyone with a pulse and are happy to go running around with no idea of how much to look for and what affordability levels the people even have. Without knowing how much house you can afford is like flying to Paris and having no idea what the money exchange rate is, where a hotel is, or what you will do when you get there. Weak agents love to waste time and apparently gas. I wouldn't show anyone a house unless they had a pre-qual letter. Not only does it reveal the financial ability of the buyer; it also shows the seller and their agent that prepared and serious buyers are involved. I always submit a pre-qual letter along with the offer. That way the seller and their agent can move forward with confidence. Sometimes in a hot market or multiple-offer situation, that's what sets us apart from the competition.

Having said all this, the pre-qual is only a preliminary qualification of what the bank believes they can lend you based on your information and credit score. It is not an approval. An approval is when the bank commits to lending you the agreed upon amount. If you really want to be a boss, get a pre-approval letter. This approval letter is basically a guarantee that you are financed and not just in the preliminary stages. Another note worth mentioning here is that the pre-qual letter gives you the upper limit of what you qualify for. You don't necessarily have to spend every last nickel you have been approved for. There is absolutely no shame in going below the limit, even very below the limit. You are the one who is going to be responsible for the payment and the taxes, so you must be the one to understand and then purchase a home with a monthly payment that works for your budget.

The bank, especially if you have stable employment and good credit, will be more than happy to stretch you to your maximum limit. You must remain in control and though perhaps flattered by a high amount, do what's right for you. Your lender won't be there to help you with your mortgage payment if you bite off more than you can chew. Many people fall for this trap and end up being what is called house poor. I have literally seen beautiful homes with shoddy landscaping, newspapers in the windows for coverings (I'm not kidding), and virtually no furniture. It's maybe OK to stretch, but at some point, it becomes absurd.

While some people advocate you getting the absolute most expensive house you can afford, my wife and I have never been a fan of that mentality. There is a lot more to life than just buying an expensive home. You want to live and thrive once you're in that home. You want to appoint and decorate your home appropriately. You want to go out to dinner, take vacations, and pay for your kids to go to summer camp. Trust me. There is more to life than a big, fat mortgage and the taxes that go with it. Remember taxes are often based on purchase price, so the higher the price, the higher the taxes.

Ideally lenders want to see your mortgage payment be less than 30 percent of your income, preferably 25 percent. Obliviously less is even better. People who live paycheck to paycheck with 40 to 50 percent going to their home payment are flirting with disaster. Why intentionally add that kind of stress to your life? My advice is find the right house in the right neighborhood with the right payment that allows you to have a high quality of living. There is absolutely no logic in your home becoming a ball and chain around your ankle. Armed with sound thinking and a pre-qualification or pre-approval letter, you can shop with confidence knowing the range of houses you should be looking at.

Back to the couple in my office
They had been married for over ten years yet had not learned to communicate effectively and be in sync with each other, at least not on the issue of home buying. As an experienced agent, I always let the bank

pre-qualify or pre-approve people before I meet with them. Financial parameters in hand, I then do my own assessment and ask several key questions. There's more to shopping for a home than the amount of money it will cost. The reason I ask a series of questions before we even go out looking is so we are all on the same page. Once we have discussed and narrowed down the options, we can move forward as a unified front. Weak agents will just run out the door with any warm body and never ask a single intelligent question. They confuse busyness with business and activity with production. They feel if they are busy running around town, they are being a good agent. They are so desperate that they never stop and consider the fact that the way they are going about it is counterproductive and a waste of time for all parties involved.

I always start by asking buyers where geographically they want to live

This may seem kind of basic, but you would be surprised at how many people really haven't thought things through or have settled their hearts on a location. It's not that people don't have opinions or desires. It's just that sometimes they haven't been given the opportunity to process and articulate what they want. It's my primary role to hone in on the bulls-eye, so we can find them the exact kind of home that best suits them. In most towns there are many options. It's as important to know what you want as much as what you don't want. So basically the questions are designed to whittle things down until we end up with a workable plan. Some people know right out of the gate and tell me what they are looking for. Other people need some help processing.

If people need help processing, I might ask the following: Do you want to buy raw land and have your home built from the ground up? Do you want rural, farm or country living or do you prefer urban or downtown? Would you rather live in the suburbs? If so which part—the older established area with mature trees or the newer parts of town with new developments? Is there a specific neighborhood you are attracted to? Neighborhoods are very unique. They all have a different feel to them.

It's almost like they have a distinct personality or vibe. Within the same region, city, or town, there can be dozens or even hundreds of different kinds of neighborhoods with entirely different kinds of feel to them.

Where to live sometimes has to do with the quality of schools, access to shopping or commute to work. All these things have to be taken into consideration. If kids are in the picture, what school do they attend and are you willing to change schools? Do you want your kids to stay in that particular school district? Do you prefer a certain distance to main arteries or freeways? What about work commute? What distance works best for you? What about family members? Is there a brother or favorite aunt or elderly parents you want to be close to? Geographically I want them to know what part of town they want to live in. From there we can narrow things down further. We want our buyers to discover and describe what is important to them. Then we can develop a game plan and design a winning strategy on where to look for a home that suits their needs. Do you notice how I don't say "dream" home or "perfect" home? Both of those terms are unrealistic and emotional. I like to focus on a home that works for them and suits their needs. You're looking for a good fit, not a fantasy.

After we're all on the same page about what area you want to live in, we talk about what specific kinds of houses appeal to you

Do you want a low-maintenance condo or townhome? If you want a condo, do you want a single floor condo that's more like a connected patio home or condos that are in a high-rise building? If you want a SFD (single-family detached), is there a particular architecture or era that is appealing? For example, if someone wants a turn-of-the century Victorian, clearly I'm not going to show them homes in a new neighborhood. Some people have a real aversion to homes built in the 1970s. Split levels were common then and the architecture to some people may feel dated. They used a lot of white and yellow bricks back then. If you hate that look, then we need to avoid those neighborhoods.

Do you want a home that's located close to the street or do you want to be pushed back off the road? Do you want a large yard or a small one?

Are we looking for a lot with trees or wide open with lots of sunshine? How about views? Do you want a house in a densely populated and built out neighborhood or a house with some elbow room that backs up to green space or the woods? Do you want a pool? If so what kind of pool? In-ground, above ground? If in-ground do you prefer beach entry with a slow slope, which is good for little kids? Do you love to do laps and prefer a rectangular pool, or do you prefer a free-flowing or kidney-shaped design? Do you want a slide, grotto, or waterfall? Clearly you will need to ask different questions for various parts of the country. In Colorado most homes don't have pools because of the weather and because at high altitude water evaporates quickly. However, when we lived in Southern California, Dallas, and Western New York, many homes had pools.

Buying a high-rise condo in Miami is much different than buying a ranch in Wyoming. An old craftsman home in Pasadena is much different than a tract home in a Denver suburb. Purchasing a duplex in Philly is different than buying a brownstone in Brooklyn. The questions asked need to be tailored to whatever part of the country you reside. How about this for some basic questions—How many bedrooms? How many bathrooms? Do you want a finished basement? Again, some parts of the country have basements while others do not. How many garage bays, two, three, four, or more? Is there someone in the family who likes to tinker and needs ample space for tools and a work bench? Do you have an RV, boat, four-wheelers, or motorcycles? What are your storage needs? Do you want these items on your property or are you ok paying for storage?

Do you prefer a single story or multistory? If multistory do you prefer the laundry be on the top floor or main level? Do you need a home office? Raising chickens are trendy these days; do you want a home where you could raise chickens? A strong agent knows what HOA's approve and which ones don't. I could literally go on and on, but you get the point. Strong agents always ask questions and pre-qualify their clients because it not only saves time, so we're not wasting effort looking at homes that don't appeal, but it also helps buyers distill what they really want. Armed with that knowledge, we can then custom design a schedule of homes to look at which fit their parameters.

If you wanted or needed a pickup truck, you wouldn't waste time looking at convertible sports cars would you? If you wanted an RV, you wouldn't look at boats. The same focus needs to be used in home shopping. Figure out what's important to you, and then go looking with confidence. Again, some people already know exactly what they want, so clearly I don't barrage them with questions. The idea is whether they know or whether they need help distilling what it is they are looking for, the agent has to be informed. Strong agents will want to know how best to serve his or her clients.

I digress - back to the couple in my office

After several questions and some conversation, I could see the woman's eyes begin to water. "Oh boy!" I thought to myself! I observed the husband's reaction. How shall I say it in polite terms? The man, though a decent guy, wasn't the most clued in dude as far as reading his wife's body language. This combined with little if any communication before they met with me created a small volcano that was about to burst. I could sense it. Her arms were crossed, and the tears came. I got up from the table and got a box of tissues for her. I asked her what she was feeling. She burst out, "He keeps talking about finding a fixer-upper in the country, but I want to be close to the mall, school, and grocery store. I don't want to have to spend half my day on the road..." She went on, but you get the idea. The husband, in total disbelief, was caught flatfooted. He didn't know what to say.

I told them I would give them some time to sort through things and that I would check on them in about ten minutes. After the emotion died down, I came back and helped them process. We continued to dialogue about their goals and their desires. They were good people; they just hadn't articulated to each other their expectations and thoughts about where to live and what kind of house they wanted. They hadn't distilled their values and what was important to them. Not that I'm a marriage counselor, but I did help them get their heads together, so they were united in what they were looking for. After the emotions settled down and they were clear on what they wanted, we preceded with a successful home search. Do you see why it's so important to pause before looking at houses and have a solid conversation? If I was a desperate or weak agent, I would have just run out the door with them and looked at houses and in so doing wasted days if not weeks.

Preferences, absolutes, and whatever's

Preferences as implied are things you prefer. They're not imperative, but you do prefer them. Absolutes are things that you must have. They are non-negotiable. And whatever's are well, whatever! They are things you really don't have an opinion on one way or the other. There is macro and micro in both preferences and absolutes however. Macro has to do with the whole country, whereas micro has to do with a specific region. Macro is do you like humidity or dry air? Micro is do you want to live in the city or suburbs? Some of these considerations will be important if you are moving cross-country whereas if you're just moving to another area in the same region or city there may be less to consider.

The macro

I recently was on a flight from Los Angeles to Denver. During the flight I struck up a conversation with the young flight attendant. Responding to one of my questions, she stated that she was based out of Miami and was going to be home later that day. "I can't wait!" She exclaimed. Not knowing much about the area but grasping her enthusiasm, I was like, "Really? What do you like about it?" Her response left me completely nonplussed. "I can't wait to get back in the humidity! It's so good for my skin!" Speechless. I didn't even know how to respond. In my opinion humidity is something to be escaped from not run toward! My wife shares my opinion and says that humidity makes her hair go crazy. Being a guy with straight hair, I can't relate, but I take her at her word.

For me the idea of living somewhere humid where your shirt always sticks to your back, windows have condensation dripping down them, and the general feeling of always needing a shower is not my cup of tea, but here she was—young, happy, energetic, attractive, professional, and a successful flight attendant—counting the hours before she was back in it. If she was thinking of moving and thought along the lines of macro, she would be aware of her affinity for humidity. If she likes humidity, then she knows what parts of the country she would like to live in and start refining her search with that parameter in place. Clearly she wouldn't be looking at dry states like Utah, Colorado, or Arizona.

Macro is do you like bright sun or is overcast OK? This might be kind of a weird question to some people because the knee jerk response would be, "Um, who doesn't like the sun?" But what I'm talking about here is do you *have* to live in a sunny or hot place? I grew up in Buffalo, New York. I really didn't know that the sky was supposed to be blue until I met my wife who was born in Los Angeles. She thought the idea of living in Buffalo was nuts. "All you have is fifty shades of gray," and that was long before the movie came out! We did live there for a few years, and she would say, "It's so depressing! You never see the sun!" She was definitely pretty fired up about the whole thing! I was like, "Uh…" I really didn't have a response. We moved to Los Angeles shortly thereafter. When you grow up somewhere you don't really realize it's "bad" weather, it's just weather. What makes it bad are your preferences and absolutes and that is a very subjective matter.

So to use the macro idea, if you hate humidity because you hate feeling sticky and you hate mold and you hate crazy hair, then Miami probably isn't for you. Birmingham, New Orleans, and Houston aren't going to be high on your list either. Preference or absolute? Clearly absolute! So then you know what you don't want and can cross off all the humid parts of the country. However, there are lots of dry spots. Do you like mountain dry or desert dry or high plains dry? Get the idea? You have to keep boiling things down until you get to what you really want.

I was recently in Austin, a town of which I am a big fan. I was staying at the Hilton on Fourth Street two blocks south of the famed Sixth Street. Sixth Street is a blast. Live music, great food, and even better people watching. I love just walking up and down the street. It's a perfect blend of locals, tourists, and college kids from nearby University of Texas. I find it entirely fascinating. The police barricade the street some evenings, and the whole section of town becomes a huge pedestrian mall and outdoor party.

One night as I was walking, my ears were assaulted by really loud metal music. I thought maybe it was some band performing in a club. It's common to hear music out in the street from such places as their doors are usually open. Nope. It was coming from Death Metal Pizza, which brought an instant smile to my face. I actually stopped dead in my tracks and burst out laughing in the middle of the street. Here was this place with amazing marketing and even better pizza. Complete with black gothic signage, graffiti, and all things metal, this pizza joint provided me the ultimate culinary head-banging experience. It's so loud inside that you basically have to point to what you want, and the guy or gal behind the counter will nod their head in affirmation and then turn and continue to thrash their head to the music while they make your pie. It was such an awesome experience. I still laugh about the brilliance of it all. And it wasn't just a gimmick. The pizza was actually really good, and this coming from a guy who grew up around some of the best pizza ever made!

Anyway, after miles of walking, many smiles and laughs and significant amounts of people watching, my watch and my body told me it was way past time for me to be asleep in my hotel bed, so I headed back to the Hilton. As I strolled away from Sixth Street, things quieted down. It was calmer, so I could notice my surroundings more clearly. I noticed a lot of things…especially the cockroach crawling along a wall that was big enough to take me on, and I'm 6'1" and 230 pounds! I was like "WHOA!" That thing kind of freaked me out. You know how you get when you're not expecting to see something?

I have a dear friend who, as a grown man now in his mid-thirties, if he sees a spider let alone a roach on steroids, he will scream and jump up on a chair, or table, or hood of a car. Its cartoon-level comedic entertainment. I mean he has a serious bug issue. I'm not judging, but it's pretty funny to see him react this way (sorry Jordan!). As many things as Austin has to offer, it would be an absolute no-go for him because he loathes bugs more than almost anything. Do you see it? The flight attendant *loves* humidity. My friend Jordan *hates* bugs. Those are not preferences. Those are absolutes. My wife hates humidity and bugs, so there are many areas of the country I can cross off!

Sometimes you don't have a choice. Maybe you hate humidity, but you or your spouse have a great job offer in Houston. At that point you have to do some soul searching and think through whether or not it's worth it. You might swear you would never live in the desert because the idea of living in a dry place with common temperatures around one hundred makes your mind go blank. However, at a national work event, you meet this amazing person and quickly fall in love. Where do they live? Phoenix! True love may make you reconsider your absolutes!

With any cross-country move you have to consider if it's worth leaving friends, family, and the predictable nature of a familiar area. Sometimes love or a job opportunity are compelling, and other times it's best to stay put. Again, all of this is highly subjective, and you just have to think things through and make the best decision possible.

Then there is the micro side of life

Once you have things narrowed down to which region of the country you want to live in, or if you're moving within the same area, then you have to get down the funnel a bit more and decide where you want to live within that region. Buying a home, like buying anything, is highly subjective. Have you ever wondered why when you go to some restaurants there are so many choices? To the person who orders the same thing every time, such a volume of possibilities is insane. To another who relishes variety, a thick menu is a thing of glory. The idea in restaurants as in real estate is the role of subjective taste. In other words, what is amazing to one person might be irrelevant to another and possibly even distasteful to a third.

Do you like trees or want to live in the forest? If so do you prefer deciduous trees or evergreens? Either of these trees makes for a very different kind of forest. Evergreens are, well, evergreen. In the winter when it snows, do you love puffy clouds of white snow laying on thick green branches? Maybe you like the year round shade an evergreen forest gives you because you find direct sunlight uncomfortable. You love the smell of pine needles and listening to the breeze blowing through the trees. Or maybe you prefer deciduous trees. A beautiful forest for you is filled with oaks, maples, and elms. You love the fall time foliage and color that comes with the change of seasons. You love to rake big piles of leaves and have the kids jump into them. You love that in the winter the sun shines through more strongly because the leaves are gone. This gives your home a cozy feeling. Or maybe you think living in the forest is nuts. You think that anyone who does so is mad. Why would you want to live in a forest? Are you a hobbit or something? Don't you know that all winter long, you have snow and ice because of the shade? You can keep it! For you, real life happens out in the open where you can see for miles. You love the feeling of open space and forests make you feel claustrophobic. You love the sun, and you enjoy the views the openness provides.

Do you like to live in the mountains or do you prefer to live in the foothills with views of the mountains? If you like to live in the mountains, do you want to be near civilization or do you kind of want to be off the grid? Would you rather live in town? If so, what kind of "in town?" There are older parts of town with large trees and classic houses. There are newer areas with pop up affordable tract houses. There are areas with large lots and custom homes. If you want to live in town, do you want to live in a neighborhood with an HOA (Home Owners Association), or do you want to be in an area with no restrictions?

Then there are SFD (single-family detached) homes as well as condos or townhomes. Which style of home do you prefer? If you have kids, do you want to live in a new development where there are potentially many young families, new schools, playgrounds, parks, and recreation centers? Or do you prefer an established blended neighborhood with all generations living together? Do you want to be near walking trails? Do you want to live in a gated country club community with a swimming pool, spa, tennis courts, café, and clubhouse?

Do you love to ride your bikes? We lived in the Santa Clarita Valley for many years. This are of California has flat areas with paved trails and rolling hills with no trails. When we first moved there, we lived in an area called Stevenson Ranch. It's a beautiful part of town, but it's in the hills, so riding a bike is tough for a family with little ones. We had to go downhill a couple of miles and cross busy streets in order to access the flat paved trails in Valencia, the neighboring town. Then, of course, we had to hike it up the hill after our bike ride, so that was fun! We eventually moved to Valencia and purchased a home in a flat area near a trail entrance. We realized family bike rides were an important value to us, and we needed to live in an area that facilitated that value.

Do you want to live on a golf course? If so, can you handle a broken window or dented exterior from time to time? Can you live with the "ping" sound that comes with every hit of the ball? What about loud golfers talking or yelling to each other? I say this from experience. We had a getaway condo on a golf course near Palm Springs. It was a nice home in a gated country club community in Southern California's Coachella Valley, about two hours east of Los Angeles. Great condo, but not all golfers are good golfers or sober ones for that matter. About twice a year, we would arrive for our weekend getaway and find a golf ball laying in our bedroom, living room or kitchen. Then it was just a matter of time until we discovered the broken window from which it had blazed through!

Living on a golf course is weird. There is a charm to it yet in some cases you are taking your life into your own hands even going into your backyard. In my opinion you should never live within two hundred yards of the tee box. You will hear that "ping" all day long, and you have the highest percentage of getting nailed by a slice or a hook off the tee. For sure I don't think it's a good idea to live on the inside of a dog-leg as people who try to cut the corner will invariably nail your home. If you've ever golfed pay attention to the homes on the course. Check out all the ball marks and dents in their siding or stucco and see all the repairs as well. It's kind of nuts. Now if you just gotta live on a golf course for whatever reason more power to you. Just know what you're getting into, and try to get a property with the lowest probability of getting bombarded.

Do you want to live on a cul-de-sac or on a side street? There are main arteries, neighborhood streets and terminal streets. Main arteries are usually large multi-lane thoroughfares designed to quickly get you from one part of town to another. Off arteries are neighborhood streets; however, not all neighborhood streets are the same. Just like the human body has arteries, veins and capillaries so to roads have different traffic capacities and flow. You have to think through the implications of each neighborhood street as they are not all equal. Most neighborhoods have a couple of different ways in and out of the neighborhood. If you live on the main access point and near the entrance, you obviously will have more traffic going by your home. The upside is you can get out and on your way quicker. If you prefer less traffic and the noise that comes with it perhaps you will need to investigate streets toward the back of the neighborhood or in terminal streets. Terminal areas are dead-ends or cul-de-sacs where the only traffic is going to be people who actually live in that section of the neighborhood.

If your home is on the outside edge of a curve, you can expect headlights beaming into your living room all night long. If you live on a corner or near an intersection, you can expect to hear cars screeching to a stop or peeling out on take-off. You will hear the engines rev as they accelerate and this includes Harleys with cored out pipes, construction trucks, and kids with tricked-out wanna-be race cars. You really have to think these things over. This is a huge decision, and you have to do your best to process well. I'm repeating myself, but it is so important to know what you want. The more distilled you are about what you want on the macro and micro level, the easier it will be to find the right home. This whole nonsense of "I'll know when I see it" is for the birds. It's as crazy as not having a preference when you are dating. "Oh, I don't know. Any woman will do." Really? I don't think so. I think we all have preferences even if they are in broad parameters. You must have parameters to filter down the choices, otherwise you will be looking for a house or a spouse forever!

Ideally you want the house that fits your lifestyle and your budget. You want a home that will accommodate the people living there. A family of five with young children will be looking at a different kind of home than a retired empty nest couple or a single professional. Again, be sure to have your list of preferences and non-negotiables ready. Really think things through. Don't compromise or you may regret it. Having said that there are some occasions where you will have to compromise as that "perfect" house may not exist or be available in the time frame you need it. In this case you just want to make sure you are mentally intact with the biggies. Sometimes if a home has eight out of ten of the big items you want, it's close enough. Other times or for some people they must have all ten. It's somewhat subjective with lots of variables. My main point I want to emphasize here is that you as a buyer really need to process well and be incredibly thoughtful about this decision because it's a big one.

The neighborhood
Here's something few people consider; you aren't just buying a house, you're buying a neighborhood. That may seem odd to consider at first glance, but it's the absolute truth. The things that surround your home have an impact either positively or negatively on your quality of your life. Perhaps you found a terrific home in a quant neighborhood and being an anti-HOA kind of person you were really happy...until your neighbor decided to paint their house hot pink and breed beagles. Yes, the small brown and white dogs with barks that seem to emerge from the bowels of the earth and are at least thirty times louder than you would expect from that size of dog. Yes, that beagle. Moreover the kennel is in the backyard along the fence, right below your bedroom window.

Maybe you found a nice home and are meticulous about keeping your yard and home in top shape. Do the people living in your new neighborhood share your zeal for all things orderly? It's painful to have the nicest yard in a neighborhood while other people are letting their lawns turn to weeds. Some people especially with young kids love the idea of being near schools. That sounds logical. Maybe the kids can walk to school. Maybe it's just fun to have a playground near your home. Whatever the perceived positive reasons, the potential negatives also must be considered. If you are near a neighborhood school, for sure at least two times a day, there will be massive activity. There will be buses pulling in and out, children yelling, running, and playing, and parents dropping off kids, which means lots of vehicles in the neighborhood.

Some schools are so poorly designed in regard to traffic flow that it is virtually impossible to go anywhere at the beginning and ending of the school day. It is utter land-locked chaos that takes a long time to dissipate. So you have to consider that when you want to live near a school. For some people it's not a big deal. They avoid leaving their home from 7:30 to 9:00 a.m. and again from 3:00 to 4:00 p.m. It's kind of like when we lived in Los Angeles. We never, if we could help it, would go on the freeways during rush hour. You just know if you live in Southern California to avoid freeways from 7:00 to 9:00 a.m. and 4:30 to 6:30 p.m. It just takes some planning. Again, I'm not here to say what's right and wrong. I'm just here to encourage you to have your eyes wide open and think about possible negatives to any home or neighborhood. That's called being realistic. Buying a home is exciting. I get that. Just don't walk around with rose colored glasses or you'll end up buying something that you may regret after the honeymoon period wears off.

There are homes that have views of the mountains, which of course is always nice. However, not all views are the same. A home can be on a hill overlooking a shopping center and have clear views of the mountains. The prospective buyers view the home during the day and marvel at the amazing views. Problem is they don't think about the fact that the shopping center parking lot lights will be glaring all night. Beyond that they may have to endure listing to traffic and car doors slamming shut during business hours. You might like a neighborhood near a hospital. You may think it's really convenient in case of an emergency. It gives you a sense of security. However, you may not think about the fact that you may be listening to ambulances and their blaring sirens day and night. You may also not realize that most hospitals have on-site incinerators that they frequently fire up. If the wind is just right, you might get some peculiar odors floating through your neighborhood.

Country living

A lot of people move to states out west like Colorado and get swept up in the romance and history of the region. I jokingly refer to this as John Denver's song Rocky Mountain High. They have seen movies, read stories, and seen celebrities establish beautiful ranches and properties in various western states. I totally get it. There is a sort of magical quality to it all. Part myth, part legend, part history, and part reality, it's my job to help people understand the reality part of things!

I had a friend who wanted to build a new home in an area called Larkspur, Colorado. Larkspur is a quaint little town with a main street that has a gas station, pizza place, bar and grill, convenience store, post office, various shops, and a large park with a great play area. Then as you go out east, the town turns into wide open rural land. Out east homes have great views but also nothing blocking the snow and wind. I cautioned him about the realities of building there which largely went ignored. They built their dream home on forty acres, which, of course, was awesome, but the very first winter he had a snow drift against his garage higher than his garage door. In other words, when he opened his garage door, all he saw was a wall of white. The snow was over eleven feet tall! If you're unfamiliar with cold parts of the country, it might snow eight inches, but the wind will blow all that snow until it hits something. The cumulative effect will be that a house, fence, trees, or embankment may end up with several feet of snow piled up against it. That's just the nature of wind and snow. Drifts are something you need to consider if you're going to live in such an area.

Living in the country has its benefits, but it also has its downsides. I know I'm repeating myself, but you have to calculate everything, so you have realistic expectations. That's a big part of what my writing is all about; thinking things through so you can have realistic expectations. My friend just kept listening to John Denver songs and really thought he wanted the ranch lifestyle. Despite my concerns based on knowledge, experience, and insight, he kept pushing forward. Beyond that I knew him well and knew his driving habits. He was an impatient and aggressive driver. I felt the distance to town and the one lane roads would quickly become an issue, which came to be true.

They also didn't take into consideration having to clear a three hundred yard long driveway. All he had was his little snowblower from his house in the suburbs. Well, that driveway was about fifteen feet long and maybe that snowblower was just fine for that kind of home. Out in the country though? Not even close. I had told him he needed to buy a tractor with a four foot wide snowblower attachment in order to clear that size of a driveway. What happened? Yes, you guessed it. Again, he didn't listen. He was a good friend but he was just kind of thick-headed and stubborn.

Another thing they didn't consider is that Larkspur is smack dab right between Colorado Springs and Castle Rock. Their home, because it was way out on the eastern outskirts, was about twelve miles from either town. They had always lived in the suburbs and had grown accustomed to convenience. When you live in a large community, you can run out for eggs, milk, or bread and be back home in minutes. You can pick up kids and drop them off with ease. Not so with country living. Unless there's a market or country store nearby, shopping is going to be a mission. Now I'm not saying that's bad and I'm not saying taking three hours to snow blow your driveway is bad, I'm just saying you have to think things through. So again, my job is to steer you into having realistic expectations and make decisions accordingly. So if you want to live in the country and if you don't mind taking forty-five minutes to an hour to get a gallon of milk, then more power to you!

Country living just takes some planning that's all. When you're in town, you can just run out and get what you need. When you live several miles from a grocery store, it just means you need to make accurate shopping lists, know how to stock up on some items, and keep track of what you have in your home and what you're running low on. You basically need to become a manager of a small store and keep track of your inventory making sure you never run out.

HOA or no HOA? That is the question!

I'm not a big regulation guy. I'm not big on someone, government or anyone, telling me how to live. It's a core American value to be independent, I get that. However, where it's important like airports and airlines, I would rather there be some standards implemented. I personally want there to be some authorities involved with air traffic control, our food chain, auto manufacturing, medical procedures, and public safety. I also like it when there are some standards and some authorities involved when it comes to my neighborhood. Now I know I'm treading out on thin ice for some of you, but just bear with me a moment. My opinions are not only based on personal taste alone but also on experience.

HOA's or Home Owners Associations govern things like landscaping, home appearance, and paint colors. They maintain common areas, walking trails, tennis courts, neighborhood parks, and community pools. Sometimes the HOA fees cover trash collection. Homeowners pay HOA's fees or dues and they vary depending on services provided. We lived in a neighborhood that had all the above amenities, and we paid $185 a month. There are some neighborhoods that provide no amenities but simply care for the medians and green common spaces that charge twenty-five dollars a quarter. Not all HOA's are created equal, and before you purchase your home, you will be given the opportunity to review the CC&Rs (Covenants, Conditions, and Restrictions) and any pertinent HOA rules. Usually if it is not to your liking, you may back out of the purchase. Just make sure you know ahead of time how this all plays out, so you don't get stuck with something you're not happy with.

While we're on the topic of CC&Rs, keep close eye out for sneaky little monthly add-ons. In some parts of the country, a developer will cut a deal with the town, county, or state and pass the cost of infrastructure to you. Isn't that nice of them? Utilities, roads, and street lighting are all added to your tax bill in the form of an additional fee. You know, builders and developers don't make enough money, so it's nice that the powers that be allow them to make you pay for their development. Sometimes called Mello-Roos, these sneaky little assessments can increase your monthly bill and it's easy to miss.

Over the years I've heard many people gripe about their HOA. It's almost a part-time hobby for some people. However, if you are a fan of order, attractive neighborhoods, and protecting your investment, you want a strict HOA. Why? Because it is just human nature to let things slide. "Give them an inch and they'll take a mile" is a saying for a reason. As soon as standards relax, then the whole thing comes undone. Self-governing is a myth. Unless there is a strict policy governing the appearance of neighborhood homes somebody, somewhere, for whatever reason, will let their home and their property decay. It's just how it goes.

Lazy people

Wasn't it Newton's first law of motion described to those interested in physics as "objects in motion tend to stay in motion and objects in rest tend to stay at rest?" In this context people who have good taste, self-respect, sound economic principles, initiative, and personal pride in their home will always care for their property. Such people need no one or nothing to motivate them to care for their home. They are homeowners in motion. Conversely those who have little self-respect, awareness, or personal pride or are just plain lazy will allow their home and their yard to deteriorate over time. They don't care about their home, and they certainly don't care about the negative impact their home's appearance is having on the rest of the neighborhood. They are selfish homeowners who are at rest. They are not in motion in any way.

The lawn and yard is usually the first thing to go. No fertilizer, core aerating, or dethatching. Not enough watering and the weeds eventually take over. Then the lawn doesn't get cut as often as it needs to. When it does get cut, they don't use a bag so the clippings just spray everywhere—on the driveway, on the sidewalk, and on the street. And there it sits, turns yellow, and rots. Then the bushes and shrubs don't get pruned because, of course, that takes work, pride, and initiative. So then you get the long scraggly plants with years of leaves and debris under them. Weeds eventually take over and become intertwined with the shrubs becoming one big green ugly mess. Combined with weeds coming up through the cracks in the driveway and sidewalk, all sense of curb appeal is lost. I'll just never understand that level of laziness and apathy. How can they not see what they are doing? Or if they see it how can they not care? It affects the beauty of the whole neighborhood as well as being a blaring siren that they are lazy and don't give a darn about their home or neighbors. For whatever reason they have become so careless and lazy, that their self-respect, pride, and respect for others has vanished.

Personally, being part of the meticulous yard club, I will never, ever understand how some people live like that. Curb appeal is the single most important thing about a home, and I will never get why people just let the appearance of their home go down the drain. It says a lot about them, and I for one really struggle with such people. It's an apathetical mentality that I just can't relate to. The third law of thermodynamics clearly states that "all things tend to decay." In other words, weeds show up all the time. Trees and shrubs die. Lawns get crabgrass. Nature itself is constantly fighting us. In order for things to fall apart, all we as humans need to do is do absolutely nothing. Since this is true then home maintenance is going to be a lifelong thing. There's no way around it. It's kind of like our physical appearance. All we have to do to let ourselves go is do nothing, eat what we want and never exercise. The third law of thermodynamics will take care of the rest. Our homes and our bodies are no place for laziness otherwise the end result is assured. Inertia, effort, and initiative need to happen otherwise things just fall apart around us. In conjunction with the yard going south other things usually follow suit. The junky car in the driveway, the flat basketball lying in the bushes, and random pieces of junk, bicycles, or unused toys strewn about.

Then the home itself will begin to show signs of neglect. The torn window screen, the peeling paint, the leaking gutters, the wood rot. It doesn't take long for a home to completely fall apart and become a candidate for a flipper TV show on HGTV. A strong HOA will never allow such an occurrence to happen in the first place. As soon as the yard appears unkempt, the owner will receive a notice from the HOA. If there is no improvement, they will receive further communication and eventually legal action from the HOA is possible. That's something some people don't realize. HOA's have limited rights over your property and can take legal action against you if you are out of compliance.

People with bad taste

Now I'm sorry to say so and I hope you don't get your knickers in a twist over this, but some people, well, they just plain don't have good taste. If *Better Homes & Gardens* magazine is the standard, they live like they have never seen such a publication. HOA's not only protect you from lazy homeowners but those with bad taste as well. Beauty is in the eye of the beholder and that's all good and well. It's just that some people really don't have good taste. They wear ugly clothes, drive horrible cars, have dated hair styles, order steak well done, flood their yard with plastic pink flamingos, mix plaids with stripes, and generally just don't get it. I'm not saying they're bad people and they may be awesome in other areas. They just don't have amazing taste.

Such people are different than the lazy homeowner. These people actually take care of things; it's just that they have such horrible taste it almost has the same effect as a lazy person's house. In some cases, it may be worse. There are two non-HOA neighborhoods I know of where the bad taste fairy struck recently. Keep in mind these are nice neighborhoods with homes north of $400,000. Both homes have to do with color of paint. One homeowner painted their home yellow. Now I'm not talking about a pastel or soft butter-cream kind of yellow that's warm and inviting. I'm talking neon, antifreeze, middle of the sun kind of yellow. It's ridiculous and blinding nature of color has the neighborhood in an outrage. The other home was recently purchased, and the new homeowners promptly had their home painted blue. Again, not soft blue, powder blue or pale-sky blue but electric blue, think Play-Doh blue. The neighbors to-tally freaked out, but again, no HOA, no rules. The neighbors can huff and puff all they want; they're the ones who purchased a home in a non-HOA neighborhood, so there you go! Usually in an HOA neighborhood, there are approved colors that are in harmony with the neighborhood. The HOA also monitors your exact location, so two houses in a row don't end up painted the same color.

Water is an issue out west as the climate in many places is dry, semiarid, or desert. Some of the concerns are legitimate, and some are exaggerated. There are some non-HOA neighborhoods where homeowners literally have stripped their entire yards and put stone down, everywhere. Some unin-formed and uninitiated people believe xeriscape is killing every living thing in your yard and putting down stone. This is blasphemy and an insult to every good landscaping idea in history. Xeriscape is the landscaping design concept that reduces water usage by limiting grassy areas and using climate appropriate plants and trees, along with moisture retaining soil amendments. This is a far cry from stripping everything and putting stones everywhere. Besides being tasteless it is usually not a good financial decision.

During a dry spell in Colorado, a neighbor of a friend of mine did just that. Stones everywhere. Hideous. The homeowners logic? Save money on water as the utility company had recently increased the cost for wa-ter. The increase? About the equivalent of five dollars to fifteen dollars a month depending on usage. So on the high side, the annual increase for their water would be about $180. $180! First of all, if you as a homeowner can't absorb an additional $180 a year your margins are way too thin. Second, their decision to turn their yard into a quarry was fundamen-tally lacking in logic. They paid $4,700 to destroy their yard and stone it. Divided by $180 means they would have to live there for over twenty-six years for the rock pile to pay for itself. Smart financial management? I think not. Then as fate would have it, the following spring was one of the wettest on record. People didn't have to use their sprinklers for months.

On the practicality side of things, some ill-advised people think put-ting stones everywhere provides a "maintenance-free" situation. I put it in quotes because there is nothing on earth that is maintenance-free. Everything has to be taken care of. In short, order homes that I observe that stone their yards eventually have weeds poking through everywhere, and it becomes even more unsightly than before. While an intelligent engagement with your yard and using climate appropriate plants especially out west is smart, those with bad taste and even worse logic don't quite think things through all the way either financially or practically. HOA neighborhoods vary on their landscape strictness. Some make you submit a landscape plan for their approval, and others have more lax approaches. For me, I like the strict HOA that sets standards and lends approval to submitted designs. I would personally lose my mind if my neighbor stripped their yard and put down stones everywhere. It's hideous looking and it would lower the value of my home and neighborhood.

Judging has to do with standards. That's why in a court room as well as any dog show, the judge will render a conclusion based on standards of either law or grooming and breeding. Likewise HOA's judge whether a landscape design or paint scheme is tasteful or not. With so many homeowners out there with embarrassingly bad taste, I personally want some protection. I personally would never live in a neighborhood without an HOA unless I was out in the country.

HOA's govern other things like whether you can park your converted school bus out front or not. Or your boat, work trailer, RV, snowmobiles, four-wheelers, dump truck, commercial van, or tractor-trailer. I am not a fan of neighborhoods where people can do anything they want and park whatever they want where ever they want. Common sense and good taste tells you parking a camper in front of a house is tacky yet, and I'm sorry to break this to you, not everyone has good taste or loads of common sense. And here's the kicker: it's not about money or socioeconomics either. I have driven through what most people would say are nice neighborhoods. Large homes with three car garages on large lots. Surely these upper class people know how to do things? Nope! Here is what I have seen:

A lifted pickup truck parked on the side of a house in three-foot weeds. At least if you're tacky enough to park a truck alongside your house, clear out the weeds and put some stone down, so it looks like a designated parking spot. A limo with flat tires parked in a driveway. Someone had enough money to buy a limo and run a business but is too cheap to rent a place suitable for his business vehicle or fix his tires for that matter. A camper parked in a driveway in front of the third-car garage taking up the length of the entire driveway. Homes where the owners don't realize you're supposed to cut your lawn every week. Other really nice homes have weeds growing through the cracks of their driveway. Five minutes on Saturday morning with a jug of weed killer takes care of that. Other homeowners leave their trash cans right next to their garage door in plain view of everyone passing by instead of putting them away.

It amazes me how people can afford a nice home but not make the effort to take care of the home. If it's a rental, there is still no excuse. I always make sure the rentals I own or manage are among the most attractive in the neighborhood. In non-HOA neighborhoods, you can walk down some streets and see an old car in a driveway covered in a bright blue tarp. Then you'll see a commercial plumbing van. Followed by a food truck or RV parked in the driveway. Then a boat a few doors down from that. HOA's will have restrictions on commercial or recreational vehicles parked in the neighborhood. It confounds me that some people can afford a house and an RV but then are too dog-gone cheap to put their camper in some fenced outdoor storage area. There are literally some people who leave their RV in their driveway all year long. I just will never understand.

As I mentioned before, some HOAs provide trash service included in your dues. This may seem odd, but a well-organized neighborhood uses one trash company that picks up trash on one day. In non-HOA neighborhoods where people are free to choose their own garbage company, there may be two or three companies picking up trash on two or three different days. In this model, there will seem to be trash cans on the street all the time. An HOA will also be sure to remind homeowners to promptly take their empty trash can off the street. If you live in connected housing like condos, the HOA will usually cover things like exterior maintenance and roof replacement in addition to looking after the common areas and other amenities. If you live out in rural areas, there are almost never any HOAs, and that's OK because that's part of country living. The idea is people out there have farm and heavy equipment on their property, and there is plenty of space, so at that point I don't care if you park a WWII tank next to the barn!

So to HOA or not HOA that is the question. In my opinion, if you purchase a home in a non-HOA neighborhood, you are gambling. If you don't mind seeing old cars with blue tarps over them or maybe you own a 1968 Camaro that you plan on refurbishing on your front lawn one of these days, then maybe the non-HOA neighborhood is perfect for you. I don't have a dog in the fight, so do what you will and do what suits your lifestyle. Just be forearmed with the information you need to make a good decision. Again, as I've stated before, you're not just buying a house, you're buying a neighborhood.

In summary here are ten guidelines for buyers:

1. Find a strong agent, preferably a top producer.
This agent will be seasoned and highly knowledgeable with deep experience. They will be strong negotiators. You don't want a rookie, inexperienced, or weak agent. Trust me. The horror stories abound. It's not just as simple as driving around and looking at houses. If it was that easy everyone would make a fortune in real estate.

2. Get prequalified with a financial institution.
You have to know how much house you can afford and then shop accordingly. Don't waste time looking at properties that don't fit your financial parameters, no matter how beautiful or enticing. Nobody looks at Range Rovers when all they can afford is a Ford Escape. Be realistic.

3. Make sure you really think through your wish list.
You want to distill what your priorities and values are. Make a list of things you must have, the non-negotiables. Then make a list of things you'd like to have and finally things that are not that important but might be nice.

You must know what you are flexible on and what are absolutes for you. If you must have a cul-de-sac and a home with western views toward the mountains, then don't compromise. Also know the difference between what can be added later and what can't. You can't add views, but you can always build a pool or larger deck.

4. Search online.
As most home searches begin online, your agent will give you a link to their real-time MLS connected website, so you can personally search available properties at your leisure. It's nice to spend relaxed time looking at things online, so you don't have to waste a lot of time driving around.

5. Go shopping.
Once all the information is gathered and priorities distilled, it's time to go looking at homes. If babies and little kids are in the picture, don't bring them. Babies in diapers and toddlers don't have opinions on homes, and they don't need to be in the mix. Even if (cross your fingers) they are well behaved, they are a distraction. If the baby starts crying because he needs a nap or the toddler acts up because she's bored out of her mind, trust me your home search is over. Get a babysitter, so you can focus. I do my best to inform people, but sometimes it just happens. The frustrating thing is that I know exactly what is going to happen. We'll look at two houses and everything will be fine. Then after buckling them into car seats for the third time, the toddler will invariably arch their back and not want to go into the seat. She will want to go play at the park across the street from the house you just looked at. Or will be suddenly life or death hungry and wasn't that a Wendy's we just passed? Or the baby will fall asleep and at the next house the mother will stay in the car, but then she doesn't get to see the house, so what's the point?

People have cut home searches short because kids were not being cooperative. What they don't realize is that I have already called all these homeowners, and many of them have left so we can enjoy viewing their home in privacy. Not only is it double work for me, but it's an inconvenience to the homeowners and a huge waste of time for every-one. All the homeowners will need to be contacted and the appointments cancelled. As you can tell, I have had experiences in this regard. Nothing derails a previously planned and thought out home search like screaming kids in the back seat. What is the point of taking all that time get pre-qualified, search online, take time off, and go out looking at houses if one screaming kid can sabotage the whole thing?

Am I heartless? No, I'm practical and pragmatic. I have kids. I get it. It's like people who stand in line and ask their little toddler who knows six words what they want at a fast-food restaurant. No problem. We'll all stand here in line while little Jimmy stares up at the menu board that he can't even read and tries to figure things out. It's really easy as a parent. "Hi, I'll have the cheeseburger, and my son will have the chicken nug-gets." Move on. This is not complicated. The same is true when shopping for homes, but it's a much bigger deal than buying lunch. You want to be clear thinking with no distractions. You need to focus on a huge pending decision you have to make. Clearly if the kids are older bring them along, but let's skip toting along the babies and little guys. Also, be sure to be well rested, hydrated, and not hungry. You need to be alert and feeling sharp.

6. View homes with a critical eye.

Don't get caught up in the emotion of it all. Try to be as levelheaded as possible, and be realistic with possible negatives. Again make sure you instinctively know your non-negotiables and your desires, and don't compromise. Take your time. Really. Don't allow anything to pressure you into looking at a home quickly. I am amazed people will take more time looking over a car than a house. A house is way more expensive and has much more significant implications for your life, so take your time and re-ally look at the house as a potential home for you and yours.

Pay attention to the direction of the home, condition of carpets, qual-ity of the woodwork, state of the yard, and everything else that needs scrutiny. You can't identify issues or potential problems to negotiate on if you blow through the house in ten minutes. Look around the neighborhood and especially your immediate neighbors. Get a feel for the area. Remember you're not just buying a home, you're buying a neighborhood. When you're really serious about a house, come back at night and walk around the neighborhood. Is it quiet or loud? Are there bright lights coming from anywhere? It's easy to overlook a local baseball diamond that has those huge, high lights. One night game will reveal everything.

7. Submit an offer on the home you select.
Your high-quality agent will walk you through this process and coach you on the approach. In some markets and on some properties, you need to be aggressive and in others you're more in the driver's seat. Make sure you know the current real estate and economic conditions, so you are aware if it is a buyers or sellers' market. Your offer needs to be realistic based on that information. If there are any issues like carpets that need to be replaced or cleaned now is the time. Any desired concession must be included in the offer. Once the offer is accepted the negotiations are over. The only caveat to this is if something pops up during the physical inspection but even then any negotiations need to be related to that particular discovery. You can't ask for money to repaint the exterior if you find a problem with the air conditioner.

With the offer you will generally submit earnest money in the form of a check. The requested amount is usually in the MLS information on the home. If you flake out and cancel the contract for illegitimate reasons, you will usually lose the money. However, if let's say a huge issue is discovered during inspection, it's been my experience you can back out of the deal and get your deposit back. Every state is different so be sure to check the local rules. If the deal goes through then your deposit is applied toward closing costs or the loan. Another good idea is to pay for any extra coverage for in-depth title searches if it's available. You don't want any surprises after you move in that the former owners cousin has a 10 percent stake in your home. In addition, I find it good practice to ask for a home warranty. Not often but sometimes after a home is sold and the new owners move in, there are weird plumbing, heating, or AC issues. Homes have systems and systems kind of get used to how the current inhabitants use things. For example, if an empty nester couple live in a home and then sell it to a family of six, the water usage will be much greater and may place a strain on the system. Sometimes the water heater, for example, will begin acting strangely because of the greater volume. A good home warranty usually covers all major items for at least the first year.

8. Pay attention to time deadlines.
Be sure to conduct all necessary inspections and financial qualifications within the designated time parameters. There is no excuse for allowing time restraints to lapse. Be sure to pay for a top-notch physical inspection whether you think the home needs it or not. There is a lot to a home and many problems can be hidden and only identified by an experienced inspector. Another source of amazement for me is that people will buy a $500,000 home but balk at paying a quality inspector $500. If the inspector finds a $3,000 problem with the AC, then your $500 is money well spent and the cost of repairs can be included in the inspection report for the seller to address. With no inspection, that repair bill might land on your lap after you move in.

9. Stay on top of your financing.
Once the inspections are done usually, the last item is your financing and the appraisal. If you have locked in financing before you even started your home search, then this should be a breeze. One thing to keep in mind during your home search time frame is to be very careful not to do anything that will negatively affect your credit score. You want to make sure you are diligent all the way through the process.

10. Get the keys and move in!
Moving can be challenging, but if you are wise in your approach and follow some common sense guidelines, your home purchase can be smooth and less stressful.

Chapter Eight

How Not to Make Your Neighbors Hate You

Your neighbors are watching you. They have already sized you up. You're the new kid on the block, and you stand out. Everyone knows the home sold, and you are the new occupants. They have judged you and formed opinions based on their observations. What I am talking about is your behavior, your actions, your patterns, and your skill at keeping a nice home. You have to understand you are the outsider, the stranger. People think this is some anthropological facet of ancient civilization where people don't trust the wanderer who suddenly appears in the village. While this was certainly true back then, not much has changed. They are unsure of you until you prove that you're "normal." You'll be an outsider for maybe six to eighteen months depending on the culture and vibe of your new neighborhood. You'll be on a kind of probation for at least the first six months. During that time the comments around the neighborhood will be like "Have you noticed the new family and how nice they keep their yard?" Or, "My goodness have you seen the new family that moved into the Ballard's old house? They are absolutely destroying it. They haven't cut their lawn in weeks, and have you noticed the toys and bicycles strewn about?"

Much of this is just standard sociology, but some of it is rooted in fear. People don't want "weirdoes" moving into their neighborhood. They don't want "scary" people invading their turf. They don't want noisy and inconsiderate people moving in near them. They don't want people moving in that will lower their quality of living or cause the appearance and attraction of their neighborhood to decline. Who could blame them? They want to keep things as they are. And so they watch you looking for clues in order to calm their nerves or confirm their fears. As a rule, I generally don't really care what people think of me. Only people with excessively weak egos run around worrying about other people's opinions. Having said that, I don't go out of my way to make people hate me either. There is a happy medium where you live your life but don't become that person whom everyone in the neighborhood hates.

That goes for your Harley

When you move into a new neighborhood, you should do your best to kind of blend in. If you're the only guy who owns a Harley with super cored-out pipes and think the sound of blasting noise echoing off the homes in your neighborhood sounds awesome at two in the morning, just be aware your new neighbors may not share your exuberance. I had a neighbor once who was super conscientious and respectful. When he was pulling out of his home early in the morning, he would glide down the driveway and down the street before turning on his Harley. Everyone loved him.

That goes for cutting your lawn at obnoxious hours

We have a new neighbor a few houses down. He for whatever ungodly reason feels that 8:00 a.m. on Saturday morning is the absolute best time to cut the lawn. Worse his Weedwacker sounds like a dying chainsaw. So we go from quiet Saturday morning with birds peacefully chirping to sounding like we're at a motocross event. The thing is it's not like he has big plans. He's around all Saturday. Not like he couldn't do it at, say, 10:00 a.m. or noon like normal people! So do the neighbors love him for destroying a perfectly peaceful Saturday morning or do we all kind of low-key hate the guy? I think you know.

That goes for your dogs barking at all hours of the day and night

This is a biggie and the single worst aspect of living in the suburbs. Close proximity should engender a sense of community, respect, awareness, and sensitivity, but sadly there are some people who just don't have a clue. I'm sure many people have secretly plotted the death of some dogs and maybe their owners. Well, hopefully not but honestly, when unintelligent dog owners create such a nuisance, it brings thinking people to the edge of sanity. I say they "create" that because that is exactly the correct word. Unintelligent owners create obnoxious dogs because they refuse to train the animal. This like all things is not complicated. Kids and puppies alike don't raise themselves. If you train them right, they will be a joy for you and everyone else. If you think kids and puppies magically turn out amazing with zero attention, discipline, love and training, then you should commit yourself to a mental hospital.

I love dogs. I grew up with dogs. I have a dog. He's a trained, obedient, pleasant, controlled, dog. As my wife and I go for our morning walks, we observe dogs behind fences barking to the point of madness, completely out of control. We observe dogs on their hind legs scratching at the glass door or window and wildly barking as if they're trying to escape a burning house. Honestly, have you ever looked at such a dog and wondered what the heck is wrong with them? It's like they've gone mental. More to the point, have you ever wondered what is wrong with their owners. Dogs don't naturally behave that way. They become that way. Why? They aren't trained, and they aren't loved. "WHOA!" some people might say. "I love my dog!" No, not really. You can't possibly love your dog without training it any more than you can say you love your kids without guidance, structure, boundaries, and discipline.

I really don't get it. It's my number-one beef with the suburbs. People who are successful and accomplished in so many ways somehow act like they've had a frontal lobotomy when it comes to their dogs. I really don't get it. We used to hang out with a couple who had two dogs. These dogs barked like mad when you walked up to the door, and they barked all night while you're there inside the house. I'm so not kidding. It's like I would be trying to have a conversation with my friend, and the dog would be right there barking. I'm thinking like "Um, dude? Your dog is right next to us… barking. Aren't you going to do something?" He would literally not even acknowledge the dog was making any noise at all while we were all going half deaf. It's like a father of fifteen wild kids who just can block out all the noise. Well, maybe he and his wife were used to it, but it was insanity to the rest of us. I literally remember being at their home for parties and watching everyone's reaction to the barking. It was glaringly obvious it was a ridiculous problem but there the owners were, without a clue.

Sometimes he would let the dogs out the back slider but guess what? They would just sit there and bark, and wildly scratch on the glass slider which I'm sure the neighbors just loved. This is a big one for me. How is it that people allow their dogs to sit outside and just wail? I counted one time that the average barking dog disturbs the peace for up to one hundred adjacent houses depending on density and location. I actually walked around the neighborhood and counted houses in every direction until I couldn't hear the annoying dog anymore. I know. I told you it was my number one pet peeve. Can you imagine? One hundred families have to sit and listen to the melodic sound of a dog barking. It's the height of inconsideration. It's incomprehensible and it's totally unnecessary.

Even more amazing is one dog died, and they got a puppy to replace it. That's always incredible to me. People who are failing at something but then turn around and keep doing it. It should be mandatory that anyone who gets a dog goes through a training program. Kind of like getting a car license. "Oh hello ma'am. You want a puppy? Ok first sign right here and pay for the training program. We wouldn't want you to take little Fido home and destroy the peace of the neighborhood would we?" We were hoping they would learn but again, zero training. Well, what do you think happened? The little puppy sat there and watched the older dog just like little kids look up to their older siblings. The big dog barked when someone walked by, so the puppy learned to bark when someone walked by. The big dog barked when you came to the door, so the puppy learned to bark when you walked up to the door. The big dog barked the entire time you were visiting, so the puppy learned to bark when you were visiting. Total madness. I don't get it. It's exasperating. His wife was the same way. Just clueless. And they're smart, successful people. It actually had a really negative impact on our relationship. We just couldn't take it anymore. I'm not saying they're bad people. They're wonderful people raising great kids. It's just that for whatever reason they are brain dead on the topic of training and controlling their animals.

Years ago we lived next to really nice people. They were great neighbors except for their dog. Their dog woke us up at least three times a week. Do you know the effect that has on people? Well, how would you like to be woken up at around 5:30 a.m. by a barking dog? Is it fun? Does it put you in a good mood? Do you like it? We didn't either. They both worked, so they let their dog out early in the morning to do her business. Problem is that because the dog was not well trained and was stuck in a cage at home, alone all day the dog became an out of control barker. That's what happens. She barked when they opened the back slider to let her out. She barked if someone walked by. She barked when the UPS truck stopped out front. She barked if another dog walked by. She barked if we were in our own backyard. If a squirrel farted in the bushes, this dog went bonkers. It was a nuisance. Our neighbors were great people, but in this one area, we had to suffer because they chose not to train their dog.

Another neighbor we were next to was not too bright. Nice people but not bright. The definition of insanity is doing the same thing over and over while expecting a different result. Their dog was named Lincoln, which, of course, with their lack of training and oversight was a complete insult to one of our famed Presidents. The dog was one of those poor neglected creatures that was left out all day, and, yes, the insecure and unloved dog barked all the time at anything for any reason. Even though the wife was home all day, the animal was just left outside. The real joy of this situation was that our newborn daughter's bedroom was right next to their property line. As any of you parents who have or have had newborns understand, you will fight a ship full of Vikings to ensure your little one stays asleep. Our daughter was woken up from her naps. Our daughter was woken up from her night time sleep. Our daughter was woken up early in the morning. Of course, this meant that when she was startled awake she cried, hard, and our sleep was of course interrupted. When you are short on your sleep requirements it has a negative impact on your entire day, your mood, and your productivity. Sleep deprived and slowly losing our minds, it became desperate. Do you see how such insensitivity and lack of consideration can make someone possible do something crazy? I totally understand when good people snap. I get it. We were at the brink.

We tried sound machines, fans, and everything we could think of, but nothing blocked out this nutty dogs incessant barking. Being only a few months in the neighborhood, I was hesitant to walk over to my neighbor's house, but we were at a breaking point. I rang the doorbell, and she answered. I politely asked her if anything could be done as the dog was continually waking up our daughter. She expressed great remorse and was kind of caught off guard like what, she never heard that animal howling all day? Amazing. She then said she would be right on it. She apologized over and over again. Satisfied, I walked back to our home feeling relieved. Twenty minutes later the dog was barking at ants crawling on the ground or whatever. My wife and I were exasperated, "Are you kidding me?" Then we heard the neighbor scream, and I mean scream, "Lincoln! Shut up! Lincoln shut up!" We could hear her from inside our house. Oh yes, my friends. Cesar Millan, the Dog Whisperer, would've been proud! The dog, of course, not new to this mindless circus completely ignored his owner. Then she would traipse down the deck stairs, grab him, and yank him inside. This new sequence of events transpired several times a day and into the night. Great! Thanks for getting right on that. What was that definition of insanity? So now in addition to listening to a barking dog, we added a screaming woman yelling "Lincoln!" So great. Thanks for all that. Big improvement. I'm glad I went over and talked to her.

Your home is your castle, your safe place, your refuge from the world. If you can't even catch a break there, where can you go? This puts us thinking people in a heck of a spot. If we say something to inconsiderate neighbors, then we risk it getting awkward. If we say nothing, then we just have to suffer with a stupid dog barking all the time. What's the fix? Well, sadly, there isn't one. You suffer. Like Lincoln's owners, you can't really say anything because they obviously don't get it. If they did got it, they would have trained the animal properly in the first place. If they were capable of raising a pleasant dog, they would have. If they had a clue, things wouldn't be this way. So there is no fix. It's just a bummer for everyone in the neighborhood. Therein is one of the major downsides of the suburbs. You are trapped with other people's irresponsibility and lack of consideration. All I can do is try to inform people. Or, of course, you can buy four hundred acres somewhere.

That ought to be enough to not hear any obnoxious dog barking. The more I think of it, that sounds like a good plan.

It's not like there aren't resources. If you can't train your dog yourself, hire someone. Take your dog to obedience school. Rent Cesar Millan DVDs from the library. Do something, anything. Just don't ignore your dog or lock it up all day and expect it to be a model citizen. It's a massive commitment similar to having kids, and as I said earlier, neither one will turn out well without discipline, love, training, and guidance.

"But don't dogs bark?" you may ask. Fair enough. I'm not talking about the occasional bark. I'm not talking about a dog getting excited when little kids are in the backyard kicking a ball. I'm talking about the mindless, incessant, ongoing barking at anything that moves. Such barking almost always comes from unloved and ignored dogs. Dogs are pack animals and need leadership. Without an alpha owner, such dogs become insecure and as a result act out in an obsessive and territorial manner, not dissimilar to kids. In short, they go nuts and make the rest of us nuts too. If you can't be home, if you can't train your dog, if you can't make the commitment, then please for the love of God and all things holy, skip the dog routine. Get some fish. They're pretty quiet.

That goes for your music

I love all music. I appreciate and listen to just about all genres at one time or another. I like Kentucky bluegrass. I like heavy metal. I like classical. I like Gospel. I like rap. I like opera. I listen to it all. I don't like any music I can hear from your house, your backyard, or your car. There's a time and place to listen to music. There's also what's called reasonable volume. It's kind of like when you were a little kid and were told to use your inside voice. If I can hear the music and especially the bass from your car ten houses away as you're pulling into the neighborhood, I'm gonna say it's too loud. Maybe they don't know. Maybe their ears are shot from years of blasting speakers in a confined area. Maybe they should ask someone in their family, "Hey, can you hear my music when I'm driving up or pulling away?" That might be a thoughtful question to ask because if family members can, so can every other house in the neighborhood. Have you heard the phrase, "Don't pee in your own pool?" It's kind of the same thing with music. If you want to blast your brains out at ungodly decibels, then cool. Just do so when you pull out on the main road. I actually told my daughter when she was in that mindless, adolescent stage to turn her sound system off the minute she pulled into our neighborhood. I'm a good neighbor like that! I suggest you do the same. It won't kill you if you don't have blasting music for two minutes.

That goes for yard care

This one should be self-evident, but you'd be surprised. Kind of like annoying barking dogs should be self-evident too! If you move into a neighborhood where pride of ownership is obvious and everyone really cares for their yard and you let your yard turn into a jungle, yes, your neighbors will hate you. Your laziness or ineptitude diminishes the attraction of the neighborhood and the value of their homes. You're going to be "that house" that stands out like a sore thumb. Prune your bushes. Remove dead branches and trees. Fertilize, water, and mow your yard. This is not complicated. If you can figure out how to buy a house, then you can figure out how to care for a yard. And when you cut your lawn, bag the clippings. You're not in the country unless you actually are in the country, then let the clippings fly. If you're in a neighborhood, then bag your clippings. I will never, ever understand people who cut their lawn and blow the clippings all over their driveway, sidewalk, and even into the street and then leave it there to rot and turn yellow. Like that's a good look? That shows pride of ownership and an awareness of curb appeal or respect for your neighbors? Really nice! It just doesn't take that much more effort to have a nice looking yard.

In order to be a responsible adult and care for your yard, you will need a lawnmower, Weedwacker, blower, and fertilizer spreader. And not some dumb hand-held whirly-bird kind of spreader. Also not a drop spreader. If you use a drop spreader and you don't walk in perfectly straight lines you will have stripes in your lawn where the fertilizer never landed. Get a broadcast spreader like a Scotts Speedygreen. That's what I use. I have an amazing lawn. These are all standard lawn-care tools. If you're really an overachiever, you can buy an edger for along the sidewalk and drive-way. However, you can also hold your Weedwacker sideways, and it does a fine job of edging along hard surfaces. Either way you should be able to see the edge of the concrete. I was walking past a house the other day that literally had almost a foot of grass growing out into the sidewalk. It's a sloppy look that offers zero curb appeal. Cut, edge, and weedwack your lawn every week. Have a set day. Then get your blower and blow off any clippings from your hard surfaces, which means driveway, sidewalk, and street. Get on a fertilizer plan and put it in your calendar. In addition, you will need shears and loppers for trimming your shrubs and trees. If you can't handle this, then hire someone. Your neighbors will thank you.

Wrapping up

So how do you live so your neighbors won't hate you? It's the exact same rule as on an airplane. Have you ever been peacefully reading on a plane or even sleeping when Chatty Kathy behind you somehow feels an insa-tiable compulsion to yakity-yak with the person next to her about abso-lutely inconsequential matters? Even worse the guy with the deep bass voice who doesn't realize how loud he is? For such people, if they were instructed to shut their pie holes, they would suddenly realize how quiet it is, and if it's quiet, then while they're waxing eloquent, they are the ones indeed who shatters that same silence. Some people, especially on planes, can't handle the silence. They are somehow insecure unless there's noise. I know people who pick me up in their car, radio blaring and don't think to turn it down once I'm in the car. I know people who leave the TV on all the time, even with guests in the house. It's just noise, noise, noise. They're addicted to it. So it is in your neighborhood. And, yes, the vast majority of this has to do with noise. Park your Harley, muzzle your obnoxious dogs, and turn off your lawnmower. Is it quiet? Is it peaceful? Then, yes, you're the one that people are starting to hate.

Chapter Nine

The Lame Agents

A broker is a go-between. A broker is someone who aids in the process of a transaction. An agent is an extension of the broker. The agent represents a client and has their best interest in mind. The agent is a dedicated advocate. They are supposed to negotiate and fight for their client to get the most favorable terms possible. They are single-minded and focused on their client exclusively. Similar to an attorney an agent, whether specializing in sports, literature, or real estate, represents another entity and negotiates on their behalf.

Unfortunately, many people, both agents and clients alike, don't really understand this basic definition. You can see the confusion within the real estate community by the terms agents give themselves. It's so weird why some just can't come out and call themselves an agent. It boggles the mind. I saw one advertisement the other day with a woman calling herself a "Sales Consultant." What does that even mean? Does she think she works at JC Penny? Does she think she's at her home putting on women's makeup parties for Mary Kay? Sales Consultant? Or is she like a corporate consultant? A consultant is someone who gives direction and ideas to somebody or some organization on a specific area of expertise. A tax consultant advises on tax strategy. A hospitality consultant works within the hotel industry. A sales consultant conducts corporate seminars and training on sales techniques. How have real estate agents suddenly become "Sales Consultants?" Consultants have no fiduciary responsibility for their clients. They simply give suggestions on how a company can make improvements to increase efficiency or profitability and then move on. So is she really just speaking to the homeowners about how they can get more money for their home and then leaving with a check for her hourly rate?

I saw another one that made me laugh out loud; "Real Estate Counselor." Seriously? Similar to the Consultant was this person truly just there to "counsel" the sellers? Did they need counseling? I mean I know selling is stressful and all but really? Counselors just talk. They don't negotiate, fight for their clients in the open market, or know how to stage a home for maximum profit. Counselors talk. Is that what you want? Someone in your home to just have a chat with? Maybe brew some fresh coffee and bake cinnamon rolls and hang out in the kitchen for a while yakking it up? "Real Estate Advisor" was another one I have seen. Really? All you're giving is some advice and that's all? Advisors, corporate, legal, or otherwise, also just get paid to talk. Are homeowners really hiring such a person to hear advice about selling their home and that's it? As the Real Estate Advisor, is that your game plan? Just show up and offer advice on how to sell the home? After you give the advice, you're leaving? No other responsibility? The foolishness literally never ends. Finally, I saw "Real Estate Practitioner" about a week ago. Practitioner? Impressive!

They are brokers and agents, and the very fact that for whatever reason they are scared to call themselves as such reveals their inability to grasp the concept entirely. Anyone having such silly terms on their business card should be a screaming indication you should not conduct any business with this person. It's grounds for immediate disqualification. It's agency. It's fiduciary responsibility. It's negotiation. It's representation. This is not confusing, and if the agent was fundamentally confused as to what his or her role was, they would not be welcome in my home. The next time I'm on a plane if the pilot can't call himself a pilot and is confused as to what he is, I am getting off the plane. The reality is many so-called real estate agents are confused as to their role, and that is precisely the problem. Precious few of them come from any business background, have run a company, have ever managed anything, have excelled in corporate sales, or have any experience in high level negotiations. They just fumble along and think you can get paid fortunes just for sticking a sign in the ground and waiting for a paycheck.

If anyone showed up at my door for a listing appointment with a business card that said anything other than "broker" or "agent," I would have them leave because I clearly wouldn't have the right person. The fact that some agents have to figure out cute ways to call themselves something other than what they are reveals a fundamental lack of understanding in the role the find themselves in and the very nature of agency. A thing by any other name is still the same thing. Are we scared to admit we're agents? Do we think the term "broker" is negative? It's just all too weird for me. So if the idea of an agent is representation, communication, and negotiation, wouldn't it behoove those thinking of buying or selling a home to find an agent who is strong in those skills? A strong agent protects their client, spots problems ahead of time, shows initiative, and fights to get them the best outcome possible.

Like all professions, there are good ones and there are bad ones. There are hardworking ones, and there are lazy ones. There are aggressive ones, and there are cowardly ones. There are professional ones and incompetent ones. In my opinion nowhere is this more true than in real estate. Second only to used car salesmen, real estate agents aren't usually held in high esteem by the general public. Yet we as a society need to buy and sell property and cars for that matter. Therein lays the rub. You need to do something, but you're not particularly fond of the key people involved. Nightmare stories abound.

I think the reason there is such a lack of professionalism in real estate is because the threshold for entry is so low. There are literally no barriers for anyone wanting to become a real estate agent. If somebody can pay some money and pass a couple of tests, they are considered an agent. So if they have the means and they are smart enough to study and pass a test, they can approach a broker and sign on as a real estate agent. The horrifying thing is there is absolutely no way to qualify if this person has any experience or is strong in negotiation, has any business sense at all, has adequate people skills, or is good at sales or communication. All they have to do is pay some money and pass a test. That's it. I have long advocated for a higher threshold of entry as well as mandatory production minimums. If an agent was told that they had to close a minimum of ten transactions a year, for example, the herd would be dramatically thinned. Better yet, if there was a higher cost for entry and more mandatory testing and training, that would prevent a lot of people from getting into real estate in the first place.

Don't get me wrong here. I'm not trying to come off as an elitist. From experience I have just seen so much incompetence due to low standards that many times I was doing the work for the other agent in the deal because they had no idea what they were doing. I remember one time in particular, if I was the least bit devious I could have sunk the agent and her clients. With the permission of my client, I pointed out obvious problems with their paperwork. I could have just turned a blind eye, and my client would have legally been able to keep their sizeable deposit. However, my client and I wanted to be helpful and ensure a smooth flow toward the closing. Then we had to smile when the commission check was passed to the incompetent agent knowing she didn't deserve even half of what she got.

Representation is a big deal. Being responsible for another's financial well-being is a big deal. An agent has what is called a "fiduciary responsibility." Meaning, they are legally responsible for all aspects of their clients' interests, including but not limited to financial, ethical, and material realms. Some in real estate have a cavalier attitude toward this whole process. I guarantee if they ever got sued and ended up in court they would get serious in a heartbeat! Over the years there have been lots of attempts at modifying the term "real estate agent." For whatever reason there has been an obnoxious trend to somehow soften the idea representation. Weak agents prefer terms like "advisor" or "consultant." Whereas there is clearly some advising and consulting going on in real estate, a consultant is not usually on the hook for their client. I know lots of consultants who blow in and blow out of companies that pay them handsomely for their advice. The consultant isn't responsible for the well-being of the company so the term doesn't quite do it for me. Consultant smacks about as corny as Subway having "sandwich artists" make lunch for you. Let's just call it what it is: agency and representation. And if it's agency and representation then negotiation and business skills are paramount. Like in any part of life, the stronger the skills the better.

This chapter is dedicated to all the lame agents out there that are confused or don't quite get what they are supposed to be doing. They are the ones who mess everything up and give this industry such a bad reputation. I have organized them into specific categories. However, oftentimes lame agents are a combination of several of these designations. You'll notice this chapter is significantly longer than the chapter on great agents. That should tell you something about the condition of the modern American real estate industry.

The Failing Agent

I start with this kind of agent intentionally as they are in the vast majority. As this is an actual statistic, you have the highest probability to encounter this type of agent. They are the ones who give the real estate industry a bad name. This may sound overly negative but it is actual fact presented by the National Association of Realtors (NAR). There is an over 85 percent turnover rate in real estate agents every five years. This means that 85 percent of real estate agents practicing today will not be here in five years. This also means that the agent failure rate is almost exactly the same as the failure rate for small businesses. And this is exactly the point. Most people who get into real estate don't understand as an independent contractor earning a 100 percent commission income, they indeed are running a small business. They fail because the overwhelming majority of agents have little if any business ownership, sales or marketing experience. According to the NAR, the average real estate agent conducts four transactions a year which isn't enough to live on, therefore they quit or become part-time dabblers. They are not professionals with a commitment to the industry or their craft. They don't possess the temperament, attitude, and skill set to succeed. Because of these reasons most agents you encounter will be statistically going out of business. They will be a failing agent.

The Cowardly Agent

Let's face it. Not everyone has amazing taste. Furthermore, not everyone is fully aware about the appearance and attractiveness of their home. They're not necessarily bad people; it's just that they're busy or distracted or overwhelmed. They may be gifted in other areas, but presenting an attractive home isn't one of them. That's where a strong real estate agent comes into play. A strong agent will give practical and possibly affordable ways to improve the appearance of the home to prepare it for the market. A strong agent will talk to their clients about appearance and attraction and why it is fundamentally essential to have brilliant curb appeal. Curb appeal is just that; how does this home look from the street, the curb? Does it scream, "My owners have no clue how to manage a home?" Or to the contrary does it proclaim "I've been the HOA green thumb award winner five times in twelve years! If I'm that nice outside, wait until you see the inside!"

I am amazed at how many people have absolutely no idea how to care for a yard. It's also troubling how many real estate agents apparently don't care to make the effort to inform their clients. There are two homes in particular that befuddle me, both with for-sale signs in their yard by large brokerages. The first home has weeds growing up through the cracks of the driveway, has visible peeling paint, a destroyed lawn, dead trees, and overgrown bushes. On top of that, whereas the entire neighborhood stained or left natural their cedar fences, this owner thought it would be a great idea to paint theirs white. White! I don't know if they were going for the "white picket fence" motif or what but they missed it, hard. It looks like a prison wall. Beyond that, it hasn't been scraped and repainted in what looks like decades as the faded and peeling paint testify to. At least if you have bad taste, maintain the object of your bad taste, so it looks decent.

The second home, by all appearances, looks nice, but their yard just needs a little work. Assuming the inside of the home is updated and in good condition, it should sell for a strong price. It just needs some yard work. So here is this nice upscale home, and their yard is at best mediocre. The bushes are not pruned or tidy. The lawn is filled with dandelions and crab grass. Just these two issues throw the whole curb appeal off. It takes it from a "Honey, stop the car and get the agent's number" to a drive-by. And here's the crazy thing: those issues are so simple to resolve and for such little money for the life of me, I can't understand why either the homeowner or real estate agent couldn't figure out how to improve the curb appeal. All it needed was about an hour of spring cleaning and raking out dead leaves from under the bushes, some fresh mulch, some trimming and pruning, and an application of a weed and feed fertilizer. With that done, hit the sprinklers for a few days, and you have a new yard. More importantly, you now have great curb appeal and are positioned for a quick sale.

You could literally fix it for less than $100 and probably get thousands more for the home and sell it quicker. That's another key principle here; you get more money for your home, and isn't that the point? Don't you want to get the most money for your home as possible? Isn't that a good investment of your $100 if you could get say $5,000 more and sell it quicker, so you could get on with your life? Apparently neither this unaware homeowner nor the Cowardly Agent understands this. I say cowardly because some agents are just plain scared to death to speak truthfully to their clients. They are horrified at the prospect of possibly making them angry or insulted. While I never go out of my way to offend my clients, I have found that people respect you for telling them the truth. Instead of speaking clearly about the issues and positioning the seller for a successful sale, the Cowardly Agent will just smile and pretend everything's great.

I am familiar with neighborhoods where there are no shortages of large homes with three and even four car garages. Unfortunately, there are parts of this area that don't have an HOA and consequently attract the worst in home ownership. There are homes with limousines with flat tires parked out front (not joking), campers, trailers of every kind, soccer nets in front yards, and portable basketball hoops everywhere. Unfortunately, if you live in a neighborhood without an HOA or with a weak one, there's little you can do about the appearance of your neighborhood. However, you can always do something about the appearance of your home. Regardless of your neighborhood, there is never an excuse to not have an amazing looking home.

Of course, as with anything, there are exceptions. The owners might be infirm or maybe have suffered a financial setback like a failed business or maybe there's a messy divorce and the home just needs to be sold "as is." Even in those challenging situations, isn't more money better than less? Someone in the relational network needs to care enough to help out and make the home have at least decent curb appeal and not throw off the vibe that it is uncared for or abandoned. The same is true on the inside. Are the owners packrats? Is there clutter everywhere? Is there too much furniture crammed into the rooms? I know I'm repeating myself here but a strong agent will help the people see things through the eyes of a potential buyer and set them up for success instead of being cowardly, addressing nothing and just watch as the buyers come and go.

While we're on the inside, are there any peculiar odors? This can be really sensitive, but it must be addressed. Some nationalities cook a lot of fish. Some cook with a lot of garlic. Both of these food items have the potential to leave a lingering odor. Now personally, I'm a fan of fish and I like garlic, but not everyone shares my opinion. When a home is closed up, the odors intensify. I can't stress this enough. Odor is the first thing that hits someone when they open the door. The smell of a home can either be an asset or an incredible turn off. There is a huge difference between a neutral or pleasant smelling home versus a pungent one. And it's not just food odor either. A moldy shower or poorly cleaned bathrooms will send off a scent. If there are toddlers and babies in the home, there can sometimes be that nursery room kind of smell. You know, it's kind of a cross between dirty diapers, vomit and baby powder? A strong agent will address any potentially negative issue. The Cowardly Agent will simply pretend that everything's great and keep moving while totally ignoring glaring and obvious issues. For that which can't be fixed quickly or affordably like soiled carpets, a strong agent will incentivize a buyer instead of allowing it to become a point of contention. A little note in the MLS stating that there will be a $3,000 paint allowance resolves an unsightly color scheme. For everything else, a strong agent will speak truthfully. A Cowardly Agent will pretend everything is perfect and avoid dealing with problems head on.

Another area you will see a Cowardly Agent emerge is in the listing presentation. Especially when it comes to price, the cowardly agent will kowtow to the owner for fear of offending them or losing the listing. If the comp's are around $300,000 but the owners want to list at $370,000, the cowardly agent will simply smile and bow to the owners request. Instead of educating the sellers on the reality of the market and the fact that not only will people not be interested in a ridiculously priced home, even if they did get the offer, it wouldn't appraise for that amount because there are no comp's to validate that price. But, of course, the cowardly agent will never do that. They will simply smile and say what a lovely home it is and watch the sellers sign the contract. The Cowardly Agent knows full well the home will never sell for that price but plays the game anyway out of fear of rejection. The cowardly agent knows that after the home sits on the market for months he or she can eventually ask the sellers for a price reduction that will get the home down into realistic range. In contrast, a strong agent informs sellers how to effectively price and position their home to sell so everyone doesn't waste their time.

You will also see the Cowardly Agent fall apart in negotiations as well. I recently presented an asking price offer on a home that listed for $429,000. The two highest comp's were at $420,000, so this home was asking a bit of a premium. The home is nice and had some appealing aspects to validate the higher price, so we didn't think it was unfair or greedy. It was on a cul-de-sac and was everything my buyers wanted. We simply requested that the four piece deck furniture remained with the house. I could tell it was a nice set, maybe worth $1,200 or so. Since we offered $9,000 over comp's, I figured it would be a slam dunk. The wife and kids were still in the home, but the husband was already transferred to Virginia with the Navy. After the agent presented our offer, the wife gave a verbal yes feeling the offer was perfectly fair. However, to my amazement, the husband demanded they keep the deck furniture. My attitude on these things is that it's just stuff. You don't fall in love with stuff. Moreover why schlep stuff all over the country. I get it that the tax payers pay for all military relocations, so it's no big deal for them, but still I thought it was a little odd that he wouldn't let it go. Even more odd was the fact that he wasn't even there but dictating from across the country. Meanwhile, his wife was stressed out dealing with the move all on her own.

I told the agent it was a bit of an insult after offering full price, and I insisted the agent go back to her clients and help them see the light. My demeanor in our verbal exchange was one that gave the hint that it wasn't worth losing the deal over a set of used deck furniture that they could easily repurchase in Virginia. The agent texted me within a few hours and said the furniture could stay with the home. Now think how things would turn out if I was Cowardly Agent. Since the Cowardly Agent is motivated by fear, I would simply have said, "Oh, OK" and backed down when I was told the sellers wanted to keep their deck furniture. Then my buyers would not only have paid top dollar for their home, but they would then have to go out and spend another $1,200 for deck furniture. Cowardly agents don't fight for their clients. They never push back. They fold their hand like a weak poker player. You can always tell when a Cowardly Agent is involved because of all the wasted time.

The Vanishing Agent

There are some agents who are so short-term minded, narrow focused, desperate, or broke that all they can think about is rushing to the close, so they can get their paycheck. Then, with paycheck in hand, they vanish into thin air. Whether they are happily bounding toward Las Vegas or some other destination is unknown, but they are simply gone. I knew agents like this in an office I used to work at. There were some agents who were hapless and low energy until they got a fish on the hook, so to say. Once they even had a faint whiff of money coming their way, they became another person. Suddenly they became optimistic and motivated. All they could talk about is what they were going to spend their money on. They made phone calls, and they made plans. Then, predictably after it was done, they disappeared.

There has been more than one occasion where I have been approached by people who have used another agent in the past but because they vanished, they wanted to work with me instead. I have developed a reputation for being steady, available, reliable, and connected. People want to work with someone who is going to be around. It's silly for the Vanishing Agent to act that way because they actually lose a lot of business with that mentality. Repeat and referral business is the cream of the crop. Such business is effortless because it just comes to you, but more importantly it's highly qualified. There is already inbuilt trust, so you can move forward with greater efficiency. The Vanishing Agent forgoes all the benefits sticking around can bring.

I learned something years ago when I was young man working as a server in restaurants. You're not going to get rich off one table. Good servers understand this principle. They know they will do quite well if they consistently provide excellent service table after table, day in and day out. They don't lose their head over one table, big tip or no tip. It's the same way in real estate. Nobody gets rich on one deal. The priority and focus should be on providing solid and consistently excellent service and over time; the money will come. Sticking around helps make that happen.

The Sign-and-Split Agent

Similar to the Vanishing Agent, the Sign-and-Split Agent (SAS) simply disappears after the contract is signed. It doesn't matter whether the agent represents a seller or buyer, once the contract is signed he or she turns into vapor. There is no communication. There is no follow up. There is no explanation of the process. There is no customer service. Gone. They are just gone. Nobody really knows where they go. We're not sure if they are actually aliens and get sucked up into a parallel universe through some hidden portal, but what we do know is that they disappear into thin air. If you have the sad misfortune of dealing with a SAS Agent, it will be like pulling teeth to get any information regarding your transaction. Plan on being in the dark and hoping everything works out, because you will not see this person again until they magically appear to collect their paycheck at closing.

The Slogan Agent

Because most real estate agents have never actually been in a business environment of any significant level, they really don't understand branding. In its basic form, branding is the methodology employed to create a lasting connection to the consumer through a memorable logo, tagline, slogan, or jingle. Branding is reinforced through consistent marketing. Branding in business is like branding on cattle farms. It is a way to put your identifiable mark on what is yours. Then everyone who encounters your business or cattle knows exactly who they are dealing with. The Slogan Agent really loves the tagline after their name. They stay up nights thinking of crafty little phrases that will bring them epic amounts of business. Here are some examples I have seen over the years:

"Consider your home sold…Colorado." So I guess he's going for "hey I'm so awesome you can think of your home as gone!" However, it's just dumb and really doesn't mean anything. Beyond that does he only do listings? From his slogan it appears that he is uninterested in working with buyers.

"The power of yes." What does that even mean? In order to promote your brand in an effective manner, it must be clearly understood. In other words, it must not only be memorable, but it must make sense. "The power of yes?" I mean is that even worth advertising since no one really knows what message that agent is trying to communicate?

"Real estate beyond the ordinary." And it was done in cursive. Wow! While attempting to be elegant and different from the rest, it just sounds cliché. What's beyond ordinary? Extraordinary? OK, so prove it. It's not really a brand, and it really doesn't say anything. It's just one more meaningless line in a thousand. So many of these sound like tired pickup lines guys have been using at bars for decades. "Hey baby, I'm anything but ordinary!" The same agent had "Professional Realtors" on their marketing. Um, in contrast to unprofessional or amateur? Every Realtor is a Realtor. There isn't any stratification. Again, what does that even mean beyond just trying to differentiate yourself to look like you're better than everyone else. "Oh, this guy's a professional. We should definitely go with him!"

"Your downtown expert." OK, so at least this one makes sense. It describes in short order what she is about. If you wanted to buy a home downtown, you know who to call. Still not sure it's branding as opposed to a description of where she specializes, but it's better than most.

"I work for you." Oh, thanks for clarifying. I thought you worked for somebody else while driving me all around town looking at houses.

"America's best real estate agent." Insert huge eye roll here. Unless you actually are and can back it up with awards, facts, and statistics, you just look silly.

"One on one service." Whew, glad we figured that out. I thought this guy was going to speak with me and everyone else in the neighborhood! Seriously. What else would real estate be but one on one? This is not some amazing revelation. It's not even worth the ink.

"We are professional real estate agents helping families find their perfect home." Again they are proud to be professional as opposed to any other alternative. Then they say they help families. So you won't work with singles or couples without kids? No empty nesters? It's funny how slogans like this sound fine upon first read, but when you actually think it through, they're ridiculous. Not only are they ridiculous, but they're also illegal. You can't advertise or verbalize which people you will work with and which ones you won't. Hmm, bet they didn't think that one through! Moreover what exactly is a "perfect" home? One that is in perfect condition without a single blemish? I've never seen one.

"Love where you live." Again, just a meaningless stupid saying that communicates nothing. What do you think people do, live somewhere they hate?

"When you're serious about real estate." So no joking around here. Only call her when you're really serious. If you're just horsing around call another agent but when you have your game face on, call her!

"The premier real estate agents in town." Oh boy, is this tiring. Premier? Compared to what? By what standards? When agents make unsubstantiated and empty-headed subjective claims about themselves, I really get bored. What does premier mean, and how do you arrive at such a lofty status?

"Real people. Real results." Oh, thank God. I was scared we were working with robots or zombies! And real results? Well, for sure they're better than fake results.

"Find out why we're number one." Number one where? Your mind? Your neighborhood? North America? Such unsubstantiated statements are trite, glib, and make me roll my eyes. They are designed to impress naïve people without providing any facts to back it up.

"Make your next move your best move." Well, thank you. I was actually considering making a huge mistake and making my next move the worst move in my life, but now that you said that, I'm going to make it my best move!

"Thinking of buying or selling? Call me!" This is the single most meaningless and tired slogan out there.

"Helping buyers and sellers get what they want when they want." Oh man, this is getting old. What if they want to stop paying taxes? What if they want a new Porsche?

"One of the most respected Realtors in town." Respected by whom? Their own children? Their neighbor? Again, unsubstantiated and subjective claims that are meaningless and convey nothing of import but are designed to project value.

"Call or text me anytime." Really? How about 2:47 a.m. next Thursday? One of my favorites!

"Personalized real estate services to home buyers and sellers." This means nothing. What does personalized mean? Does she sew the sellers initials on their shirt cuffs?

"Experience taken to new heights." Ugh, what does that even mean? Does she take her clients up in a hot air balloon?

Are you getting the point? I literally could go on all day. It is amazing how many non-thinking real estate agents are out there that just keep putting these meaningless slogans on their business cards and marketing efforts. It's exhausting. I mean why even do it if it means nothing? Moreover stupid sayings that mean nothing are a poor reflection on the agent. It reveals they don't really have a grasp on high level business. Do people honestly think such dumb sayings are going to have a positive impact on their business or bring in new clients by the droves?

How about we just skip the corny and meaningless slogans? They are so tired and only reveal the lack of thinking and business acumen in many real estate agents. I really don't know why real estate agents put these dumb slogans on their marketing materials, business cards, and websites. I honestly don't know why. It's like they get indoctrinated when they go through training or something. I just don't get it. As for me I don't have any cheesy slogan on my business cards or marketing. I don't want to participate in outdated and silly vestiges from the 1970s. I wish everyone would follow suit, especially the Slogan Agent.

The Technology Agent

More than at any time in history, technology has become a main staple in an increasingly large portion of our daily lives. The same is true in the real estate industry. There are legitimate and helpful additions to the process, and there are deceptive strategies to give the illusion that the agent is working hard on behalf of their clients. I say deceptive because some technology is designed to mislead people into thinking something is true when it is not. For example, some agent's websites show listings as if they are theirs when they belong to someone else. This gives the impression that this agent is a top producer when in fact they are hijacking other agent's listings and falsely misleading people into thinking they are their own. In literature, that is called plagiarism. I don't know what they call it in real estate.

Some agents subscribe to a paid newsletter service that simply adds their name and picture to the top of it as if the agent created, designed, wrote, published, and mailed the information. These newsletters are filled with tips and trends along with local market statistics. They are either mailed or e-mailed directly from the publisher. The agent literally never touches them. It is designed to make people believe that this agent is not only a prolific writer, which reveals a level of intelligence and organizational skill, but also truly has their finger on the pulse of the real estate market. In reality, this agent could be golfing or eating a cinnamon roll at Dunkin' Donuts while someone else writes, edits, prints, and sends the newsletter. While no one can argue the efficient nature of such endeavors, I am generally against such things because they lack integrity and are intentionally misleading, false, and deceptive. It doesn't pass the straight face test. In other words, if someone actually asked them if the they wrote those newsletters, they would have to contort their facial expression to not reveal the truth. It's just nonsense and it's unnecessary. If you want to write a newsletter, then write a newsletter. Do the work. I personally write not only books (New Home Construction Tips and Traps, coming in 2018!) but also all my own online articles which I post on my Facebook page, P.Johan Real Estate. I have also written over 150 articles on LinkedIn.

While I am anything but a Luddite, I do find that technology is great, but in the final analysis, we are in a people business. Many agents get this wrong. They say when asked, "Oh, I'm in the real estate business." The truth is nobody is really in the real estate business. Nobody is in any kind of business. We are all in the people business. Even pastors fall into this trap by thinking ministry is about theology. While good theology is important, you are dealing with human beings and a pastor better be great with people. A restaurant manager is not in the food business but in the people business. People prepare the food, people deliver the food to the table and people eat the food. Good food notwithstanding, in order to succeed in the restaurant business you need to be able to connect with people on a deep and meaningful level, both your staff and your customers. Regardless of vocation, people are involved, and if that is true and it is, then we must be exceptional with our people skills.

I have found that some agents who really focus on the benefits of technology do so to compensate for their lack of people skills. Not all, but some are incredibly awkward and uncomfortable to be around, but, boy, do they have all the bells and whistles! The ones I have been familiar with not only lack people skills but they have also been lackluster in their appearance and communication skills as well. Again, while technology is clearly important, it is not the end all be all. Technology can't negotiate a great price or terms. Technology can't provide you with market understanding, and technology can't do the hard work that's necessary to get deals done. Technology can't engender trust. Technology has no face. It is a tool and should be used as an additional supplement to enhance effectiveness, not as a replacement or crutch.

The Part-Time Agent

This is a tough one. They may be good people, but this kind of agent just doesn't do enough business to be proficient at it. Having said that, just because someone does real estate part-time doesn't necessarily mean they are only partially competent, but for many it's a challenge to juggle multiple jobs with any sense of excellence. Worse, because their time and attention is split, their availability is spotty. Real estate can be a fairly random occupation where your schedule has to be flexible. You need to be available to your clients and accommodate their schedule if at all possible. Beyond that much of real estate has to do with speed of communication and speed of action. The full-time agent is able to communicate quickly with his or her clients, is available to show houses on short notice and get an offer in fast. They are not distracted with outside pursuits. Can you imagine losing your dream home because it got scooped up by a full-time agent while you were waiting for your Part-Time Agent to finish his shift at Home Depot?

A lot of agents are part-time initially because they are transitioning out of one career and moving into real estate. It takes a really skillful and adept person to pull this off, and most are unable to do so. Remember, the failure rate for Realtors is 85 percent so not only are they juggling their main job and their part-time job, but they are pressing into a new business with an extraordinarily high failure rate which makes it even harder. Would you want a surgeon operating on a loved one if they were "part-time" or if it wasn't their main focus? There not only is an issue of availability and focus but also of commitment. How committed is somebody if they aren't willing to put all their eggs in one basket? They are asking you do so with your home and using them as your agent. Why aren't they willing to do the same?

The Dabbling Agent

This is one of the most agonizing aspects of real estate. There are enough dabblers roaming around every community in the United States that eventually they will stumble upon some unsuspecting soul and convince them that they are indeed a real estate agent. "Oh yes. I can help you with that!" Whereas the Part-Time Agent might at least be working toward full-time, the Dabbling Agent really has no intention of doing so. They dabble. They dip their toe in the water but never really commit to jumping in. They're busy with other things, and real estate is not even close to their top priority. They're the guy who "makes an appearance" at a party and then splits the first chance he can. The Dabbling Agent most likely has a lot of irons in the fire, so to say. He does "a lot of things." He's a go-getter kind of guy, but not really. He has lots of ideas and lots of imagination and seems to always be busy, but he rarely commits to something. He just dabbles.

It's weird that in other professions a strong commitment is required for success or even entry for that matter. There is no dabbling. There has to be a commitment to education, perhaps apprenticeship, or residency, and then eventually that commitment pays off. Proper sushi chefs in Japan may apprentice for up to twelve years before mastering their craft. They definitely don't dabble in sushi! Did you ever hear of anyone "dabbling" at nuclear medicine? Have you ever heard someone say at a party, "Yea, I'm kind of dabbling with getting my PhD?" Ever seen anyone dabble at being a Special Forces soldier? Real estate, unfortunately, is the kind of industry where dabblers can hide in the shadows and not really commit. For some it's a hobby that they do if they feel like it. They "do" real estate when they're bored, when they bump into someone, when the moment strikes them, or when they need a little extra cash. For the Dabbling Agent, real estate is a hobby up there with flying kites, doing puzzles, and making origami.

The Desperate Agent

Again, and I know I'm repeating myself, remember that 85 percent of real estate agents fail and drop out within five years. You really need to keep that in the front of your mind if you are attempting to understand the real estate industry. Because the vast majority of real estate agents are failing in some degree, there will logically be a high percentage of them who are desperate for business. By and large the Desperate Agent is broke or, at least for whatever reason, acts like it. They wear desperation like a cologne that permeates everything they touch and everywhere they go people get a whiff of it. The impetus for all activity of the Desperate Agent is anxiety and fear. They are anxious, and because they are anxious, they are not thinking straight. Their messy thinking clouds their judgment and creates a context whereby the desperate agent becomes irrational and illogical. The Desperate Agent has many sub-categories that I have outlined below:

The Desperate Agent doesn't respect themselves, their life, or their family. They are basically indentured servants who will do anything for the one in power, and the one in power is the prospect, the almighty prospect. The prospect is the maybe, the hopeful, the almost, the possible buyer or seller. The Desperate Agent lives in a constant state of panic and anxiety cloaked in what they think is good customer service. Such agents believe that inconveniencing themselves and their family is the way they prove they are hard workers. They are always ready to go.

No sacrifice is so great that they will not make on your behalf, almighty prospect. They will miss their son's baseball game. They will rise from the dinner table. They will skip church on Sunday for you. They will stay out all day Saturday with you. They will cancel plans, cut vacations short, and pass on date night. They will gladly abandon those they love for your attention, all powerful prospect. They don't respect themselves. They only respect you, the omnipotent prospect. For you alone hold the keys of their income in your hand, and they will, in exchange, do anything for you.

The Desperate Agent is horrible at qualifying. An experienced, top producing agent qualifies prospects because they don't want to waste time. They know time is money, so they don't waste effort on someone who either isn't serious or is unable to go through with a transaction when they could focus on prepared and ready buyers and sellers. The Desperate Agent, on the other hand, will never qualify a prospect. They won't educate and inform their clients on the process. They won't ask for a pre-qualification letter from a lender. They won't ask questions of buyers in order to clarify what kind of home they want. Can they afford to buy a house? Doesn't matter! Do they know what they want? Doesn't matter! If the buyers are a couple, are they both in agreement on what they are looking for? Doesn't matter! What matters is that they are in the agent's car driving around looking at houses, any houses. In the agent's mind busyness equals business. Frantic activity and spending time driving around is what agents do after all. In their mind all this panicked running around equals progress and a paycheck. In reality those things may or may not bring income. What is certain, however, is they are so desperate, their anxiety overrules the common sense foundational action of prequalifying candidates, so they could have a specific, focused, and targeted approach to finding a home.

The Desperate Agent will gladly surrender their income. It's one of the most pathetic things about real estate. The Desperate Agent, in an attempt to secure any deal, will gladly whisper to the prospect that they will chop their income as a sort of bribe. On the selling side, they will gladly take a lower listing commission just for the pleasure of having their name on a sign in the front of someone's yard. On the buying side, they will happily tote potential buyers around town and even buy them lunch. To cinch the deal, they will tell them, before their second ice tea even hits the table, that they will give the prospects half their commission after closing. The unsuspecting prospect then allows their mind to wander, elated at their good fortune. They marvel at the fact that they not only get a new home, but that they also get a nice cash bonus! They begin mentally planning on what they're going to do with their newly discovered windfall. Half way through their chicken chimichanga, they have already found several worthy expenditures that they can apply their portion to.

Indeed the Desperate Agent will gladly surrender their income to you, oh mighty prospect. And then here's a thought: How is this weak agent, this desperate person, going to negotiate on your behalf when they can't even negotiate for their own income? How is someone so weak going to suddenly become strong in representing you? How are they going to fight for you when they can't even fight for themselves? If they fall down on their own income, which is an expression of their personal value and contribution, they will assuredly fall down on everything else. I've seen it time and time again. The Desperate Agent falls flat on their face and quickly surrenders in negotiations because their desperation, anxiety, and fear manipulates them instead of focusing on their fiduciary responsibility to their client that they supposedly represent. They will sell their client down the river and surrender everything behind the scenes just to get this dog gone deal closed.

The Desperate Agent is afraid. It really comes down to this simple fact. They are scared, they are nervous, and they are anxious. If they would ever pause, get off the treadmill of their insecure life, and take internal inventory, they would realize that everything they do, at least in real estate, is motivated by fear. Fear of rejection. Fear of not closing the deal. Fear of not producing and wondering what other agents in the office think. Fear of driving around for days and not getting a contract signed. Fear of not having enough money. In fear there is no rest. In fear there is no confidence. When fear rules, strategy, smart thinking, and tactics all go out the window in exchange for the path of least resistance.

The Desperate Agent is envious but unaware. He is envious at those who succeed. He is jealous of the top producing agents in the office. He is convinced that there is some secret they are employing to achieve their success. The sad thing is that while he is distracted with his conviction that the issue is external, he is fundamentally unaware that the issue is entirely internal. The issue is completely his to own. That desperation he wears like a cologne is actually a repellent. Think of mosquito repellent. You spray it on your arms, and when a mosquito comes near it, they actually turn and fly away. They are repelled. Desperation does the same thing to prospects and potential clients. Experts say that dogs can sense fear and anxiety. I think people can too. People can discern the anxiety a desperate agent projects. Most of our communication is nonverbal. Our body language, gestures, energy, and facial expressions along with our overall demeanor communicate much louder than our words. People pick up on the desperation, and it makes them feel uncomfortable. When people are uncomfortable, they walk away. The Desperate Agent is unaware that his demeanor and attitude is actually a repellent not dissimilar to bug spray.

The Desperate Agent is nonconfrontational. I've already touched on this elsewhere in the book, but it deserves its own section. Well-adjusted people understand that confrontation is part of life. It's not negative. It's not toxic. It's not something to be avoided. It's just part of life. Weak, anxious, and fearful people avoid it like the plague, and nobody avoids it more than the Desperate Agent. Because deep down inside in places she doesn't ever reveal at parties, this terrified agent will do anything to avoid a confrontation. She is a people pleaser. Oh sure, everyone thinks she's great. Her neighbors think she's awesome. Teachers at school and parents at the playground all think fondly of her. Her friends or the one's she thinks are friends, will never tell her the truth though. Deep down a terror resides. This gnawing existential rash continues to chafe at her and affects everything she does. She can't confront her own demons, so how is she supposed to confront anything else? She can't fight for her own emotional and mental freedom, so how will she negotiate the best deal for you? She will not rock the boat. She will not make waves. She will make sure everyone loves her. Of course, everyone will love her because she always loses, she always surrenders. The other agents love her because she always gives in during negotiations. Clearly a criminal will "love" the bank that always smiles and hands over the money. She falsely misinterprets feigned temporary affection for earned dedication and loyalty. She buys her relationships by not confronting anything or anybody.

The Emotional Agent

There are so many of this kind of agent I could probably right a whole chapter on just them. From time to time, I conduct financial management and investment seminars. My favorite thing I always say at my seminars is "panic is not a strategy." So many agents really don't get this. At the first sign of any kind of challenge, the fear mechanism kicks in, and they go straight into an emotional tailspin. It all just turns into panic central. I don't get it. Well, actually I do get it. Most agents have no background in negotiations or high-level sales, so they are in over their heads. They were told they could make great money, paid some fees, passed some tests, received little if any training, and they were released on an unsuspecting general public.

Seriously, let me say something clinical here. Psychologically speaking, when a person is in over their head and is in an area where they know deep down in their soul they don't belong and that they don't possess the skill set to do the job correctly and competently, they have a subterranean anxiety. You know what I mean? They're pretenders. They're posers. They have what is called imposter syndrome, and because of that, they are fear based, lack confidence, can't be logical in the face of challenges, and freak out at the smallest little thing. Their entire emotional construct is rooted in fear. Fear of people finding out that they're actually not that good at real estate. Fear of rejection. Fear of not making money. Fear of looking stupid. Fear of not succeeding. Fear of having wasted time and money to get into real estate in the first place. Fear of failing. That deep-down fear creates intense mental anxiety and roils around like boiling lava within the core of an active volcano. The only thing it takes for that fear to manifest and come exploding up is a problem or challenge because such events threaten to tear the mask off and expose them for who they really are. That's it. Kaboom! Logic and creative problem solving is out the window. Well developed professionals know that life and business are filled with problems and challenges. That's why you stay levelheaded and figure things out. Not so with the Emotional Agent. All she knows how to do is freak the heck out at the first sign of things getting complicated.

Sometimes the Emotional Agent has personal problems. While a pro can compartmentalize, the Emotional Agent cannot. Like a hunter dragging a dead dear out of the woods, they drag their negative energy, fear, and personal issues into the office with them. Unfortunately the carcass is in the car with her clients as well, metaphorically speaking. I don't fault anyone for struggling, and I sure know what it feels like to be in a tough spot, but when agents allow their personal desperation or issues to interfere with a transaction, it can really add unnecessary stress and waste a lot of time and energy. I recently had an Emotional Agent text me in a panic. She had received a loan cancellation notice from my buyers lender. Even though my client was a physician, had great credit, and was fully capable to execute the transaction, the agent just freaked out. You see, what happens is when you live scared and are fear based, your entire perspective on life is anticipating things going wrong. Then like a self-fulfilling prophecy, anything that pops up will trigger panic as that person expects impending doom.

Now if you're crazy by yourself, I say be as crazy as you want to be, but when I'm involved, the unnecessary drama is completely unwelcomed. Though she cognitively knew my client was financially able and knew that I was a strong agent, she took the loan cancellation as a signal to freak out instead of being logical or rational. First of all, if it was an issue, I would have known about it ahead of time and contacted her as clearly I have a vested interest in my buyer's financing. Second, all that happened as it often does, was that my buyer was shopping around and found a better loan. Instead of using intelligence and logic, she allowed her fear-based emotional structure to manipulate her and create a completely unnecessary negative whirlwind. I don't respond to everything right away. I have what is called a life. I am also running a business and have other transactions I am working on. I also have my priorities in order and don't drop everything just because someone texts me or leaves a voice mail. I'll get to it in a reasonable time period but in the middle of dinner isn't it. Few things in life are so dog gone important that it merits that kind of attention. Panicky people with no control of their emotions are rarely successful because their fear-based decision making sabotages momentum and strains relationships.

Here's the real kicker. In her freaked out state of mind and because I didn't respond to her text in less than three and a half seconds, she called my client directly. I don't need to tell you how inappropriate it is for an agent to contact someone else's client. It's a huge no, as in like, never! Can you imagine what would happen in the legal world if an attorney directly contacted the client on the opposing side without permission? There would be hell to pay. But there she went, filled with fear, freaking out and breaking protocol because all she can see is failure and collapse. The Apocalypse was happening, and she shifted into life-saving mode. Here's the weird thing; this type of person doesn't even know what to do with themselves if things go smoothly. They can't possibly. It's like they're addicted to chaos. I can't imagine living with such a person, but frankly some people are just plain nutty. They have to have drama. If it doesn't show up, they create it. That's how they feel valued or something. I don't know it's all too weird for me. I'm just saying it's out there, and I've seen it more times than I care to remember.

The Drop Everything Agent

Although I touched on this before, the Drop Everything Agent or DEA is worthy of its own category as an extension of the Desperate Agent. The DEA will, as the name implies, drop everything for a prospect or client at any time. They are so anxious for business and have their priorities so out of whack, that they believe the way it works is to be available 100 percent of the time. As I noted before, such people don't respect themselves or their family, so how is it they think their prospects or clients will respect them? The bottom line is the DEA will end up attracting horrible, disrespectful people that will waste their time, make no deals, and bring in no money. You attract what you are in life. That is a very clear principle. It is the law of attraction. If you disrespect yourself and your family, you will attract disrespectful clients and prospects.

The DEA while intending to exhibit eagerness, will actually exude desperation when they always answer the phone and then frantically tear out the door. They will split regardless of what they were doing at the time, just to drive around and show houses to any passerby who happens to attain their phone number. The perspective buyer may or may not be qualified. The perspective buyer may or may not be serious, but there goes the DEA, running out the door, dropping everything and everybody to go taxi around perfect strangers all over town. Such agents believe that the drama they create, the sense of panic, the harried pace, the running around is what makes things happen. This is what agents must do if they want to make money. Yet oddly enough such agents are rarely successful because they have no game plan, no logical strategy. All they do is answer the phone and run. Does that sound strategic? Panic is not a strategy. Not having a plan is a recipe for disaster in our personal financial lives and in our real estate careers. As I've said before, busyness isn't business. The DEA doesn't really get that.

The Buy Your Business Agent

While I am completely fine with taking advantage of every opportunity to expand one's business, there is this thing, particularly in real estate, where agents take the lazy way and try to buy their business. There are only two ways to make money in real estate: earn it or buy it. When I say earn it, I mean doing it the right way, the long-term way, and the sustainable way. This is the old fashioned, hardworking way of doing business, one person at a time and one deal at a time. This is where relationships mean something and honesty and integrity do too. Then there are the agents who buy their business. They rent billboards and park benches and plaster their face all over town. They pay for mailing lists and subscribe to lead generation companies. They pay young guys to cold call and badger people into listening to their pitch. I know agents who pay over $10,000 a month in such endeavors.

Now from a business perspective, the math may work. I mean if you spend $10,000 a month on some campaign and make $40,000 from that effort, then you are operating, at least on paper, in a sound and profitable manner. That may be true, yet why is it that such people who take shortcuts come across as shysters at least to me? They just churn through people and count their money. It just doesn't feel right. Maybe I'm old fashioned, but I rarely see this type of method work long term. In addition, there are dumb things like monthly or quarterly flyers mailed out to homes offering free nachos at your favorite Mexican restaurant with the agents face prominently shellacked on the flyer. I mean really think this through. Does anyone who is undecided on which agent to use choose somebody because they can save a few dollars on a plate of tortilla chips with melted cheese? Seriously, what is the point?

The Designation Agent

In contrast to the learning agent, which you'll read about in the chapter on great agents, the Designation Agent has taken a few courses as well but then slaps them on the tail of their last name as if they actually mean something. Folks, let's talk straight here: there are very few designations that mean anything to the general public. PhD is one that I think most people relate to, and the other is MD. Maybe MBA gets some attention. Beyond that the list gets short really fast. Every industry has certifications that only make sense to those in that industry. It's like an inside joke where only people privy to the context enjoy a laugh. To anyone on the outside, the humor escapes them. The same is true in each industry. Engineers have designations. Astrophysicists have designations. Preachers have designations. Horticulturalists have designations. Most of these only mean something to others in that field.

I saw a sign the other day that made me shake my head. It was a major national real estate brand, and after the agents name, she had the initials CRS, CDPE, GRI. Now do you think the average person walking down the street has any idea what the Sam Hill those initials mean? Do you actually think someone would drive by and say to their husband, "Whoa, sweetie. Stop the car. I have to get this agents number. They are CDPE qualified!" It's utter nonsense. CRS means Council of Residential Specialists. CDPE stands for Certified Distressed Property Expert, and GRI is Graduate Realtor Institute. Do you honestly think anyone even knows or cares what the Council of Residential Specialist is? Is it so important for the ego that some agents feel they have to jam such initials after their name as if they mean anything at all?

Moreover, especially when the general public has absolutely no idea what they stand for or what they mean, what is really the sense of slapping those initials after an agents name? This agent most likely felt that the more initials she could attach to her name, the more impressive and smart she appeared. In reality, it has the opposite effect. It can come off as pretentious as well as confusing, if not irrelevant. Beyond that it just cluttered up her sign with meaningless letters that have no strategic value. Take the classes, learn, and get the certificate, sure. Just don't add it to your business card or sign. Nobody cares, and it just takes up space.

The BFF Agent

The BFF agent is that guy who comes across as your long-lost uncle or old college roommate. They are your BFF, your, as kids nowadays say, Best Friend Forever! They are your pals. They are your new buddy. They are exceedingly sappy and complimentary. They want you to go golfing, have drinks, and then come over for dinner. Whereas clearly some clients do indeed turn into friends, many are just grateful for professional representation. The BFF Agent might be a really nice person deep down, but the cynical side of me has just seen this move overplayed. The reason I say so is because the BFF Agent is rarely the same after the close. In other words, it's just schmooze, schmooze, schmooze! It comes across at the very least usurious and at worst sleazy. You don't need to schmooze people. You don't need to bribe people. You don't need to be ridiculous and be the over the top gregarious long-lost uncle. Just do your job, be amicable, and see where things go. It's a professional relationship that may or may not develop into something else.

The Longevity Agent

How many times have you heard someone say, "I've been doing this for twenty-five years…" You can talk to a preacher, a plumber or a paralegal, and somehow the span of years seems to creep into the conversation. Many people inform you of the years they have been doing something in order to provide you with the mental conclusion that they are an expert. After all they've been doing this thing for decades! The implication is that they are amazing at what they do, yet this equation is not necessarily true. Do you know any politicians or members of Congress who have been in politics for many years and are still as misdirected and ineffective as ever? Are there builders who have been in business for years but still build homes with shoddy quality? Are there teachers or professors who have taught in schools for decades but in reality are horrible communicators and virtually every student that has the misfortune of being assigned to their class dislikes them? The answer is yes to all, so clearly longevity doesn't actually mean anything except the person has been able to avoid getting fired from their job. There are scores of people in virtually every industry and in every vocation that fly below the radar even though they are grossly incompetent. If anyone truly knew how horrible they were, they would be fired but they hide in the shadows or behind their union.

Just because someone has done something for a long time doesn't necessarily equate to excellence by any means. As a matter of fact, sometimes longevity can be a hindrance. The old saying, "You can't teach an old dog new tricks" might apply here. Maybe a young, energetic, passionate recent graduate is a far better fit to teach your child than the old, bitter, crabby, cynical woman who has a guaranteed slot in the school system due to her "longevity." Maybe some career Senator needs to get back in the real world to rediscover how it feels to be a regular citizen instead of remaining in the government bureaucracy. You need to discover what the agent has actually accomplished beyond just hanging around for decades.

The Shoe Budget Agent

I so wish I was making this one up, but it's real. I will never forget the transaction I did with an agent who revealed a new sales strategy to me. I had the listing, and she brought the buyer. She was perfectly pleasant and upbeat and equally clueless, unprofessional, and inexperienced. Of course, she was one of those who didn't do enough business to develop any experience or skill and, for that matter, didn't take the whole thing that seriously to begin with. After several delays and mistakes, I asked her why she was struggling so much with the contract language and time deadlines. No matter how good of an agent you are, the entire process is somewhat limited to the skills, competency, experience, and intelligence of the other agent. She revealed to me the shocking reason that explained her incompetence. She in almost gleeful abandon admitted all she likes to sell is one or two homes a year to fund her Nordstrom shoe budget. There you have it, and I'm not making this stuff up. She said it so matter-of-factly that it caught me completely flatfooted. I'm usually quick on my feet, but this was a new one for me. In utter disbelief I asked her to repeat herself, convinced I misheard her. She explained that her husband had put her on a spending budget, and in order for her to facilitate her shoe obsession, she got her real estate license and needed to just sell one or two houses a year. I didn't know whether to be embarrassed for her insatiable lack of awareness and shamelessness or be impressed with her categorization skills and goal-setting ability.

I was stopped in my tracks by the lunacy of what she so glibly stated. Here I was being a full-time professional, expanding my knowledge base, enrolling in continuing education classes in order to achieve higher levels of certification, and taking my career very seriously in order to feed my family and reach the highest levels of accomplishment possible. In contrast, here she was, wanting to buy shoes at Nordstrom. I suppose if she was an amazing agent I might not have taken issue, but in reality she was horrible, as anybody would be if they only did something once or twice a year. Try golfing twice a year, and see how you do. Try working out twice a year, and see how you feel. Try balancing your bank accounts twice a year, and see how things turn out. There she was in all of her incompetent glory, eyes on the prize, and completely and blissfully unaware at how horrible she truly was. I told her at the end I may have well kept both sides of the commission since I did most of her work for her. Shoe budget indeed.

The Cynical Agent

I don't care whether you call it energy, the law of attraction, or karma or whatever, but one thing is certain that mean-spirited, angry, or cynical people usually aren't successful. I read a bumper sticker once that said, "If you're not cynical, you're not paying attention." Part of that may be true, and the more you pay attention to politics, government waste, and the like, there's plenty of reasons to be cynical. The longer you live, the easier it is to become jaded. I suppose a little cynicism does show you are paying attention and are aware at the inconsistencies in life. However, like its cousin sarcasm, cynicism can quickly become toxic and repellent. I remember one older agent had a favorite phrase she used all the time as her go-to response to any problems in a transaction. She would blurt out, "Buyers are liars." It's a cute little rhyme that's easy to remember and proposes to be witty, but in reality, such statements reveal more about the person that utters such nonsense rather than the buyer they are attempting to malign.

I understood why she said it. Buyers sometimes can be fickle or indecisive. They can change their mind or get buyer's remorse. Buyers can flake out and not show up to agreed upon times. Buyers can sometimes be working with you, and then after investing hours showing houses, they decide to buy a home with a "really nice agent" they met at an open house last weekend. However, that's exactly why I always spend a lot of time prequalifying buyers, so we don't waste effort. I spend time with clients, discussing their desires, and I only work with people who are prepared, able, and ready to move forward with a real estate transaction. Maybe the issue wasn't with the buyer but with her? There's a novel thought! Maybe she ended up with horrible buyers exactly because she didn't put in the effort early on to make sure everyone was on the same page. The Cynical Agent will often avoid accountability and instead project blame on everyone else.

Or maybe she was so dog-gone manipulative, pushy, and demanding that she made people feel uncomfortable causing them to back out. Maybe the longer people were around her, they picked up on her passive-aggressive toxicity and felt slimed. Do you know that feeling? Slimed is when you just feel icky. Like how you feel after being with a noxious person, and you wish you could give your soul a bath. That's the feeling. The weird thing is that people are just that; people. People don't like to be pushed, they want to enjoy house hunting. People want to be dealt with graciously. People don't like to be manipulated or bullied. People want to feel good about their decisions and that those decisions were thoughtfully and harmoniously arrived at. Buying a home is a big event, and it should be filled with strategy, intentionality, thoughtfulness, and careful consideration. Too bad this agent forgot what it feels like to be a person preparing to make a big decision. The Cynical Agent can't really engage in empathy because their jaded nature assumes the worst in everyone.

The Lazy Agent
So here is the sad truth. Many agents are just plain lazy. That's the straight honest truth. On the listing side, they think that the sum total of their efforts is sticking a sign in the ground and then kick back and wait for a paycheck. On the buying side, they think that the sum total of their efforts is to show half a dozen houses, put in an offer, and wait for the money to show up. My dad worked in a factory his whole adult life. He used to come home and vent at how frustrating it was working with some people who had zero drive, passion, or initiative. Being a grateful immigrant with

a massive work ethic, this was his number one angst at work. He thought it was a horrible thing to be lazy. He thought it was tragic and embarrassing to be thought of as lazy. He felt such people had a complete lack of pride, self-awareness, and healthy ego. They would do just barely above the minimum threshold of work and nothing more. I suppose in every industry there are lazy people who just do the bare minimum. To us hard-chargers who are strategic about establishing goals, living life with passion, and achieving our desires, it's impossible to comprehend the lack of motivation some people have. Yet there they are. Doing the least amount of work possible. Getting in the way. Not contributing. Never improving. Blaming everything and everybody while making excuses for their own lack of production. I have discovered two kinds of lazy: benevolent lazy and malicious lazy.

The benevolent Lazy Agent. What I mean by benevolent is that these agents are actually quite nice. They certainly mean no harm; they just aren't particularly driven or motivated. They won't take the initiative mostly out of ignorance not out of malice. They won't work particularly hard either mostly because they don't think they have to. They usually are not particularly skilled either. Perhaps they haven't been properly trained, so their activity and expectations are very low. The benevolent Lazy Agent can be a really nice person. They just don't get it. I have one perfect example of a benevolently Lazy Agent. I had listed a home and she brought the buyer. After a few weeks we were getting close to the appraisal deadline. The agent texted me and asked for an extension because she didn't know the status of the appraisal. Extensions to contracts occur sometimes, and both parties have to sign off on it in order for it take effect. Now I'm always happy to extend the time periods or the length of the contract itself if there are extenuating circumstances. That's life. I get that. What I'm not OK with is going through the extra effort, tracking down my clients for signatures, and delaying progress all because the other agent is lazy or incompetent. She stated in her text to me that she was worried. I have found one thing that combats worry really well—action! Why worry about the unknown when a quick phone call can give you the answer?

I replied, "Did you call the appraiser?"

I was amazed at the next text; "No, I usually don't do that."

Flabbergasted I thought, "Well gee whiz, there Cowpoke—ya think ya maybe should?"

As I often do with incompetent or lazy agents, I take the initiative to solve their problems, knowing they are incapable of making progress themselves. I called the appraiser and had a lovely ten minute conversation. The appraiser gave me all the information I needed. I thanked her and then called the buyer's agent and told her, "I just called your appraiser. She said she appreciated the reminder. The appraiser was overworked, but everything is done, and was just sitting in a pile on her desk. It will be in the file by morning." It just needed somebody to care enough to find out the status of things, investigate, and push a little. The appraiser wasn't a bad person by any stretch. She was just swamped, and when people are swamped, paper piles up on their desks and things fall through the cracks. It took me calling and spending a few minutes with her to grease the axles and get things moving again. Complicated? No. Time consuming? No. It just took some initiative.

Then the agent flooded me with texts about how amazing I was and that I exhibited good team work. Of course, the reality is I am not on her team and she was lazy but whatever. At that moment I didn't think I was particularly amazing. I just showed a little initiative, picked up the phone, and handled the situation. It's not like I climbed Mount Everest or ran into a burning building to save someone. I mean think about her mentality; her paycheck depends on the process going smoothly. It is her job to be involved every step of the way. She needs to be on top of signatures, inspections, financing, appraisals, deadlines, and a host of other items as a buyer representative. It's her responsibility, and it's her job, and it's how she protects her clients and her personal income. They actually went past the appraisal deadline due to her inability to pick up the phone. Can you imagine if I was a hard nose or had a better offer come in? I contractually could have cancelled her offer and gone with somebody else, and her clients would have lost out on the home they really wanted all because she just couldn't figure out how to call an appraiser and do what I did in less than ten minutes.

The malicious Lazy Agent. This person is just plain ignorant and arrogant. They won't lift a finger to be helpful. They will show no initiative. They are self-absorbed and frankly don't care about anyone else. Thankfully, I haven't encountered many of this kind of agent, but they are definitely out there. They are all smiles to their client, but once the contract is signed, they are miserable to work with. I never understood this kind of person. It takes both agents on both sides to work together to get the deal done. I really don't get why some people intentionally make it hard. I was in one transaction where the guy flat out told me he didn't care about what he was supposed to do because he knew that I had a reputation for being a hard worker and that I would pick up the slack. I was astounded. It was a really weird situation for me to be in. He was correct I had a good reputation. He was also correct that I would not let a deal die due to his attitude and laziness. People like that never make it long term. Eventually that kind of pathetic attitude brings about the failure they so deserve.

The Just Doesn't Get It Agent

There are some agents who just don't get it. They are horrible at communication. They dress like a four year old when their mother is out of town and their appearance is, well, not sharp. You know, the kind of guy who wears black and blue and doesn't realize they not only don't match, but they look like a walking bruise? That guy. I'm not saying you need to look like a living Ken or Barbie doll, but an agent has to understand they are not in the real estate business but in the people business. If you're good with people, if you come across as put together and professional, you have a much higher chance of succeeding. Current hair styles and updated fashion show that you know what time and day it is. You're alert, on the ball, and ready for action. You exude a comfortable confidence.

Showing up with shaggy hair, bushy sideburns, and canoe paddle ties probably won't cut it. That is unless you're really going for some wicked retro look. I say get a haircut and go shopping. Men, let me speak directly to you. If you're married, take your wife with you. Better yet bring your teenage daughter if you have one. Otherwise borrow one from a friend, neighbor, or relative. Most women are way more in tune to these things than men. Prospects and potential clients will size you up within seconds and if they determine you're not sharp, you lose business. That goes for the guy that walks around the office in shorts and a T-shirt. Does that look really project professionalism and engender trust? It's not just about appearance or people skills. It's also about motivation as well. There are people in every profession under the sun who shouldn't be doing what they're doing. Such people just don't get it. They don't look right, act right or perform well. They just don't get that they don't belong there and that they're better suited for other things. There are people behind pulpits of churches, wheels of police cars, and lathes in factories that are doing it for all the wrong reasons. Real estate is no exception.

The Partnership Agent

Remember when Sears and Kmart merged? It was like the idea here was if two outdated and failing stores got together, they would create what, an amazing new brand? The answer is no. Logically and painfully no. It's like two peasants getting married and hoping to give birth to a prince! It didn't create anything new or amazing; it was just two failing stores now under the same corporate umbrella, and both are still failing and currently clos-ing stores. The same is true in some real estate partnerships. Oftentimes two underperforming agents will join forces in hopes they will somehow defy the principles of logic and become a powerhouse together. No, it's just two failing agents under one name just like the Sears and Kmart merger. The Partnership Agent doesn't realize that the reason for their failure is because they are not good at what they do and adding other people to the mix changes nothing.

Another form of partnerships in real estate are "teams." Though there are highly functional teams you will read about in the next chapter, there are many more poorly performing teams. Oftentimes the "team" will be led by a lazy or disconnected agent who assembles a group of newer agents with promises of easy money. The head agent will buy leads and have the "team" follow up on the leads. Generally the commission is split 50/50. The leads are usually weak buyer leads and the morale of the so-called "team" is often low with high turnover. More often than not it turns into a boiler room kind of mentality led by an absentee head agent. It's not really a team at all which is why I put it in quotes, but a bunch of people trying to find the shortcut. The lazy head agent is trying to get out of working hard and the people attracted to such agents don't want to go out and do the work themselves. They are just happy to be like small chicks and wait for the mother bird to feed them worms. Remember, the law of attraction means you attract what you are. A lazy agent attracts and assembles a lazy team.

The Obsolete Agent

Isn't that a horrible moniker? The word "obsolete" is a sad word to me. It means that something used to function or work well but doesn't anymore. It's a word of yester-year, of a day gone by. It's how it feels to be a cassette tape player in a downloading world. Obsolete. It also means stuck in the past. It's not necessarily an age thing, but it often is. However, I believe it's more of a mentality. It's a stuck mind-set that doesn't want to move forward and stay current. When there are new and improved technologies and methodologies out there that make you more efficient, why wouldn't you want to learn about them? One reason I suppose is that it takes a fair amount of effort to move forward. Another reason is that it's hard to let go of things that have historically worked really well. Especially if they've worked really well for a long time. Also, we can become suspicious of new technology. There was tremendous suspicious of the TV when it first came out. For that matter, in earlier years when a voice came out of a box called a radio many thought it was demonic. How, after all can a person's voice be in the room without them being present? Of course, there is evil and mischief afoot!

I have a dear friend, Dick Huntrods, who, at ninety, has taught me things about technology and computers. I think it's great! He was an aerospace engineer during his working years, and you would be hard pressed to find a sharper person. After nine decades, he is still curious, interested, and interesting. By contrast, I know people in their forties or early fifties whose best days are clearly behind them.

When there are proven statistics that the vast majority of all home searches begin online, why wouldn't you have a robust website and Internet presence? Why wouldn't you become proficient at Internet marketing? Why wouldn't you provide potential buyers a resource that allows them to have an active role in looking for their new home? People value time, privacy, and efficiency. There are few things more efficient than sitting in your bed with your pajamas on, laptop open, looking at homes! The Obsolete Agent would rather you come into the office and watch him scroll through homes he in his infinite wisdom has selected for you. There are many examples, and there are many models of obsolete real estate tactics that I reference elsewhere, so I won't repeat myself here. Just be alert to an agent's methods. Keep on the lookout for current and efficient strategies and be aware of those that resist them.

The Rookie Agent

Everyone who has ever signed up to do anything for the first time was a rookie. No problem there. I was once a rookie. You were once a rookie. In real estate I happened to learn quickly and won Rookie of the Year award in my first year with Prudential California Realty. Actually it wasn't even a full year. I started in May, and by the end of the year, I had outsold every other rookie in history by over 200 percent and that in only eight months. OK, good for me. Not everyone has the same rocket like success right out of the gate. For most people starting at something new is a struggle, and it takes years to accomplish any measure of success. This is certainly true in real estate. The problem is that in many brokerages a rookie will struggle to find support. People are busy making money, and they are not going to stop and help a newbie. The brokers or owners are busy doing their thing as well. They have a company to run with many complexities.

It can be really lonely sometimes starting out. It seems like everyone else knows what they are doing and are running full steam ahead while you're hardly out of your chair. Remember what it felt like to be a freshman in high school? Thankfully, the first brokerage I worked with catered to entry-level agents and provided sensational Mike Ferry training. This enabled me to hit the ground running, however this certainly isn't the case at every brokerage. In addition, I had owned several small businesses by then as well as launching new divisions in large companies. Clearly, I wasn't the average rookie or real estate agent for that matter. My business background gave me a significant advantage.

In all things there has to be a season of apprenticeship. As a society we don't talk much about it, but for thousands of years, it has been the mechanism that has allowed for older generations to pass down skill, information, talent, and techniques to the younger generation. This is especially true in the trades. Regardless if you are a cabinet maker, a plumber or a machinist, everyone starts as an apprentice and is connected to an old timer that knows the ins and outs of the trade. The proven idea here is that someone shows you the ropes and that eventually with time and experience you go out on your own. I was fortunate, but, as I said, many offices just don't provide adequate training or apprenticeships for new agents. They are left to their own devices to figure things out. I never understood this brokerage mentality. Don't you want your agents to succeed? Don't you want your people to have the best training and to set them up for success? If people are properly trained and supervised, they make more money and the brokerage makes more money.

For whatever reason many offices forget about new agents. Many seasoned agents and brokers have forgotten what it's like to start out and have limited skill and knowledge. It's kind of like some sort of weird survival of the fittest thing. They just throw the rookies out there. Problem is, and it's no fault of their own, rookies can really make a mess of things while they're figuring things out. If you're a buyer or seller, you need to make sure you're not working with an unsupervised rookie as there are countless things that need to be done right. Even a new server at any restaurant works with a trainer for a while. We're not talking about ordering burgers here. We're talking about the largest physical investment of your life. It needs to be handled by someone who knows what they're doing. If you want to work with a rookie, just make sure they are supervised and closely aligned with an experienced agent. Too many things can go wrong in a real estate transaction, and such missteps can be very costly.

The Whiney Agent

Back in the old days, there used to be a thing called "floor time." Some offices still operate this way. This was a mechanism where certain agents were on a rotation, and either worked the front desk or fielded incoming phone calls. This was the broker's way of providing opportunities to low performers. I say low performers because top agents are too busy making money and closing deals to be sitting around an office staring at a phone hoping it rings or waiting for someone to magically walk through the front door. In every office, the Whiney Agent will always be on the rotation. The Whiney Agent will complain if she perceives too much time has gone by since she last held floor time or if other people are crowding the schedule. If she would apply half the determination she exhibits in securing a spot at the front desk to her overall career she might actually be out conducting business instead of staring at the phone. I say whiney because there's, well lots of whining going on. Her worldview is that she is somehow being overlooked or short-changed. "If only" are her opening comments on just about everything. She blames her lack of production on everything and everybody. It's never her fault. It's always out there, external, somewhere, in the big nebulous universe where responsibility lay. She's too busy nagging the broker for more floor time to actually do some self reflection.

The Ego Agent

Some agents honestly make me gag. They think they are God's gift to real estate and that if you by chance are lucky enough to be in their presence, well, then it's a great day for you! They become some weird cliché that a Saturday Night Live skit could be based on. They somehow believe that just because they have had a measure of success in real estate that they are now a household name or celebrity and should be treated as such. One agent after shaking hands with an out of state friend of mine stated her name and then said, "Perhaps you've heard of me." She did so with a straight face. My friend was not able respond in like manner. I'll never understand it. It must be a deep personal insecurity of some kind trying to be masked over by projecting a false sense of power. I'm not saying they're not good agents, and some are even top producers. It's just that the air they put off is obnoxious. I remember the number one guy on our office. He really loved himself. I mean his office was literally shellacked with memorabilia, pictures of his smiling face, newspaper clippings, plaques, and awards. It was a shrine! We actually caught him one morning with Windex and paper towels as he was cleaning his trophies! My buddy and I laughed out loud. Sorry. Sometimes I just can't take it. We kept joking that maybe someday we would walk in, and he would be in his office lighting candles and bowing to his awards.

Anyway, within two and half years, I had surpassed his volume and had collected a significant amount of plaques and awards as well…which I left in boxes under my desk. This is one part of the industry I never really understood. Agents will trip over themselves to go to national conventions and local events just for the opportunity to have their name called and stroll across some stage to receive a plaque. I don't know if their parents didn't praise them enough when they were children or what the issue is. I was top 6 percent sales in the nation and never went to such an event. I was too busy working. The plaques and trophies arrived, and I simply put them in a box, which, of course, drove the former number one guy insane. It just blew his mind that I didn't put the stuff up on the wall and build a shrine to myself. It's just not my style. There are people who know they're good, and there are people who have to convince themselves that they're good.

Another weird way ego emerges is with some agents modifying miniscule items in contracts just to show they're in charge. The first time this happened I was flummoxed. I asked a fellow agent about this guy and she said, "Oh yea, that's just the way he is. He wants you to know he's the boss." Are you kidding me? This agent intentionally added or deleted ridiculous and unnecessary things from the contract, all of which need a round of signatures, just so he could flex his little muscles? Wow! So everyone is inconvenienced and the time periods get delayed all for his Napoleon-like mentality. Amazing!

Check your ego at the door. You're not curing cancer, you haven't won a Nobel Prize, you aren't saving children from a war-torn country. I say keep your head down, stay humble, focus on serving and helping people accomplish their goals, and things will turn out great.

The I Don't Know Who I Am Agent

As I mentioned before, if any agent came to my house and had any stupid thing on their business card like Sales Consultant, Real Estate Counselor, or Real Estate Advisor, I would immediately show them the door and maybe give them a swift kick on the way out. This isn't a joke. We're dealing with people's most costly asset, and they deserve a professional who is clear on what their role is. A broker or agent of any kind represents the interests of another. A Sports Agent fights for their athlete to get them the best salary and benefits package with the best team. They don't just give "advice." They don't just "counsel" the athlete. They are not "consultants." They are agents and they are clear on their role. They serve their clients by getting them the most money and in so doing they also win. That's called "everybody wins."

I remember one client who had the sad misfortune of having an I Don't Know Who I Am Agent try to sell their home. They were a discount agent who worked for far less than the standard commission, and, yes, they had some cheesy title that didn't mention broker or agent. The homeowner was exhausted with endless showings and no results. During the three months his home was listed with the confused agent I sold four houses in his neighborhood. He fired his agent and called me. My commission was going to be around $7,000 more than his confused agent, but I told him

I would be able to get way more money for his home, so we would both win. Well, I did sell the home in short order for $39,000 more, which, less my $7,000, means he pocketed an extra $32,000 just for working with an agent who understood what it means to be an agent and fight for their clients. I never have been nor am I now confused as to what my role is.

The Gushing Agent

This agent comes to your home armed with so many canned compliments that it's embarrassing. "Oh, your taste in décor is fabulous!" to "Wow, are you in interior design?" and my personal favorite, "This is the most beautiful home I've ever seen!" The disingenuous flattery is designed to do nothing more than lower your defenses, manipulate your emotions, and endear yourself to her. I think we all know the difference between an authentic compliment and bloated rhetoric or fluffy phrases. We also know within realistic parameters the actual level of attraction our homes have. We know if we are amazing at decorating or not. We know if our furniture is top shelf or looks like it came from a garage sale. All the phony compliments in the world shouldn't move you.

Some poor unsuspecting souls got snookered into working with The Gushing Agent because they were just so dog-gone nice. Nice? You want your kids' kindergarten teacher to be nice. You want the nurse looking after your elderly mother to be nice. You want the person grooming your dog to be nice. In real estate you want someone who is tough, has sound business skills, knows high-level negotiation, and thoroughly understands handling your home, and consequently your money takes more talent than just being nice.

The Fluffy Agent

Similar to the Gushing Agent, the Fluffy Agent adds fluff to everything she does. Her marketing is fluff, her speech is fluff, and the way she handles challenges is fluff. I don't know about you, but I'm super over being lied to and being talked to like I'm in elementary school. It's not that I'm necessarily skeptical although that's part of it; it's just that I'm a grown man, an adult, and I can handle the truth. I think most people would feel the same way. I really don't know what it is about real estate, but somewhere somebody felt that appropriate marketing of homes had to include super-fluous and fluffy language. Maybe such agents wish they were Harlequin Romance novelists or something. I don't get it. Literally, no other industry uses language like the real estate industry.

"Pulling up to the driveway you'll know you're home. As you walk through the custom front door, you will be warmly greeted by an inlaid Italian marble mosaic that will make you think you're in your own chalet in Tuscany. The soaring ceilings give you a sense of space which blend seamlessly into marvelous and sweeping cathedral ceilings in the great room. This elegant home is an entertainers dream complete with butler's pantry and wet bar which can be accessed from within this gorgeous home or from the placid backyard. As you walk outside to the oversized deck you will be greeted by a serenade of chirping birds and falling water from the nearby fountain. From the spacious deck you will enjoy endless miles of views and feel you are on top of the world. Walking back into the home adjacent to the great room is the gourmet kitchen suitable for a five-star chef..."

Barf. It goes on forever. Insert hard eye roll here, and what the heck is a "gourmet kitchen" anyway? I get so tired of it all. I read an ad the other day by a Fluffy Agent that said, "Experience luxury and quality like no other." Really? You've done an exhaustive search of every home in the world, and literally no other home in the world has luxury and qual-ity like this house? Wow! How about we just take a Marketing 101 class at the local community college and learn to effectively and accurately communicate the attributes of a home without all the meaningless and unsubstantiated words. How about we skip the poetry and stick to facts and avoid flowery speech and exaggeration. Man, I'm so done with fluff. It doesn't end here, though. The Fluffy Agent even has a way of speak-ing about negative things too. It used to be a "price reduction" when you lowered the price of a home for sale. That turned into a "price adjust-ment." If that wasn't good enough, now it's "price improvement!" It's just meaningless industry jargon that is utter nonsense. The only thing that needs improvement is the quality of agent who actually knows how to price a home correctly, so they don't have to lower the price and figure out a fluffy way to say it!

The Any Price Agent

Everything for sale has a price. A fast-food burger costs between one to five dollars depending on the chain and size of the burger and ongoing promotions. A "gourmet" burger at an upscale restaurant can cost anywhere from ten to fifteen dollars. Would anybody think of buying a cheeseburger for fifty-two dollars? I mean even if it was coated in some exotic Russian caviar, it would still be a stretch. Yet that's what the any price agent does with your home. He will excite you with the prospects of you making much more money than you anticipated. Of course, his pricing is not founded in reality, but he won't let you know that. It is a deceptive and despicable scheme that more often than not unsuspecting homeowners falls for. It just sounds so appealing. As a matter of fact, many sellers choose the agent who suggests the highest list price. The Any Price Agent is one of the worst kind of agents because not only are they not truthful, but they also waste your time by promising something that will never, ever happen. They will fawn over you and your home making you think you are special and your home is uniquely attractive. Real estate is competitive, and smart homeowners should interview at least three agents. Unfortunately many naïve homeowners only listen to projected sale price, and consequently the agent who promises the highest price gets the contract.

All he wants is for you to take the bait and sign the agreement. He knows full well that the home will never sell at that price, but rest assured he will lead you to believe it will. Does he have some unknown powers? Is he in possession of some pixy dust? Does he have some kind of mental ability to brainwash prospective buyers into grossly overpaying for a home? Every home has a reasonable range it will sell for depending on quality, condition, upgrades, and comps. Anything dramatically over that range will cause buyers to be turned off because it's a fifty-two dollar cheeseburger. After a few weeks and very few showings, the Any Price Agent's magical prowess will seem to grow stale. Not to worry he will briskly appear and "consult" with you about the progress or lack thereof. He will reference how astonished he is that the home has not sold yet and that he is concerned. He will walk through the home with you one more time to see if he can discover a smoking gun that would point to any reason why your home hasn't sold. He will say that the overall market is acting strangely and that it is unpredictable right now for some reason. After mulling around a bit, he will, with Academy Award level skill, regretfully inform you that "we should probably lower the price."

He will blame the economy, flaky buyers, and even the President of the United States. He will deflect and cajole. He will do and say anything but tell you the truth. The truth is he knew he was listing your home for way too much money. He knew he was being deceptive and flat out understood the price was unrealistic. He did so just to butter you up, so you would hire him and sign the contract. He knew full well that there was no chance your home would sell for that price because people don't overpay for anything, especially big ticket items like houses. He knew the comparable homes in the area sold for much less and that your home is nothing special, but he lied to you to gain your business knowing he could always beat you up later to lower the price all while deflecting the real issue. At best The Any Price Agent is an incompetent amateur with no business skills. At worst, they are sneaky and deceptive. Do you have any idea how bad an agent looks when they list a home for $285,000 and have to reduce it all the way down to a reasonable $218,000 if that's what other similar homes are selling for? Think logically for a moment; why would any agent list it that high? It's just ridiculous. Nobody is going to buy a cheeseburger for fifty-two dollars!

The Association Agent
Some agents and even some brokerages connect to a group, cause, or category through their marketing. They will say things that connect them

to the military, religion, golf, or even cats. Though there is nothing inherently wrong with doing so, the underlying assumption is based on a less than perfect idea. They are attempting to artificially bond with people and gain their trust based on common values, interests, or hobbies. What they are saying is, "Hey I like golf? Do you? Let me sell you a house!" Does any thinking person actually believe that just because someone golfs it automatically qualifies them to be an amazing real estate agent? Once you really think about it, it's kind of silly isn't it? Yet this strategy takes advantage of a fundamental principle in sociology and anthropology. It has to do with principles of community, gathering together, and trust. People like people who are like themselves. When there is common ground, there is an embedded trust level that borders on irrational though it's just a fact of society.

I was born and raised in Buffalo, New York. As I have lived in different areas and have encountered people from my hometown, there is an automatic affinity, familiarity, and trust. We talk about the Buffalo Bills, chicken wings, pizza, high taxes, and bad weather. There is an instant connection. The crazy thing is that it is completely illogical. Just because someone is from my hometown doesn't make them an amazing person does it? But that's how we are as people. That's how we connect to others. We hang out with people like us, that do the things we do, and who are similar to us. The Association Agent uses their alignment or history with something in an attempt to endear prospects to them. They are wanting to leverage their associations as sociological tools for people to trust them without reservation. There are many examples of marketing in code or by using hints.

I remember one lady who advertised with a picture of her holding her cat? Not really sure what she was going for there. "Hi everyone! Use me as your agent on your next sale or purchase because I like cats!" Another woman had a picture of her next to a horse, presumably hers but who really knows. There she was with her Wranglers, boots, and cowgirl hat, holding the reigns, standing next to Mr. Ed. The reality is she could have easily gotten dressed up and went and posed next to somebody's horse and had someone take a snapshot. It's not really that complicated. I know I'm showing my cynical side, but trust me I've seen it all, and these things happen every day of the week. What was her angle? She was wanting to associate with people who have an interest in buying land, farms, or ranches. She was wanting to communicate, "Hey fellow equestrian friend, look at me and Mustang over here! Because I am standing next to a horse, I am the best qualified person to find you that dream horse property!"

For our Mormon friends, you may see an agent wearing a BYU sweatshirt or a picture of his family in front of the temple in Salt Lake City. "Hey all you Latter Day Saints, I'm your guy for real estate." Is there anything wrong with that? No. Does being a Mormon automatically make you an amazing real estate agent? Not necessarily. Then there are those who pull at the patriotic heart strings of average Americans who state, "Former soldier now proudly serving ABC Realty in our community." Clearly there are skill sets in the military like discipline, honor, and hard work that can translate into any line of business. However, just because someone served four years in Hawaii at the naval base, doesn't automatically make them an amazing agent. One Association Agent had "Air Force Colonel (retired)" on his business card and marketing. Now, emotions and patriotism aside, what logical thing does that have to do with real estate? Nothing at all. A military career while noble and filled with leadership opportunities doesn't really correlate to being a brilliant real estate agent. What the retired Colonel is trying to say is, "Hey fellow active and retired military members! You can trust me with your home. I put in twenty years!" Or perhaps he's attempting to draw on people's patriotic heart strings and make them feel obligated to give the old Colonel some business. Or maybe it's an authority thing. I don't know.

Christians do it too. I saw a sign the other day on my morning walk that was coded. The brokerage had a "t" in the name, and they made it larger than the rest of the letters and made it in a bold style. So they were turning the "t" into a cross. Wink, wink, "Hey fellow Christians! I go to church and that makes me an amazing real estate agent!" The so-called

Jesus Fish is the most overused code ever. The "ichthys" is an ancient Greek symbol that looks like a fish. Early Christians under persecution used this symbol to communicate to other believers where they were meeting. Again, I get it. There's nothing inherently wrong with using an association to draw more business. I just bristle a little bit because the underlying premise is faulty and a bit deceptive. Just because someone is a Christian, and maybe even an awesome Christian, does not mean they understand business at a high level and are qualified to help you with your largest personal investment. I know lots of Christians who I wouldn't buy a basketball from. And I know lots of Christians who are absolutely amazing. The same is true of golfers, cat lovers, equestrians, Mormons, and veterans.

The Last Name Agent

As the title implies, the Last Name Agent relies on having a certain last name above and beyond any skill or talent. The son of a recognizable and famous local business person is certainly at an advantage. The wife of a well-known and powerful attorney will clearly be able to gain clients. These kinds of agents will benefit from name recognition in the community and the celebrity status that may bring. If, for example, a local CEO of a well known business has a son in real estate, it is not unreasonable to think that there would be some pressure for anyone in the company to use his son as their agent. If the mayor had a daughter in real estate wouldn't that have an impact on her business? Such people don't earn their business, but simply gain clients not by virtue of their ability, competency or hard work, but by their last name. I am not implying they are all bad, but some are just plain horrible because they didn't earn their business. They didn't prove themselves or come up through the ranks. They found a shortcut. They are entitled and were simply handed everything as they rode the coattails of someone in their family. They can hide behind their last name and the amount of business that generates.

It's kind of like when you see the same last name in multiple positions in a real estate brokerage or business. There's dad in his early sixties and there's his son in his late twenties, same last name. Dad's clearly preparing to hand off the business to junior. Sadly, not everyone has the same tenacity, hunger or skill that their parents do. Once they are in charge and are out from the safety net and shade of their older family members, they fall flat on their faces. Clearly many family run businesses thrive and children who grow up in such a culture do develop high-level skills early on that set them up for success. It's just that it's not a given. Similar to the Association Agent, the Last Name Agent leverages aspects of their lives in order to increase their business. Beyond all this many agents in the office may resent junior because he did not arrive at his status through ability or hard work but merely through genetics. Perk after perk will be given to the son to prop him up while other agents have to go out and scratch out a living. Naked nepotism has a way of chafing regular people who lack such privilege. Unfortunately it is a bit disingenuous because your last name, famous or otherwise, proves nothing but bloodlines. It reveals nothing about someone's ability or skill level. However, because such agents are related to others who are well known they may accomplish significant business levels despite their actual skill.

The I Really Don't Deserve This Agent

Maybe I have a chip on my shoulder. I grew up in an immigrant home where there was no plan B. You had to work your butt off to succeed at anything. I suppose that's why most immigrants are successful in America precisely because there is no plan B. There is no backup. There is no rich uncle that will bail you out. Growing up nothing was handed to me. I started working when I was eleven. For a few bucks, I cut neighbor's lawns, raked their leaves, and shoveled their driveways during winter. I delivered the Buffalo News. That was back in the day when kids delivered newspapers. I had a large wooden box at the end of my driveway and every morning the box would be filled from some unseen person who drove around all night and filled the boxes all over town. Then I would grab my sack which I slung over my shoulder, rode my bike down to the box, and filled my sack. Weighed down with dozens of rolled up newspapers I, in a completely precarious manner, began riding through the neighborhood. The weight of the sack on my right side made the ride entirely off balance and yes I wiped out more than once.

After that my parents signed New York's mandatory "working papers" for kids who wanted to get a real job after fourteen years of age. Off I went to the local Italian restaurant to wash dishes and bus tables. On and on it went. Immigrants know how to work and we're not scared to get our hands dirty. Having said that, yes, maybe I have an issue. Maybe I need therapy. Maybe I need to cut people some slack, but I was raised that you enjoy the fruit of your labor after you've worked hard. Nothing is handed to you so I always chafe when people get a free ride.

Similar to the Last Name Agent, I have a problem with some agents who succeed entirely based on some inside angle or relationship. There's one lady I know. She does a ton of business. On paper she's a rock star, but when you meet her she's obnoxiously awkward, doesn't make eye contact, hardly acknowledges you, and is as cold and uncomfortable as a Siberian winter. When I first encountered her I was fundamentally un-impressed. Being fairly new to the brokerage, I asked the office manager who the awkward lady was. I was told she was a top producer. I was like, "No way. Impossible." The office manager assured me she did an insane amount of deals. I smelled a rat. You see, in life, you don't succeed if you lack communication or people skills, especially in sales. It just doesn't happen. It would be like a really mean person succeeding as a kindergar-ten teacher. It just doesn't work that way! So when there is great success with poor communication and people skills, you can bet there is an inside angle or hidden story. Turns out her husband is a mortgage broker and feeds her all the business she can handle. I knew it! I knew there had to be an angle. I guess her husband was in the military so they milk that angle as well.

Is there anything really wrong with that? Not really. It's just that it's dis-ingenuous. Anytime someone is handed something they haven't worked for, they know they don't deserve it. They act sheepish or in this case cold. They know they are posers. Psychologists call it imposter syndrome where someone is acting as if one thing is true while being scared the truth will come out that they really aren't who they are projecting themselves to be. The I Really Don't Deserve This Agent constantly has to hide so people don't catch on to their little secret angle. The weird thing is if they were just cool and admitted to everyone what the truth was, I don't think most people would care. However, when you live a lie and try to hide your little secret and pretend you're something you're not, people sense it.

Chapter Ten

The Great Agents

There is really something special about people who are at the top of their game. Whether it's sports, entertainment, or business, such people draw our admiration and respect. They are the top producers and usually the top income generators. They are not average, and they don't do things the conventional way. They employ unique methods and strategies that propel them to the top. They are tenacious, committed, zealous, assertive, and driven. They usually possess an indomitable spirit and firm work ethic. Their goals are usually far beyond the average person's ability to even comprehend, and their strategy, discipline, and drive allow them to achieve incredible objectives.

Real estate, like any industry, has their superstars. While not every great agent will grace the cover of a magazine or be a keynote speaker at some conference, their impact is noteworthy. They are the ones who generate the most business, last the longest, are the best at what they do, and hold up the industry. Since 85 percent of real estate agents drop out within five years, the remaining 15 percent are largely comprised of great agents, and maybe 1to 5 percent of those are at the superstar level. Though there are many overlapping qualities, it is worth pointing out several types of great agents in this chapter. Some great agents may be a blend of some if not all these qualities, but top producers for sure will have many of these aspects in their arsenal.

The Expansion Agent

While there clearly is value in a focused, local strategy, there must also be room for expansion. I am always amazed at how lazy or unmotivated some agents are. I had a client whose mom needed to downsize. She lived in San Dimas, about sixty miles away from where I lived. My client had used my services several times and had a high level of trust for me. She wanted me to help her mom sell her home and find a condo for her. In exactly this moment, you will reveal what kind of agent you are. For most agents, the two voices that emerge internally are, "I don't know anything about San Dimas, but I'll figure it out!" or "I have no idea where San Dimas is. I don't know anything about that market. I don't belong to their association. I'm gonna tell them sorry; I don't work in that area." In this situation, "I don't" turns into "I can't" and "I can't" leads to lost income and lost service to those who trust you and want to work with you.

At the time I was working in the Santa Clarita Valley located in northern Los Angeles County. My client's mother lived in San Dimas about an hour drive south and east from where I did the majority of my business. I had a decision to make. What did I do? Well, I figured it out! Each area of the country belongs to a regional or local association that oversees real estate licensees and the MLS (Multiple Listing Service). Such associations provide access to the local database for all real estate activity in addition to providing ability to open lockboxes. Lockboxes are those bulky things you see hanging from doorknobs of homes for sale. Inside the lockbox is the key to the home. Though many associations use the same lockbox company, these days there still are several other options available. Some lockboxes open with a Bluetooth code, some are combo locks, and still others have to have a pager-type device inserted into the face of the box. Agents generally belong to the association of the area where they live and conduct business. Their codes or technology to access lockboxes only work in their territory.

I looked into which association was over San Dimas, and, yes, there was some effort and cost involved, but I joined that association and was then able to conduct real estate business in that area. I researched, studied, and became proficient at the new system and the new market. We listed her home, sold it, and found her a perfect little condo. Happy client back in Santa Clarita because mom was well looked after. Happy mom because she was able to downsize and use an agent the family trusted. Happy agent because those two properties brought in over a million dollars of business for me. The story doesn't end there, though. The mom had a brother in the area who wanted to sell his primary home and three rentals and move to a new development near Temecula, a community about seventy miles south of San Dimas. So what did I do? I figured it out. We listed and sold four properties to the tune of $3 million. I joined yet another association and researched yet another community. I was now working over two hours from home and doing a lot of driving. They bought a home for $650,000 in Murrieta. Was it worth it for happy clients that like and trust me? Was it worth it to now have the running tally of nearly $5 million in sales? Um, yea! The story still doesn't end there! Remember mom? Her mom, which was grandma to my original client back in Santa Clarita, needed her home sold because she was going into an assisted care facility. This generated another $500,000 in sales.

So just from that one client in my town came all this business, if and only if I was willing to expand and learn new territories. Almost $6 million of business came in because I agreed to help my client, was committed to growth, and was motivated enough to figure things out. Six million dollars in sales would be an amazing year for most agents. For me this was just the result of respecting the family of one of my clients. I'm here to tell you that there were plenty of agents in the Santa Clarita Valley who never left the valley, ever! Many agents wouldn't even leave our valley for the big valley, the San Fernando Valley, just ten miles south of us. This huge tract of land in Los Angeles County famous for creating "valley girls" and the backdrop for many movies and TV shows was also a place I conducted a fair amount of business.

Many agents couldn't be bothered, yet, in contrast, there I was making far more money in just one family network than most agents make in a whole year. Beyond that I had very happy clients because people want to do business with people they know, trust, and have had positive experiences with. People don't want to reinvent the wheel and go through all the effort to find somebody else. They just want things handled. Have you ever heard the expression, "I've got a guy?" When you have a plumber, a babysitter, a dentist, a golf coach, or a financial advisor who you have rapport and experience with, you kind of want to stick with the "guy." People also like to recommend their guy. Many agents sell themselves short in this area. They don't really understand the relief that comes with actually being a trusted "guy" for real estate. Fixing a leaky pipe is a big deal. Selling or buying a home is a massive deal. People are busy and stressed, and it's one less thing that they have to worry about if they know there is someone who will take care of their real estate needs, especially when it's their mom, uncle, and grandmother!

I conducted business hours away from my hometown. I learned how to sell real estate in the Coachella Valley, where Palm Springs and other iconic golf communities reside. I helped buyers find land in San Louis Obispo, three hours northeast of Santa Clarita. I worked in "The Valley," Orange County, and San Diego. All told I increased my business in a few years by over $10 million by being willing to figure things out in a new area. This is low hanging fruit. That's not to say it's easy. What I mean by low hanging is that it's there if you just want to reach up and take it. If you're lazy, unmotivated, or distracted, then I guess you can walk by it. I never did. I was always hungry, and I was always happy to help my clients. I considered it an honor that they would trust me with their extended family members. By expanding my knowledge base and learning how other areas operate, it opened up an opportunity to earn significantly more income.

Even better, when word got out that I knew those other areas, local real estate agents back in Santa Clarita gave me their out-of-area business. I would gladly pay them a 25 percent referral fee and earn the rest for myself. Think of that. It's standard business to earn 25 percent on out of town referrals. Living in Los Angeles if I had a client moving to Atlanta, I would find a fellow RE/MAX agent out there on our corporate website, and then my clients would have someone waiting for them on the other side of their move. I, in turn, would earn 25 percent of the Atlanta agent's commission. It's a great system. Your clients are well cared for, and you get a little something in return. However, think if I would have referred my business in San Dimas. Think about how much money I would not have earned. I only would have received 25 percent of the initial sale and wouldn't have even known about the other family member's properties. It pays to show up, work hard, figure it out, and provide exceptional service to your clients.

In addition to expanding geographically, I also expanded in the kinds of real estate I was involved in. I had a high net worth client who was a great guy. He had several rentals that I managed. I had assisted him on his primary residence as well as purchasing and selling invest-ment properties. One day he approached me to find him a business to buy. He wanted a package that included the business operations, land, and building. I didn't know the first thing about buying a busi-ness. I didn't even know where to start looking, but I figured it out. You know initiative and drive are two key traits that will take you far in life. I was approached by another client who wanted to start purchasing multi-unit properties. Again, I didn't know the first thing about apart-ments, duplexes, triplexes, and quads, but I figured it out. Beyond that I have been asked to find commercial office space, working farms, and ranches as well as raw undeveloped land. I also expanded into helping clients with leasing corporate, office, warehouse, and manufacturing space. Each time I started with very limited knowledge but pressed into it and learned all I could.

It's a great feeling to investigate an area you have limited knowledge of and end up with a satisfied client, increased income, and a new pool of knowledge along with the experience to be able to do it again with confi-dence. The bottom line is, for those who possess an expansion mental-ity, nothing ever gets turned down. The Expansion Agent figures it out, expands, grows, serves their clients, and makes more money. It's a big world out there, and there's plenty to learn, explore, and expand into.

Regardless of initial ability, the Expansion Agent learns all they can and goes for it!

The Resourceful Agent

Basically the idea here is that an agent is a resource because of their vast pool of knowledge and experience. A Resourceful Agent not only has a deep understanding of real estate and the local market, but they are also a wonderful help for newcomers. They know where the great parks and restaurants are. They know the weather patterns throughout the year. They know all the local events, hiking trails, and natural attractions. They can help recommend schools and even teachers, as well as dentists and doctors. They know where the best shopping action is along with health clubs, golf courses, and recreation centers. Beyond local interests The Resourceful Agent has an arsenal of contacts for everything. I have a team of people who partner with me on every real estate transaction. They are all high-quality people, and I couldn't go far without them. There is no second guessing, and there is no hesitation. They are all sharp, and in exchange for their high level of competency, I give them my unwavering loyalty. I don't shop. I don't look for a bargain. I find great people and deal with them exclusively. They never have to worry about me. Listen, I'm way too busy to play games. I communicate clearly to everyone on my team and tell them they have my exclusive loyalty. No need to ever wonder. That's how trust is built, and that's how you have high impact teams of people who work well together and get things done.

The most important person in my real estate world is Lori Moran. I literally couldn't do anything without her. It's hard to explain everything she does, so let's just say she does everything! Seriously. She just handles it in stride like a pro and makes it look easy. It also helps that we laugh like old high-school friends when we're together, which makes it even better! When I have a listing, I use Unified Title. Dan Osinski in Business Development is my go-to guy for anything I need, and Stephanie Hayes along with Lisa Key are my title geniuses. I never have to be concerned about the process knowing these two bright ladies are on the job. When people ask me for a home inspection referral, I never think of anyone else but Chris Behan of Pillar to Post. He is not only brilliant at what he does but he is also a thorough communicator. He is very patient and takes great effort in explaining the inspection results to my clients. I hope to not only be resourceful in the transaction process but also for many other things like painters, drywallers, landscapers, roofers, interior designers, plumbers, you name it. A real estate agent is one of the first relationships people make in a new town and as such can be a tremendous help assisting the newcomer into their new life.

The No Drama Agent

Any time you have high-dollar items like houses combined with low quality, poorly trained agents, you can expect drama. Frankly, many people are in way over their head. With little or no business skill or negotiation experience, emotions quickly get out of control. I cannot tell you how many times I am accosted by an emotional, out-of-control agent simply because I pushed back on terms or price because it wasn't favorable to my clients. You would have thought I slapped their mother the way they acted. Such agents always freak out because they simply have no other tools in their bag but emotion. Not so with great agents. The No Drama Agent understands business and negotiations on a high level. They also have a keen understanding of human behavior and possess a high level of emotional intelligence. They know that emotion has no role in trying to get your clients the best arrangement possible. They know that in corporate negotiations as in real estate negotiations, a cool head always prevails. The No Drama Agent doesn't take anything personally. They are not reactive or defensive. When confronted with a challenge or obstacle they focus on solving problems not on enflaming emotions. They understand this is business, and they have to be strategic not emotional.

Even if they are going through a hard time personally, they don't drag that into their professional lives. Their clients deserve a levelheaded negotiator who will fight for them with a clear mind. I'm sure many of us have been desperate or struggling at one time or another. It's just that you don't want your actions to amplify your inner anxiety. Be cool under pressure. Stay professional. As the saying goes, "Never let them see you sweat." There have been seasons in my life that I have been under such duress that every day was a mission just to get through. I'm sure many of you have had seasons like that. That's just life. Compartmentalization is a great skill here. Do your best to not drag it into the office. When you are with people, be present and be professional. If you have to excuse yourself from the conference table and go into the bathroom to wipe the sweat from your brow or the tears from your eyes, then do so. If you need to go sit in your car and scream for a few minutes, have at it. Just don't drag it into your business. People who are preparing to make huge decisions deserve an agent who is emotionally stable and ready to help them achieve their goals.

The Top Producing Agent

In sales you hear this term "top producer." It means that, um, someone is a top producer! They are usually national award winners and have a list of achievements on their business card or marketing material. They will generally be a well-oiled machine, a real pro achieving incredible levels of sales. Excellence, high standards, drive, and passion lead these men and women to the front of the pack. They are the experts who generate the most business, make the most money, and have the most clients. They are not dabblers or part-timers. They are utterly committed to their career, and it's just that. A career. They dominate not only due to their longevity and being a common staple in their community, but they remain at the top because of their strategy, business acumen, and overall mastery of the real estate industry. They are not your normal everyday agent any more than a Super Bowl champion is anything but an average athlete. They are at the top of their game, and it takes a special kind of person to achieve that distinction in an overcrowded industry filled with every kind of agent imaginable.

A Top Producing Agent arrives at their lofty position by being smart and strategic. They learn early what to focus on and delegate the rest.

The Top Producer will do only what they alone can do and delegate other functions to competent people. More often than not the Top Producer will have a considerable support structure that enables them to focus on generating business. You see, the average agent who does four deals a year, which is an actual statistic, does everything themselves. They have the time. They are also not making a lot of money, so they can't usually afford to pay others to assist them. The top producer, on the other hand, may do forty, sixty, or one hundred transactions or more every year. The kind of mentality and structure needed to accomplish these levels of sales is drastically different than the kind you need to do four in a year. In order to achieve such levels, the Top Producing Agent has a keen understanding that they are running a small business. They have the mentality and temperament of a full-time business owner. Running a business is far different than doing something as a side hustle four times a year. The Top Producing Agent runs their business efficiently and with intentional strategy. They develop not only a methodology but also a team that functions with specific duties. As I mentioned before, the Top Producing Agent will focus on what they alone can do and find others to do the rest.

A huge part of real estate is correctly processing the piles of paperwork. There are deadlines that must be adhered to and demands that must be met. Though it's important, paperwork doesn't earn you money; going out and finding clients does. Therefore, most Top Producing Agents delegate the responsibility of managing the paperwork to a Transaction Coordinator or TC. The TC is a paid member of the team who thrives on details and is highly organized. As they are usually paid per transaction, the more successful the agent, the more income the TC generates. In turn the agent, freed up from the load of paperwork, can now go out and generate more business. Top Producing Agents have other people on their team as well. Some Top Producers may only do listing presentations and allow for someone else on their team to focus on helping their buyers find an appropriate home. I'm sure many Top Producers will help family, personal friends, and special clients find a home, but that will be the exception not the norm. The reason for this is representing a buyer takes a lot more time, and that time for the Top Producer can be better used elsewhere. He or she focuses on efficiency and maximizing profit while ensuring their clients are well looked after. In addition, the listing agent is usually a more skilled agent than a buyer's agent. Communicating effectively, presenting a listing proposal, explaining marketing, negotiating, and going through contracts is much more complicated than simply driving someone around and looking at houses. Clearly, intentionality has to be engaged when looking at houses as well. As I've mentioned elsewhere, buyers need to be financially pre-qualified and understand exactly what type of home they are looking for, but beyond that the buyer's agent is merely driving clients around town. In the vast majority of cases, the Top Producing Agent will focus on listings because that is where their skill and experience can really shine.

The Aware Agent

It is essential to have an agent who is aware of potential problems and then has the ability to design a strategy to address those concerns. On the buying side, the Aware Agent can foresee potential issues with a home and then use them to negotiate a lower price or better terms. To clarify, I am not advocating that an agent confuse his or her role with that of a property inspector. Inspections, done by a certified and experienced professional, are vital to a smooth process. I am talking about little things that an aware person notices. A dead tree, a stain on the carpet, peeling paint, and chipped tile are just some of the things that should be noticed and then used as leverage in negotiation superior terms. Beyond physical items the Aware Agent will bring external items to the buyers attention like road noise, busy nearby schools, traffic, freeway access, proximity to shopping, and a host of other items that are important to know. Especially when the buyers are from out of town, the Aware Agent is a great resource for the newcomer.

Many agents don't get involved with things like this because they are more interested in just getting a sale and moving on. They feel that it's not their responsibility to find faults in a home or point out concerns about the location. However, this mentality is shortsighted and unprofessional in my opinion. The Aware Agent wants to find things in a home that allow for potentially more favorable negotiations on terms or price. If the average days on market is forty-five days, and a home they are looking at has sat for three months, then they know the home is stale and perhaps a better deal can be negotiated. The clients are better served than with the kind of agent who just opens a door and lets buyers figure things out.

On the listing side, an Aware Agent is important as well. An alert agent can point to things in the house or on the property that need to be addressed in order to attract a full price offer. I think most people tend to turn a blind eye on certain parts of their home or property. A fresh pair of eyes and ideas from an Aware Agent can really help improve the offering of a home. Weeds in the cracks of a driveway, a dead bush, a torn window screen, a leaking faucet are all things most people can live with, but to a buyer, they can all become a bit of a turn-off and impact the offering price. Things like this are easily and affordably addressed in order to make the home look sharp and sell for a solid price. It's about creating a wonderful home buying or selling experience for your customers. An Alert Agent will create happy customers, who in turn will tell others about their amazing real estate transaction.

The Generous Agent

Unfortunately there are a lot of greedy people out there. There are those who act like scared little squirrels and run and hide all their acorns. Such people believe the world is a hostile place of lack, limitations, and shortages. They believe it's a dog-eat-dog world, and they must do everything they can to get theirs and keep theirs. They are small-minded and fear based. Their decision making is reduced to how they can gain more. They are inherently selfish and self- absorbed. Such is not the case with the Generous Agent. This kind of agent has learned to tap into a life flow that knows deep in their heart that limitations and shortages are an illusion. They know full well that the universe is an abundant and beautiful place. They understand that there is more than enough opportunity, customers, and money to go around. They do not live in fear. They are not anxious. They are rested and peaceful knowing that because of their big hearted efforts, things will turn out just fine.

The Generous Agent is conscientious of everyone who makes their success possible and rewards them accordingly. Though it often is, this doesn't have to just be a money thing either. It's about remembering people and respecting them. It's about spending time with the office receptionist or administrator and getting to know them. It's about remembering people's birthdays and their children's names. It's about being aware of the people around you and especially those who are on your team or who help you in your endeavors. I buy Starbucks gift cards for my title officer and her assistant. I even give one to the receptionist. That blows some people's minds, but who do you think the title personnel will be more than happy to work hard for, the Grinch Agent or the Generous Agent? I don't give people gifts because I'm looking to receive something in return. I give gifts as an expression of my gratitude and to thank people for a job well done. It's human nature to have a special place in your heart for such people, and consequently I always receive top notch service.

Life operates this way. All of life responds to the law of the harvest. It's about sowing and reaping. It's about planting seeds and harvesting a crop. Some stingy people sow few seeds and consequently reap small harvests. I am generous and plant seeds of love and appreciation everywhere I go. It's no surprise to me when good things come my way. I tip generously when I dine out as well. I go out of my way to give someone a compliment or a word of encouragement. Again, it isn't always about money or a physical gift. Sometimes the nicest thing you can do for someone is give a forgotten person a hug and listen to their story. This also isn't some glorious fountain of generosity that suddenly emerges once a person is wealthy. Physical wealth follows spiritual and emotional health. There were many years when my wife and I were really struggling financially but we would still do nice things for people.

I am generous to my clients as well. It depends on the situation, but I always give amazing gifts. Buying or selling a home and moving can be stressful. Even in the best circumstances, it's challenging. Wouldn't it be a great idea to give clients a gift of a full-body massage and day at the spa? Or how about a three day cruise? Or limo service to and from a concert including fine dining? Or a first-class flight to Vegas for two days including a $500 casino voucher, food credits, and suite? I often give gift baskets filled with tickets to local attractions to my out of town clients. You know how fun it is to land in a new location and have an agent who finds fun things for you and your family to do? I put a significant amount of time and effort to customize a gift for my clients. I listen carefully and ask a lot of questions and can usually figure out how to knock my client's socks off!

Clearly the level of gift depends on the size of the deal, but why not have fun with it? You can be as creative as you want to. I have a teenage daughter. I can offer free babysitting for one year to my clients who move here from out of state. I, of course, pay my daughter for her time, but do you know what a relief it is to have a solid babysitter in a new town? It provides the parents an opportunity to go out and enjoy a quiet dinner or event without worrying about the kids. Other times it's making sure the vacant property is looked after, that the lawn is cut, or the drive and walkway are clear of snow. Sometimes it's getting some rooms painted before clients move in. Sometimes it's merely an expression of my appreciation. Sometimes it's a gift that brings tears to my client's eyes. I have even worked for free in certain situations of incredible and heartbreaking hardship.

We live in such a calculated society where everyone it seems is figuring out how to get more out of their job, their pension, their retirement, or their customers. Many companies like the airline industry, for example, continue to be punitive to their customers with smaller seats and horrible policies in a desire to extract more profit. When you give generously out of a happy heart, it just blows people's minds. I love it! I believe we live in a limitless universe. I believe the more I give, the more I receive. I believe as I tap into this abundance mentality more is given to me. There is more than enough to go around. The Generous Agent is a full-hearted person who gives away their money, gifts, time, attention, and love. Such agents know they are successful because they are tapped into a major life principle and flow of the universe.

The Communicating Agent

While this should be self-evident, you would be surprised how many agents are horrible at communicating. Lame agents take hours and even days to respond to requests or questions. They have forgotten what it feels like to be dependent upon someone for information and direction. They don't take into consideration the importance of a home purchase or sale and the potential anxiety silence creates. Beyond that it can be off-putting even disrespectful to those making such a big decision. A great agent is a Communicating Agent. They are aware of the pressures and emotions while in a real estate transaction. They realize that questions need to be answered promptly and that there are deadlines where things have to be accomplished by. They know that communicating information in a timely manner keeps clients in a positive frame of mind. Armed with current and helpful information, they can confidently move forward with the process.

It takes empathy and awareness as well as good business sense to stay in touch with your clients. With most people having smart phones that can receive texts and e-mail in addition to voice mail, there is no excuse for not promptly communicating to your clients. Most people understand that real estate agents have a life and don't expect you to drop everything for them. Most people are reasonable and understand there are meetings and lunches where responding is inappropriate. However, if hours or days go by, clearly there is a problem. I will even text or call my clients even when there is no new information. "Hi Madison. No new developments. We're still waiting to hear from the other agent but I just wanted to touch base and say hi." Such messages are worth their weight in gold when you are a client just waiting to hear something. It puts people at east and lets them know you are on the job and that they are not forgotten.

The Learning Agent

In every industry there are people who don't lift a finger to improve their knowledge or skill set and others who constantly are on the lookout for opportunities to improve. Would you like to go to a dentist that graduated from dental school in 1973 and hasn't learned any new techniques or done any continuing education or certification since? It's the same in real estate. If you line up two agents, and one business card says "Agent," and the other guy has eighteen certifications on the back of his card, which agent makes a stronger impression? There are classes and certifications on virtually every real estate topic under heaven, and smart agents know that continual improvement is not only a way to stay sharp, but it's also a way to get more business.

Some of the certifications out there are Distressed Property Expert, Investor Agent Specialist, Military Housing Specialist, Foreclosure Specialist, Luxury Home Specialist, and Short-sale Specialist. When you see such designations tastefully presented on someone's flyer or business card, it tells you that this agent is very committed to their career and consequently your objectives. Beyond formal studies it's also important to be they type of person who is well read and up to date on current trends and new technology. The Learning Agent is a life-long learner who is always hungry for new and fresh information and skills.

The Team Agent

Oftentimes a top producing real estate agent generates so much business that he or she can't possibly do it all themselves. In order to continue to grow, they expand and bring in other people to help shoulder the growth. This is in stark contrast to two failing agents who join together to create a team which I mentioned in the previous chapter. The Team Agent organizes their business in order to maximize efficiency and capture a larger portion of the market. Oftentimes the other team members have specific roles or specialties, like being a dedicated buyer's agent or relocation agent. Other times they just share in the general work load. There may be personal assistants who take care of many little details that frees up the Team Agent to be more efficient. There will most likely be an administrator or team manager who is the hub on the wheel. Regardless of their role, they know that together they can generate much more business than they could alone. They often have a distinctly unique culture and group personality which is reflected in their marketing. They are like a mini-company within the larger company or brokerage. There are many highly effective, top producing teams in virtually every city in America.

The Do What It Takes Agent

Some agents will not lift a finger to help out a buyer or seller. They leave everything to their clients to figure things out on their own. Great agents will look for every opportunity to be a blessing to their clients. They will problem solve, show initiative, and take matters into their own hands. They will make arrangements for carpet cleaners after they move out if need be. They will assist in having utilities turned on before their out-of-state clients arrive. The will make sure the lawn and yard is maintained on their vacant listing. The Do What It Takes Agent will do what needs to be done in order for the whole process to run smoother. They will drive documents that need to be notarized a couple of hours if necessary. They focus on getting things done.

I often preview homes for clients to determine if it meets their exact requirements. I also do that because sometimes things look different in person than in a photo online. Also, if there are negative aspects like power lines behind the home, agents will usually omit that from the picture and take a photo from an angle that obscures the negative item. Part of that I suppose is good marketing. Part of it I feel is deceptive. I would rather people just shoot straight with me, so we don't all waste time. We're going to see the power lines sooner or later, you may as well just come out with it up front. If a home looks like it's close to the desires of a client, sometimes I will preview it by myself to see if it is indeed a good fit or if there is something that needs to be addressed. In this way I don't waste my client's time, and when we do look at homes, it's more stream-lined. This particular home seemed to fit well with my client's desires. The listing agent happened to be conducting an open house and was posted up in the kitchen. I informed the agent I had clients and that her listing seemed like a good fit. She was all grins. Upstairs in the master bath I smelled mold. It was a hot day and the air conditioning was on, but the bathroom window was open, which was a glaring sign that something was wrong.

I walked downstairs and said, "What's with the moldy smell in the master bath?" She, looking for an Academy Award for Best Actress, said with feigned shock, "What smell?" I confess I don't generally suffer fools gladly nor do I have patience when I know people are lying right to my face. I looked right at her and said, "Give me a break. I can smell the mold and that's why you have the window open even though you have the AC on and it's ninety-five degrees outside." With that I promptly walked out. The point is I would rather go by myself and encounter lame agents and their stupid tricks alone than with clients. They don't need to be exposed to such sophomoric behavior, and besides it's a total waste of time for them. This is a big thing to consider. The Do What It Takes Agent knows their clients have obligations. They know they have jobs and lives to deal with and wasting their time doesn't serve them well. "Yea but don't you spend a lot of time previewing homes," some lame agent might ask as if I'm working too hard? I mean what are we getting paid for? Lazy agents will just never get it.

A friend of mine had their rental for sale. He listed it in May. At the time I was in process of selling my interpretation company and was preparing to get back into real estate. I had gotten crushed and lost more than I care to remember in the real estate collapse of 2008. I had rentals, my personal home, a property management company, a thriving real estate operation with multiple team members, and I was studying for my brokerage license in order to open my own shop. Then it all crashed. I had over $6,000,000 of listings out there that represented almost $200,000 in income, but the buyers vanished and the bottom fell out. Over the course of eighteen months, we blew through our savings and investments and liquidated everything.

That's the thing about this business. Real estate is cyclical. There are ups and downs. When you are 100 percent commission sales, you don't sell and you don't eat. That's it! There's no salary or draw. There's no base income as in some sales jobs. Nothing. You must have reserves or a spouse to support you during the lean times. I didn't have the luxury of spousal support as my wife was home with our baby boy. It was all on my shoulders. I was as they say, all in. We lived conservatively in a 1,900 square-foot home in a nice neighborhood in Los Angeles County. We had ample reserves, but it just wasn't enough for this once in a lifetime financial storm. Limping and wounded I took a corporate sales job and then launched a company that I ran for several years. After enjoying high double-digit annual growth, my company was acquired by a major market leader.

Healthy once again I wanted to get back into real estate. I renewed my license in July . During a conversation in late September, my friend was telling me how frustrated he was with his agent. Now it was autumn, and the "hot" time to sell was largely over. Kids were back in school, and interest in the home had died way down. Moreover, winter was soon approaching. The agent had recommended price reductions throughout summer that accomplished nothing. To weak or lazy agents the only viable strategy is to give away their clients' money by reducing the price of the home. This, of course, also reveals that they don't know what they're doing and didn't price the home correctly to start with. Or there is something about the appearance of the home that needs to be addressed. Either way, a proactive and experienced agent will address such issues so the home can sell quickly and for top dollar.

I asked to meet him at his rental. We stood at the curb and the problem was glaringly obvious. Like elephant on an elementary school playground obvious. You could barely see the home from the street. Their suburban neighborhood was fine. Their home was fine. It's just that it had zero curb appeal. Dead grass, overgrown, and unpruned bushes along with too many trees created a horrible first impression. That in conjunction with a lazy agent made for a bit of a disaster. Many years ago I had a landscape architecture firm that designed, installed, and maintained residential landscaping. I love landscaping and am never afraid to get my hands dirty. I walked him through the front yard and told him what trees needed to be removed, which bushes needed pruning, and gave him a strategy to tidy up the place.

He said he was going to fire her and hire me. Not the first time that's happened! I told him to give me $500 and two days. I brought my chain saw, yard tools, and had a dumpster delivered. I cut down trees. I pruned bushes and raked out year's worth of debris and leaves. I repaired the sprinklers. I put down fresh soil, graded it, and topped it off with new sod. I planted some flowers and added fresh mulch. The home could now breathe and be visible from the street, complimented by nicely appointed new landscaping. Overgrown and crowded landscaping made the home feel like it was suffocating and stagnant. Besides that you actually had to walk sideways from the driveway to the front door. The junipers were that overgrown!

The second day I was on my hands and knees laying down sod when a woman pulled up and got out of her car. She explained that she was a nurse and worked at the nearby hospital. She said she put in an offer on another home in the neighborhood but preferred the location of this one. "Are you the owner?" I laughed and said, "No. I'm the real estate agent and currently the landscaper!" She grew excited and asked if it was back on the market. She told me she couldn't believe how much different the home looked and how much brighter it was with all the trees and over-grown bushes out of the way. Long story short, she cancelled her other deal and gave us a full-price offer. Which by the way was $5,000 more than what it was previously listed for! So let's review shall we? Lazy agent has home for sale all summer long and can't get it sold during the busiest time of the year for real estate. Lazy agent gets fired for her incompetency which she fully deserved. I get hired and execute a strategic game plan. I do the work. I'm not lazy. We earn a full-price offer before the landscap-ing is even done. My friend got an extra $5,000 less $500 for landscap-ing materials and plants. I'm sure some may think I'm nuts, but I like to work, and besides he was a good friend who was in a jam. Regardless, the Do What It Takes Agent gets things done. They will either do things themselves or have someone on their team do it, but the great agents are always looking to add value and be helpful.

The Empathy Agent

The reason I have enjoyed success in business over the years is that I never forget what it feels like to be a consumer or a customer. Do you know what I mean? Some doctors have been doctors for so long that they forget how to treat people like they would like to be treated if they were sick. While their technical skill may be fine, their bedside manners are horrific. This goes for police officers, teachers, pastors, and, yes, real estate agents. It's easy to get locked into a professional mentality where you focus on the technical aspects while ignoring the human aspects. People like this have an emotionally disconnected attitude and even indifference toward their clients which can be interpreted as disrespect. Some agents have poor people skills and struggle to connect with people in a meaningful way. Their communication style is ineffective and just comes across as robotic or scripted.

Truly effective professionals always stay in touch with what it feels like to be on the other side. Developing and maintaining a type of vocational empathy is really key to having ongoing success. Empathy is basically being considerate of the other person in the equation and being mindful of their emotions, heart, thoughts, and experience. I call it being customer centric. In other words, I have always tailored my actions, communication, sales, and marketing with the customer or client in mind. The Empathy Agent knows how it feels to walk in their customers' shoes.

The Connecting Agent

Great agents are Connecting Agents. They intrinsically know how to connect to people and be relatable. They are sociable and pleasant. They know how to strike up a conversation and are openhearted toward people.

You would think in sales this would be a no-brainer, but you would be surprised. That's precisely part of the problem. Many people get into real estate not only lacking in basic business and negotiation skills, but having a minimal if any understanding of sales in general. There are plenty of agents who are awkward, painfully introverted, or lack people skills, yet here they are "selling" real estate. I have said it many times that no matter what you do you are in the people business. It's the only business on the planet. We're not in the real estate business. We're in the people business. We work with buyers and sellers, both of which are human or at least I hope they are. Some agents and business people for that matter lose sight of that most simple fact. Knowing how to connect with people will almost always equal success.

I found myself at Discount Tires getting a new set put on my car. Sitting there flipping through magazines but totally aware of my surroundings, I noticed a young lady who came and sat a couple of seats over from me. With nothing but empty chairs between us and nobody else in the room, I asked her if she's getting new tires too. I mean duh. Of course, she's getting tires. She wasn't there to get a massage. The name of the business is Discount Tires after all! What can I say? It's the first thing that came to my mind! She smiled and nodded her head. I, uninvited, said, "I'm a real estate agent, so I am running the wheels off my car." While it was true that I was indeed a real estate agent and while it was true that my tires needed replacing, it may not have been entirely accurate that I ran my wheels off my car, but, again, that's what came to my mind! It doesn't need to be perfect. Just open your mouth and get moving. Stick your neck out a little. To my absolute delight and unexpectedly so, she replied, "Oh really? I just got married and my husband and I want to move out of our apartment." It's kind of like when you've been sitting in a boat for hours with a line in the water, and all of sudden the bobber gets pulled beneath the surface of the lake! Wake up! It's go time! I almost had to slap myself. I was kind of laughing on the inside. "Is it really this easy, this real estate thing?" Well, it isn't, but sometimes you do have situations like this that just come out of nowhere.

They became my very first clients, and I found them a perfect little starter home in a nice neighborhood with tree lined streets. Of course, it isn't always this easy, but one thing is for sure; if you don't open your mouth, no one will know you are a real estate agent. There are some secrets you should keep to yourself. Your profession as an agent isn't one of them. Pass out business cards, shake as many hands as you can, and let everyone know you are in real estate. Great agents always connect with people, and let them know they are in the business of real estate.

The New Home Development Agent

In most growing metro areas across the nation, there are new developments emerging. Such developments can be built out by a local builder or by large national companies. Sometimes it will be just one builder or it can be several. Great agents know where the new developments are and have already built relationships with the builder's staff. Great agents also have researched and know where future developments are going to be. They will have copies of all the available models and be up to date on open lots. Many agents will over their entire career not ever bring one buyer to a new development, and for the life of me, I can't imagine why. Builders make it so easy. You simply go with your clients, introduce yourself as an outside agent, and fill out a card with your client's name. That's it! Builders pay the commission, and you serve your clients well. Everybody wins.

In one development I brought eleven different buyers totaling over $5 million in sales. Over time I had such an amazing relationship with the builder's agent that she offered me a premium lot at a discount, and I ended up having a home built in that development. I hadn't planned on buying a home; it was just that after spending so much time in that development, knowing the staff, and being very familiar with the area and the builder, it just made sense. There is something wonderful about a new home in a new development, and the great agents know how to tap into that part of the market.

This concludes our chapter on agents. As you no doubt observed in the previous chapter that there are way more categories of bad agents than there are of good ones. This falls in line with the 80/20 rule. Eighty percent of the business is done by 20 percent of the agents, and 80 percent of the income is earned by the same. You can bet that in order to dominate in the over-crowded real estate industry, you have to be a great agent.

Chapter Eleven

The Rental

I have personally participated in the rental market, and I have run a business that had a property management division as a service to my clients. There are many opinions on the matter, but I will primarily focus on the practical aspects.

There are many kinds of investors with varied strategies and personal preferences. Some invest and rent out land, farms, or horse arenas. Others rent out office space. Still others only invest in three-bedroom, two-bath homes, so-called bread-and-butter homes. I have one friend in Los Angeles who purchases old factories and warehouses and converts them into individual office spaces with a common receptionist and office manager. People rent out offices, and there are different price tiers for month to month or long term. Sometimes my friend, if the space allows, builds out retail or restaurant space at street level with the offices internally or on upper floors.

The first thing you have to determine is what kind of investor you are. Most people start with residential housing. However, even in that category, there are different kinds. There are attached homes like condominiums, townhomes, duplexes, triplexes, and quads. In condos there are multi-floor, high-rise, and ground level single story. An investor can purchase an apartment building or convert an old hotel into rentals. These are all examples of attached housing. Then there are single family detached (SFD) homes, which are a standard fixture in the suburbs. So even in the residential space, there is a significant variety. Once the determination is made that, for example, you want to be a rental owner in the residential arena, the pros and cons of each type of rental must be understood. Then there are different markets, price points, and neighborhoods. You have to know the peculiarities of each area. Being realistic and writing down a pros and cons list will help you make an informed decision.

SFD or stand-alone homes are nice but require interior and exterior maintenance whereas a condo or townhome has an HOA that takes care of at least the exterior. Do you want to own duplexes in a distressed part of town, so you can buy them cheap? They may be cheap, but you may struggle with other issues. Do you want to purchase luxury housing and rent to business executives? You'll probably be able to charge a handsome sum for the rent, but the home may sit vacant at times, and you'll have to carry the note. Do you want to purchase vacation property near tourist sites or ski resorts for daily, weekly, or monthly renters? That will most likely be amazing during peak season, but what strategy will you employ to attract renters in the off season? Do you want to rent homes near a military base and take advantage of frequent turnover? Homes near a military base will most likely rent quickly, but what if there are cuts to the defense budget and they downsize the base? Do you want to own a large home near a university and divide it into multiple rentals or make it available to a fraternity or multiple roommates? Homes near colleges are great, but the wear and tear will most likely be significant. Do you want to pick up a small apartment building and contract with the government to offer low-income Section 8 housing? Though you will receive steady rental checks from the government, the process may be complicated. As you can see, there is plenty to think about and process.

There are different kinds of properties in different kinds of neighborhoods and different kinds of markets and different kinds of strategies. There's no right or wrong path. What you chose has to do with budget, personal taste, objectives, and long-term strategy. Beyond that sometimes an opportunity will reveal itself, and although it's outside your parameters, it may be something to consider. Of course, you can just wing it and see what happens. Lots of successful people have done that, and things have turned out just fine. Of course, there are also plenty of nightmare stories out there as well. I highly recommend having a business plan and a sound strategy based on your personal objectives and desires. The key here is once you determine that you want to be an investor, just do it. What you end up with is not near as important as the decision to move forward. One thing is for sure, nothing happens if nothing happens. So make something happen!

By the way I try to avoid using the grossly outdated designation of "landlord." I mean honestly are we in feudal Europe? Do we live in Elizabethan England? "Hark! Who goeth there? Is it Sir James the Landlord? I beseech thee. Why dost thou come to the castle this fortnight?" Just use the title of property owner or rental owner. That works just fine. Most people don't have "lords" in their lives who they must bow down to in deference. I find it distasteful and condescending. You're not a lord or a knight for that matter!

Do the math

There needs to be a period of due diligence where you investigate not only specific properties but also your finances, rental projections, and general market indicators. Regarding finances, you not only need to know what loan amounts you can qualify for, but you also need sizeable reserves for vacancies and repairs. Part of your due diligence is to understand the market as a whole. You must be an expert in anything you invest in. If you are investing in stocks and choose Disney, for example, you should educate yourself and know that they not only run theme parks and retail locations but they also have TV and radio channels for kids in addition to having a significant presence in music and movie production as well as owning ABC and ESPN. You would research all of Disney's holdings and have a working knowledge of not only their business strategy but also what percentage of the market they capture. The same is true in real estate investing. You must become an expert in local economic conditions and trends. If the local Army base is expanding, then you know there will be a surge of new arrivals that may need housing. Also, if a large manufacturer is closing and moving to Mexico, it might not be a good idea to purchase a three-bedroom home two blocks from the factory. A growing university in town will provide ample students that need off-campus housing.

Beyond trends you must also calculate supply and demand and existing inventory. If there is a glut of rentals in a certain area of town, it might not make sense to scoop up duplexes there. It may be a good idea to interview active investors. You need to know how long it takes on average to fill a vacancy, how long renters generally stay for, and what the current rents are. The more information you acquire, the better. Knowledge is power. Once you've determined what part of town you want to invest in and what type of investment you want to purchase, it's time to go shopping. This is the fun part! So let's say you've settled on investing in three or four bedroom homes in a middle-class suburb. Beyond determining what kind of investment to purchase, you must also determine what condition you are looking for. Some investors look for beat down properties, so they can remodel them and then rent them out. This way they make money not only by renting out the property, but they also have equity in the home from the improvements. Other investors don't want to involve themselves with construction or repairs but just want to find a home that's ready to go, so they can put renters in there as soon as possible.

Regarding remodeling or repairs, if you have the tools, knowledge and skills then do it yourself if you're so inclined. If not, then have a pro do it. Many years ago we rented a home from a do-it-yourselfer. He had done significant, what he felt were improvements, to the home. And yes, he was very proud. However, within short order his newly installed granite tiles started popping off the bathroom counters. He had put the tile adhesive directly on MDF or medium density fiberboard. This material is often used as sub-counters or shelving in many newer homes. It's basically sawdust glued together and it's very smooth. Well, in order for mastic or tile adhesive to adhere it must be troweled over a rough surface. He, though well intended, obviously didn't know this. He was basically trying to stick tile onto a mirror. They all popped off and made quite a mess. He was a retired Air Force pilot and while he certainly enjoyed his military career, he wasn't exactly a home improvement pro. He probably should have stuck to flying planes and just hired a pro to do home repairs, but you know how some guys are. There were many other things he messed up pretending he was a contractor, but it would take a whole chapter. Suffice it to say, things didn't end up well and he had nobody to blame but himself.

While we're on this, topic let's talk about condition and quality. Some investors put in total garbage as far as quality is concerned and then are outraged when they have to replace everything all the time. You get what you pay for. If you put down a cheap carpet on a thin pad don't be shocked if it only lasts three years. Old-school investor thinking is that renters are slobs, so an investor with such a belief puts in the cheapest of everything. Cheap carpet, cheap linoleum, cheap fixtures, and cheap cabinets. Everything is on the cheap. Their mentality is that the renters will ruin everything anyway, so you might as well not spend a lot of money on it. I have always taken the contrary approach. I purchased a condo in the Coachella Valley near Palm Springs many years ago. It was located in a gate-guarded country club with swimming pools, tennis, clubhouse, restaurants, and golf course. I purchased it new and had the builder put in cherry cabinets, beautiful black granite counters, and large travertine tile for the flooring. The kitchen appliances were stainless steel, and the home was located on the third fairway.

My mentality as an investor is that I will only offer properties that I myself would want to live in. You attract what you are. I wanted to attract quality renters, and the only way to do that is to offer a quality home. I hear so many investors share nightmare stories, and I just laugh. I have never had a problem, not one. Other investors are so dog-gone cheap that they attract the wrong kinds of renters. If their premise is that renters are slobs that ruin properties, then they attract the kinds of renters that live up to their low expectations. It's like a self-fulfilling prophecy. I am the exact opposite. I believe that many renters are perfectly fine people with families, jobs, hopes, and dreams. If you treat them with respect and give them a quality home to reside in, they, in turn will respect you and your property. Remember renters are consumers, and they will generally select the best looking home in their price range. My homes are beautifully appointed, and the yards are impeccably maintained. Again, remember that renters are just like anyone else. They like nice things, and they like to be treated with dignity. Especially in a down market or competitive market conditions, my properties will always stand out compared to the cheap investor's rentals. As an added bonus, I have far less turnover because my renters love my properties and are in no hurry to leave. Beyond that because I am fair-minded and reasonable, we develop perfectly pleasant working relationships with our tenants.

HOAs and CC&Rs

Make sure you inform yourself of the CC&Rs (covenants, conditions and restrictions) especially in the multi-family and attached markets. CC&Rs are generally overseen by an HOA (Home Owners Association). You might get in a jam if you purchase a condo in a high-rise only to find out later per the rules that will be legally enforced, that the condos are only to be used as a primary residence. There may be age restrictions, pet restrictions, and any other limitation you can think of. Even if you purchase a single-family detached home, there still may be HOA restrictions that you will be responsible for regardless of who lives in your property. Do your homework. Due diligence is the most important part of the process. There is absolutely no excuse for getting into a tough situation.

Negative and positive cash flow

Part of your major consideration is what rents are going for and what your projected monthly cash flow will be. Positive cash flow is obviously the ideal; however, it is not the only consideration. You would need to get professional CPA advice on this, but if, for example, your income was high and you needed deductions, you might benefit from a negative cash-flow rental. Again, I'm not an accountant, and you would have to speak to a pro to understand various strategies. Just know that there are multiple paths you can go down. Having said that, the best case scenario is to have a positive cash flow, meaning there is money left over every month after paying the mortgage, taxes, insurance, maintenance, and any HOA dues. Any leftover monies should be kept in a separate account and saved for inevitable repairs or replacement of items. It's important to have a cushion.

As I mentioned, you may not have to overly fixate on positive cash flow depending on your income situation. Other considerations to remember are that the mortgage is being paid down, so you are building free equity. Beyond that in a hot market that brings steady appreciation to properties, you may rent out a place for say a $200 monthly loss, but that is irrelevant if the property appreciates $35,000 a year! With that kind of annual appreciation, you most likely won't care about being negative $2,400 every twelve months. While we are on cash flow, please know that owning rental property is a rich person's game. Well, maybe not rich, but you need to have a steady income apart from the rentals, and you need to have ample reserves for the eventual costs and repairs associated with owning a rental home. In addition, you will need reserves in the event the property stays vacant. Your life will be increasingly difficult if you are depending on a $150 a month positive cash flow to pay your own personal bills. If the market changes or if the property remains vacant for a month or two, it could sink you. That's why I say it's a rich person's game. Better said it's a stable person's game. Before getting involved with rentals, you should be financially stable with plenty in savings.

Where do I find renters?

Once you've researched, done your due diligence, selected a property, and made your purchase, it's time to rent it out. So how will you and prospective renters find each other? Now is the time for marketing. In many areas, a sign in the front yard or an ad in the paper or on Craig's List does the trick. Sometimes you can find someone by just letting your social networks know you have a rental available or by mentioning it on social media like Facebook. Part of your strategy in purchasing a specific property is having a type of renter in mind. If you purchase a large home with seven separate guest suites near a major university, it's kind of obvious that you are looking to rent to college students. If you purchase a bread-and-butter, three-bedroom home near an elementary school, you're probably thinking a young family might be perfect.

There are laws that govern such things, and you have to be careful to get legal counsel about this topic. However, if you did happen to own a large divided home near a campus, you might be able to advertise in the university paper or website. You could ask administration if there are any boards you could post flyers on. Most schools have such options readily available. You could even contact the university housing department or develop relationships with a key administrative staff member. If you were near a military base, you might investigate options there as well. If a company is dramatically expanding and making a bunch of new hires, it might make sense to befriend someone in the HR department. Whatever situation you find yourself in, expand your marketing to include options beyond a sign in the front yard or window.

Interviewing potential renters

Your investment property is purchased, and your marketing is in place. Your phone rings, and now you have someone interested. You will most likely meet at your investment property as they will want to see it first-hand. You show them the property, and they express interest. What now? Clearly before this point you will have needed to purchase real estate applications and rental contracts. You must research and get legal counsel on this. Sometimes specific terms must be drawn up by an attorney, and other times prepackaged applications and contracts from an office supply store will suffice. You must determine your terms. How much of a deposit do you want? In many places one month's rent is standard. Some investors like two months. Whatever you want just be aware of the impact it will have on the prospective pool of possible renters. If your rent is $1,200, many people are able to make a one month deposit, but $2,400 for two months may eliminate many from proceeding. It goes without saying, but especially for the deposit and probably first month's rent, be sure to have certified funds like a cashier's check or money order. The last thing you want is for someone to give you a deposit on a personal check and have it bounce after they have the keys.

Along with a contract and terms, you will want to secure a process for checking credit. No matter what they drive or what clothes they wear or how nice they seem or how cute their baby is, always, and I mean always, conduct a credit check. This is a financial matter not an emotional one. You are looking for payment history and the exhibition of responsibility. Having said that, life happens. If someone has blemished credit, give them a chance to explain. You can't judge bad credit with too sweeping a brush. The real estate collapse of 2008 claimed many victims. Lots of good people lost everything. Houses were foreclosed upon, cars were repossessed, and credit was crushed. It's perfectly fine to listen and be reasonable. Economic downturns, loss of a job, or declining health are among the many reasons people may have credit blemishes. There are lots of good people out there who hit some bad luck. Many people are completely worthy of a second or even third chance. Regardless, do what's comfortable for you. If you want only renters with really strong credit and that is a logical criteria for you, then stick with that strategy.

You may if the law allows want to conduct a criminal background check. Not sure how you would feel if someone had great credit, but you didn't know they were a convicted felon. Again, seek legal counsel if you are able to do this in your area, but the bottom line is the more information you have, the better. You may be able to just ascertain this information from questions on your application. Of course people can lie but at least it gives you a feel for the person. Like credit, just because someone may have a less than perfect past shouldn't necessarily block them from a preferred future. Listen to the story and if it's reasonable then perhaps you can be comfortable moving forward. If not, then pass and move on. Remember, it's your property and it's your call. Don't do anything that makes you feel uncomfortable or will potentially keep you up at night worrying. If you're renting to a young soldier, for example, you may want to get the name of his commanding officer. Nothing puts the fear of God in a young military member like knowing that you have his boss's name and number! All your research and fact gathering is designed to mitigate risk.

So here you are standing in the kitchen of your rental, and they say they are interested. Don't ever be a sucker and do the old "Gee, you two look swell. Sign here and the keys are yours." While you may think you're an amazing judge of character and maybe this method works for you, it is a better idea to do some homework. Remember once they sign, you lose some rights and some power. The time for homework, due diligence, and investigation is before they sign the contract. There's a difference between having an informative conversation and coming across like an interrogator for the FBI. Relax and just talk. People will be more than happy to share their story and speak openly about their work history or challenges they may have had in the past. If you feel someone is being shifty or evasive, you don't have to rent to them. Let me be perfectly clear. Never get desperate. Many rental property owners create their own disasters and unnecessarily increase the stress in their life because they got desperate and rented to the wrong people. Some landlords seemingly rent to anyone with a pulse and wonder why they have so many problems.

If they like your property and can afford the rent and you feel good about your conversation with them, it's time for the application. The application will give you the information you need to do a credit check and investigate their work history and references. Follow through! It's easy to get lax and just gloss over this part. You have to be diligent and cover your bases. This is a major investment you are turning over to a complete stranger. You better get all the information you can. Having said this, do this part quickly. If you are a procrastinator, your prospective renters aren't going to wait around forever. Especially in a competitive market, they may go elsewhere because they have options. I'm not sure there is a magic timeframe, but whatever time you need, communicate that to them and respond promptly. I don't think it should ever take more than three days. If there is a cost to credit checks and you want to be reimbursed for your time you can charge a reasonable application fee like $25. Or you can just skip a fee and consider it a necessary expense.

The rental agreement

After investigating and reviewing their credit, if you determine they are a good candidate for your property, you will meet again and have them sign the rental agreement. Be sure you are happy with the terms of the agreement because you and they will be bound by them. Included in the agreement are terms for payment, lease duration, and delineation of expectations. You want to be clear on who does what and when. You can have a lot of flexibility with this as it's up to you and them what works best for both parties. For one of my renters, we shared the same bank, so they just set up an auto withdrawal and had it transferred into my account every month. It couldn't have been easier. I never had to be concerned with a late payment or if the check was in the mail.

You can accept credit cards if you want. I know that may sound nuts but it's convenient and the small fee may be tax deductible as a legitimate expense of doing business. It may give you a competitive edge in a tight market because there are many people who almost exclusively use credit cards in order to capture miles or points on their favorite rewards card. You can use a mobile device like Square or PayPal, both of which provide you with a card swiper you plug right into your smart phone. You can have them drop off or mail you a check, of course, or you can have them deposit it into your bank account. I have a friend in the music business. For him it's either feast or famine. When he was renting sometimes he wanted to pay six months in advance when he received a big check. Usually his landlord gave him a slight discount for paying ahead of time. There are no rules here. Whatever works best is what is best.

A big part of the terms of any rental agreement is the delineation of responsibilities. Have this in writing. This not only protects both parties legally and ethically, but it also allows for accurate expectations, so it can be a harmonious experience for both of you. Everything that has to be done in a home will have to be done in a rental home. This means lawn and yard maintenance, snow removal, light bulb replacement, and dealing with clogged toilets to name a few. It's funny how such banal items become the downfall of so many in the rental ownership world. I always get asked, "What about toilets clogging?" I don't know where this fixation comes from. Honestly, it's weird to me that people are so hung up on toilets and calls in the middle of the night. There are a lot of investors who frankly have enough money to buy a rental but don't possess the business skill or have the temperament to be a rental owner. There are plenty of people who make poor decisions out of ignorance. My role is to make sure investors have as much knowledge as possible so they can avoid the traps and pitfalls of the rental game.

A successful investor knows how to conduct business in a professional manner in order to establish realistic expectations. I provide a plunger at all my rentals. Good plungers, not those cheap, stupid burnt orange looking things that don't work. I tell all my renters cleaning up after yourself is part of being a responsible adult. I'm not your mother and you're not twelve. If you have a job and a car and maybe a family, you can handle a plunger. That goes for spiders and that goes for light bulbs. Light bulbs are not expensive. Nor are they complicated to install. They can handle that too. If you prefer, you can leave a box of bulbs in the garage. I usually tell my renters and have it in writing that all expenses under twenty-five dollars are their responsibility. We can all be big boys and girls and exhibit adult level responsibility. I don't get calls at 2:00 in the morning.

Regarding lawn care and snow removal, this is negotiable. If you want your property cared for professionally so you never have to think about it, then do so. Otherwise quite often renters will be more than happy to care for those items for a slight reduction in rent. On the other hand, if you are highly particular and want your property cared for in a specific way, you may want to do it yourself or have a professional company do it. Who cleans the carpet upon vacating and who cuts the lawn among many other things must be clearly outlined in the agreement. Again, there's no right or wrong here; it's whatever you agree upon and whatever works best for both parties.

Property condition

Here is usually where things can get wonky. Condition, as with beauty, is in the eyes of the beholder. Upon vacating you may discover the home is in relatively the same condition as it was before you rented it. There may be normal wear and tear, or there may be some significant issues. A friend of mine protected himself and the renter by using video. He recorded every room with the new renters in it, zooming in on the condition of the home. When it was time to move out, they simply reviewed the video and compared the current condition to how it looked in the video. This may seem excessive or even a bit creepy, but guess what? He never had a problem! If agreed upon you may, for example, conduct quarterly inspections though you wouldn't have to necessarily call it that. There may be various rules or laws governing this so do your homework. Again, whatever is legal and whatever you both agree upon and have in writing in the rental agreement is fine.

Another big issue here is the original quality of the materials used in the home. I have dealt with cheapskate rental owners, and they always seem indignant when the renters moved out because of the condition of the home. One guy was notoriously cheap. He put in the cheapest carpet with the thinnest pad. He proudly told the new renters "this is brand new carpet." After a couple of years of the family living in the home, the carpet was shot. Not because the people were extraordinarily rough on the flooring but because it was so cheap that it literally fell apart under normal usage. A lot of rental owners do this and then pretend to have some moral high ground when the property looks beat down after renting it out for a few years. You have to be realistic and know the quality of the materials you are installing and you have to know how long such quality should last. As the saying goes, "The bitterness of poor quality lasts longer than the thrill of a bargain."

If at the end of the lease there are holes in the walls and cigarette burns in the linoleum, you have issues, and that is what the deposit is for. However, this probably won't happen because you're smarter than that and aren't going to rent to those kinds of people. Speaking of cigarettes we never rent to smokers. Cigarettes have nicotine, which is basically oil. I remember years ago when I was painting the interior of a home. I rolled the paint out on the wall, and it began to run down to the floor like water. The paint began to streak. I was like "What the heck?" Years of smoking had literally coated the walls and ceiling with a film of oily substance that water-based latex paint would not adhere to. Remember, oil and water don't mix. Beyond that smoke is well, smoke. After fires homes are treated for "smoke damage." Homes are never treated for clean air damage. Smoke will stick in the carpets, the drapes, and the drywall. It gets into the vents, the furnace, and every nook and cranny of the home. The smell and the oily substance will never leave. I'm not interested in my properties being ruined by someone's bad habit.

Property management companies

You may want to hire a property management company. Not all property management companies are created equal though, and you need to be very careful about going this route. A good property manager will look after your investment as if it was their own. You need someone who is alert, aware, disciplined, professional, detail oriented, good at business, and tenacious. This is not the role for a passive personality or someone with a lazy character flaw. The general duties of a property-management company are to market your home and secure a good tenant which includes conducting credit checks and any needed investigation. Beyond that they collect rental payment, deposit it in an account that is not comingled with other obligations, and then forward you the remainder of the money less their fee.

They also should be in charge of caring for the home and making sure it looks sharp. This would include yard care and snow removal, regular interior and exterior maintenance, as well as repairs. Listen, don't be a slumlord and don't do business with property management companies that act like slumlords. So many investors and managers fail on this point. That's why people roll their eyes at an investment property when talking to their friends and say, "It's a rental." It shouldn't be that way. Like I said before, my properties are among the best maintained homes on the block. It's a horrible look to be an apathetical, absentee owner who only cares about collecting rents. Whether you use a management company or not, you should have great pride in your rental home and assure it always looks great. There is nothing worse than living in a nice neighborhood and then have some carless slumlord of a guy buy a home, rent it out, and let it go down the drain. It's disrespectful to the neighbors, and it's a dumb financial policy as a nicely maintained home will rent for more and eventually sell for more. Speaking of neighbors, develop relationships with the neighbors. Don't be a stranger. When I am involved with my own rentals or managing properties, I always introduce myself to the immediate neighbors. I want them to know who I am, and I want them to have my phone number so they can call me if they see something unsightly or if there is a problem. Sometimes a neighbor will know someone who would like to rent in their neighborhood, so that saves me time and money because now I don't have to advertise. Beyond making sure the home always looks good, the property manager is also charged with inspecting the property upon the renters vacating and refunding the deposit. If there is damage then a portion of the deposit would be used to make necessary repairs and the remainder returned to the tenant.

Property management companies generally charge a percentage of the rent or perhaps a flat rate. Whatever it is it can add up and be a drain on your net profit. While it may be a deductible expense, it is nevertheless an expense that will impact your bottom line. I hate to say this, but there are many inferior property-management companies out there with extraordinarily weak managers. Frankly many of them are lazy. They simply collect the rent and maybe drive by your property once or twice a year. It is residual income, which means they collect their fee every month like clockwork whether they work hard or not. It's real easy for some managers to be lazy or lax.

The other day I had a client who needed to rent a property that was outside the parameters of what I had available. I found a small rental on the MLS, managed by another company. I contacted them and scheduled a viewing with my client. Their so-called manager was 15 minutes late and then blamed the traffic. That's always my favorite line. "Oh you mean the same traffic that we just drove through but managed to get here on time anyway?" Blame anything but by all means don't blame yourself and your horrible time management habits. That's usually enough to make me leave, but I figured I'd give peace a chance. Then she hurriedly went up the stairs and opened the door to the condo. Funk. Straight funk. It was a bachelor pad and smelled like it. Like junior high boys that don't quite understand hygiene yet! The owner was away for some time and so the place was rank. I walked straight through and opened up some windows. Gee, like maybe somebody else should have done had they been a professional and been here early? Then she said that the advertisement was wrong and that the garage wouldn't be available. My client was livid. That was the only reason they were interested. To add the final icing on this amazing cake of incompetence, the manager started telling me my fee if my client took the place. Nonplussed. No words. I interrupted her and said we could talk about that later. You never discuss payment in front of clients. That should be self-evident. I apologized to my client in front of the manager and asked her to head down the stairs, and that I would meet up with her shortly. I then laid into this so-called manager about being late, showing a stale and smelly home, false advertisement and discussing payment in front of clients. I mean how unprofessional can you be? The levels of gross incompetency out there never ceases to amaze me. Now think this through; this person is paid to manage this rental. Paid! The owner of the condo was going to move out in a few weeks and rent out his home and this is the genius he picked to take care of his most expensive asset? And she can't even figure out how to get somewhere on time? Do you see what I mean?

I knew of one investor that while the so-called manager was happy to collect monthly fees, they didn't so much as ever even drive by the home. Much to their chagrin, after years of neglect, the investor discovered rampant termite and roof damage that ran into the multiple tens of thousands of dollars. In addition the old brick fireplace was pulling away from the

house. I cannot stress this point enough. You must have property management that is active throughout the year, not just one that focuses on
getting a renter in the home and then falls asleep on the job. This is especially true if you are an out of state investor. The checks roll in, and they
collect their fees. They may not have high standards on the quality of
renter they allow to live in your home. There are many nightmare stories
out there. Only do business with a property-management company that
you respect and that comes highly recommended by existing rental property owners. You want the management company to live up to your high
standards. Make sure your expectations are in writing and that everyone
is perfectly clear on what you want. You're the boss and you're paying so
make sure they are with the program!

The accidental rental owner
I just sold an investment property for dear friends of ours. They purchased
the home several years ago as their family home. After a few years and
a few more babies, they decided to find a larger home. Problem was
that they couldn't necessarily qualify for the larger home they wanted,
but their lender told them a creative way to pull it off. If they could rent
their current home and show rental income, they would then qualify for
their new larger home. They did and they did. They were so happy to
move into their larger home on five acres. Their kids adjusted to their new
surroundings quickly, and it was a very positive experience. That is until
the realities of being a rental owner emerged. They soon discovered that
they lacked the business sense and the needed temperament to be rental
property owners. They rented to problem people, got calls in the middle
of the night, and the property was vacant for months at a time. Paying
two mortgages almost broke them financially. Long story short, they are
great people raising great kids and are great friends. They're just not cut
out for being rental owners, and they would tell you that themselves! After
a couple of years of almost unbearable stress and tension, they decided
to sell and free themselves from that burden. We sold the rental for them,

and they could not be happier. The accidental rental owner season of their lives was over.

There's lots of people who will say, "oh, we'll just rent it out" when planning on what to do with their home after they move out. Problem is, it's just not that simple. Owning and managing a rental is simple, but it certainly isn't easy. It's a major effort and major responsibility. It takes intentionality, planning, strategy, finances, and keen business sense. This is not something to slide into without great consideration. If you are motivated, interested, and have the finances and temperament to become an investor, I can tell you firsthand that it is an exhilarating and rewarding experience. Besides having someone else pay off your homes, gaining tax benefits, and generating an income there is just something intangibly wonderful about owning multiple properties. It's a great feeling!

Chapter Twelve

Flipping Properties

There are many TV shows lauding the concept of flipping houses. The perky hosts are usually excited, motivated, and skilled at virtually every aspect of construction. They seemingly know how to do anything and enjoy every minute of the process, and are totally energized. While this all may be true, what is also true is that they have tons of support and financial sponsors that certainly make things a whole lot easier. All the cheering and high-fiving may be more for the cameras than for reality. While you may also be excited and motivated, you need the appropriate skills, resources, and temperament in order to successfully flip properties for profit. There are almost endless details to consider, and it takes not only business acumen but also a significant understanding of construction, contracting, and design. It is also very important to have your finger on the pulse of the market. Some strategies are perfect in certain situations that can be disastrous in others.

I have flipped many properties. I have also been a licensed contractor with substantial knowledge of every manner of residential construction. In addition I owned a landscape company many years ago, and I have also been a national award winning real estate agent. This all funnels into a significant advantage for me in flipping homes. I not only have the construction knowledge and the business skill, but in addition I have keen insights into local markets from a real estate trending perspective. If you are ill-equipped, your "investment" can turn into a money pit and become an unintentional divestment producing negative and frustrating results.

I cannot stress this enough. Be sure to have all the appropriate skills or know those who do before even considering flipping houses. Nothing is worse than committing months of effort and significant amounts of finances only to break even or lose money.

We recently watched an episode of *The Deed* where an ill-prepared woman lost several months of her life, created incredible strain and stress for herself in addition to losing over $100,000. She was in way over her head. It's important to not only come prepared but also to not bite off more than you can chew. Flipping properties is not for the faint of heart nor is it for the inexperienced. Leave emotions and dreams out of it. You must have sound thinking and clear strategy employed in order to be successful in flipping homes profitably.

Calculations and due diligence

The whole idea of flipping is that you purchase a distressed property, make improvements, and then sell it for a profit. Hence, flip! It doesn't necessarily have to be a distressed property, but more often than not, it is. In aggressive markets I have purchased homes that are just kind of tired but not really distressed by any means. The homes were just dated and worn. New landscaping and fresh paint inside and out along with new flooring, counters, and fixtures can turn a tired home into something attractive that receives a strong offer. Generally speaking, whether the property is distressed or just tired, in a flip there are efforts made to improve the property to substantiate a higher sale price. There are three distinct phases in flipping a property: purchase, improvement and sale. In order to succeed in the flipping game, these phases must be done strategically.

Before you make an offer on a property, you must have all your calculations pretty tight. While viewing a property take notes on what needs obvious repair, what is tired, out of style, or obsolete. Observe what needs replacing and think about what other improvements you would like to make. After this first visit begin to make your initial calculations, do some homework and investigate. You may have to make some calls, and you may have to visit some stores or shops to get ballpark prices on things. If you do not have the skills to do the improvements yourself, you will have to pay somebody to do them. Beyond that if you don't know how to organize the improvements and the flow of the work that needs to be done, in addition, you will need to pay a general contractor or GC. The GC may charge you 10 percent of the project, so if all the improvements cost $80,000, you will need to tack on an additional $8,000 to your expenses. This, of course, erodes your profit, so if you can do the GC work yourself, you will save that portion of the expenses. Clearly the more work you do yourself, the greater the profit. Having said that, if doing it yourself means the project will take seven months, then remember you have seven months of mortgage, insurance, taxes, maintenance, and possible HOA dues.

For me I not only have done the vast majority of the work, but I have also had my real estate license. In this way I minimize my expenses and maximize my profit. Because of my background in construction, I don't need to ever pay a general contractor and I don't need to pay skilled workers to do most of the improvements. Beyond that I receive commission income from the purchase that I can put toward the repairs. After everything is completed and the home is ready to be put on the market, I save half the commission representing myself, and if I find the buyer, I save the entire commission.

After conducting some initial homework and maybe this only takes an afternoon, plan a second visit. I am always surprised at how many things I pick up on my second visit in addition to what I observed the first time. Give yourself plenty of time to really investigate and take accurate notes. Here is where you want to tighten things up. If you are not skilled in the trades needed to conduct appropriate repairs or improvements, you will need those people with you in order to gain accurate estimates. This can get cumbersome especially if there are multiple projects that need to be done. Some people are a bit sloppy and even careless before presenting an offer, knowing they can get out if anything significant emerges during the inspection phase. While it may be possible to get out of a transaction if a physical inspection reveals undesirable issues, why waste the time and effort only to stop a couple of weeks into the process? You want to get as much information as you can before you make an offer.

Again, if you are skilled in construction or have a partner who is skilled, you will have a distinct advantage. Otherwise bring along a GC. If you are going to function as the general contractor, you may have to schedule a parade of people to come to the home with you. On any given flip, you may need to have a plumber, electrician, drywaller, carpenter, and land-scaper with you. Scheduling this can be a bit of a nightmare, so clearly the less outside help you need, the better. Whether you plan on doing the work yourself or are hiring people, get your bottom line estimates on repairs and improvements. There is always what I call some fluff room be-tween estimates and the actual final numbers, but you just want to make sure that your numbers are based on facts and not mere guesses. These facts and estimates will generate for you a working budget that will serve as a guideline for expenses. When the job is complete, you may come in at, under, or over budget depending on your initial accuracy, changes, or discoveries.

You must have fairly firm numbers on what it will take to make money on a property. This is not easy as much of this is speculation, and there are always surprises that come up. However, a professional can usually esti-mate within fairly tight parameters. Don't be light here, and don't minimize what you think things will cost. Assume things will cost more. Assume some things will go wrong. Assume there will be some costly surprises. Assume there will be some things you didn't even think about. Assume all those things, and pad your estimates accordingly. If none of it happens, con-gratulations, you make more money. When you are estimating for repairs and improvements always, and I mean always, have a range and then plan for the high end of that range. Don't be naïve. If you are working with oth-ers, ask for best and worst case scenario pricing. This will give you a range. Also, make sure you have documentation that explains the range. You don't want to give people license to gouge you and take the high end of the range just because it's available. For example, you may have a low-range price on exterior painting, but the high end will accommodate repairs and replace-ment for discovered wood rot on the trim, soffit, or fascia. Some things you only discover once you're into a job.

Stuff happens, and if you are prepared, you will thrive. If you are oper-ating on razor-thin margins hoping everything will work out, you are invari-ably skating on thin ice. This is not Las Vegas or Atlantic City. This is not gambling. This is the use of calculated business strategy to generate a proposed profit. Be smart and be thorough. Your primary calculation will be based on knowing what the spread is between purchase price and the eventual estimated sales price. This will provide you with a gross profit es-timate. From this number you will subtract mortgage payment, insurance, and taxes along with maintenance of the property, possible HOA dues and all the costs of improvement. In addition you will need to subtract Realtor fees and closing costs unless you are a licensed real estate agent. In that case, as I mentioned before, you will receive the commission on the buy-ing side and be able to save on the selling side. Closing costs however are usually fixed and have nothing to do with being an agent.

You must also be sure that the home is clear of liens, back taxes, or anything else that would cloud the title. If there are title complications, you'll need to add those numbers to your expenses. As I referenced, part of your calculations must unfortunately include taxes on your profit. Tax strategies are endless, so make sure you get professional advice before you get involved with flipping properties. Your financial and tax situation is unique, so make sure you get the facts. In some cases, you may just want to pay the capital gains tax and move on with your life, and other times you may want to conduct a 1031 exchange whereby your profits are rolled over into another similar investment property in order to possibly defer taxes. Again, have a good CPA in your corner, and have all the facts before you dive into an investment property.

The purchase
Suffice it to say after doing your homework the next thing you need to do is purchase the property at the right price. The right price is an

appropriately discounted price that takes into consideration the condition of the property. In addition, the right price has room for all the expenses while still maintaining a significant margin for profit. This is one of the most important details in the flipping process. You must really have your business hat on here. This is not an emotional purchase nor is a property something you fall in love with. This is a money-making vehicle. As such it's just straight business. And if it's just straight business, it's about numbers, and no number is more important than the purchase price. Be prepared to negotiate the price if needed and have reasons backing up why you are offering a lower price. Here is where you must have a thorough understanding of median sales prices in your market. If someone is asking an above median price for a below-quality home, there is room to negotiate, providing it is not an aggressive market or one that has extremely low inventory.

At this point you will already have your financing in order. Whether you have cash, get a loan, combine family money, or have investors, you want to know what your purchasing power is. Cash is usually best but not always feasible, so you may have to get creative. As a side note, if you are purchasing distressed properties at auction, oftentimes the terms are for cash only, so do your homework ahead of time and come prepared.

Comps, listed homes, pending, and sold.
You must have a recent comparative market analysis (CMA) or comp for short. Comps are detailed reports generated by the real estate agent. The comp will reveal homes for sale, those which are pending, and those which have sold. All three of those groups of homes yield key portions of information and insight that you can use in establishing the value of the home you are looking at and what profit you may project. You don't necessarily care what a home sold for two years ago. Usually a ninety-day search will suffice.

Pending sales are not much help because the actual agreed upon sale price is not made public. The ill-informed or unscrupulous agent may push back on your lower offer citing a home similar to theirs at the same price is pending, but that is nonsense as you have no idea what the actual offer is nor do you know what concessions were made. If the property you are looking at is $200,000 and the pending home was listed for $200,000, those sellers may have accepted an offer of $175,000. In addition maybe the seller gave a $5,000 concession for paint and carpet reducing the actual sale price to $170,000. The only thing pending homes indicate is days on market or DOM. If everything that is for sale slips into pending in less than a week, then you know the market is hot or that inventory is low or both. This then tells you your property is in a desired area and you can expect a quick sale once improvements are completed and the home is listed for sale.

Homes that are currently for sale are largely irrelevant for your purposes as well. We don't care what someone lists their home for. That means nothing except as a base line of current pricing. For example, if there are four homes for sale in the area and they are all roughly the same, they should have roughly the same price. However, if two are at $200,000, one is at $165,000, and one is at $215,000, you need do some investigation. Sometimes there are reasons why and sometimes it's just unrealistic sellers represented by weak agents offering an unreasonable price. And again, just like homes that are pending, there are many variables to current homes on the market. They may have to reduce their asking price or the home may sit there, get stagnant and expire. There just isn't really much helpful information here except in knowing your competition. Your home could justify a higher than average price if it was really improved well, but you would still have to be in the range of current home prices in order to remain relevant and competitive.

The sold column is the only one that matters when viewing comps. The sold properties will give you a range for price per square foot, which is one of the easiest metrics to evaluate a home. Homes across the country can be anywhere from $65 to $300 a square foot with luxury homes or penthouses fetching much higher than that. You will want to establish what the average is for the area you are looking at. Whatever the dynamics make sure you are comparing apples to apples. For example, at the time of this writing, I am investigating a possible flip. It is in western New York in the area where I grew up. I am very familiar with the neighborhood and know that homes are selling for around $100 a square foot. The property I am looking at is listed at a price that yields a square-foot price of $56. In good condition, this 2,400 square-foot home should sell for around $240,000. Right now it is being offered for about $135,000 because it is distressed. On paper there looks to be about $100,000 available between offering price and the average per square-foot sales price in the area. Clearly this will catch the eye of anyone interested in flipping a home. In addition, those looking for a personal residence would be enticed as they can enjoy embedded equity right on day one.

The home has been abandoned even though it is in a very nice neighborhood across from a large treed park with two lakes and walking trails. It is near the New York State Thruway and near the University of Buffalo. It has a perfect location in a great part of town. From the pictures online, it looks perfect for me. There are downed trees and branches all over the large quarter acre property. The three skylights have been leaking for some time, and there is significant water damage to the ceiling, walls, and flooring. The property is dated and looks like it has never been improved since construction in the early 1980s. If I move forward with this home, I will simply tear out the skylights, nail in joists, add plywood to the roof, and have a roofer match the shingles. Then we will clearly have some drywall repair and replacement. The entire home needs updated flooring and light fixtures. The kitchen and bathrooms need to be gutted. The interior and exterior needs a fresh coat of paint, and the home desperately needs some nice landscaping to enhance its curb appeal.

I am estimating it needs about $40,000 on the high end to bring this home up to speed. I am planning on offering $125,000 as this home has sat abandoned for some time, and as it is winter at the time of this writing, I doubt this property is being looked at. So my calculations put us at $165,000 total costs. And as New York and Colorado have reciprocal agreements for real estate agents, I can use my license to purchase the home netting $3,750. So I subtract that from my total and end up with total all in costs before sale of $161,250. At an average per square-foot price of $100, our projected sale price will be $240,000 providing a gross profit of $78,750, from which I will subtract selling commission and closing costs. However, as I will be representing myself, I only have to pay the buyers commission of $7,200, so our projected pretax profit looks like it will be a little over $70,000. It will take us about forty-five days to complete, so this looks to be a profitable venture. I am waiting on a little more information and will most likely be making an offer within days. As I grew up in the area, I have friends who can make arrangements for viewing the property and getting estimates. Though the online pictures were helpful, my friend went through the property and Facetimed me during the walk through. I was able to see everything just as if I was walking through myself. I share all this to show you how you should view a property in order to offer the right price.

Also, be aware of competition. Speed is needed here. There is no shortage of others wanting to do the same thing you are doing. There are hobbyists, newcomers, contractors, and professional flippers all going after the same thing. It's like five people having five hooks in the water going for the same fish, so prepare to move quickly. Again, as I've said before, it is a distinct advantage if you can do most of the due diligence and estimating yourself as you will save time. Otherwise if you need to parade a bunch of people through the property in order to get firm estimates, the experienced flipper or contractor who knows what things cost on one visit may scoop up the property. Remember there are many variables that go into a fair price for a home. It is your responsibility to be aware of them all before you make an offer.

Improvement

Assuming you bought it at the right price and did all your realistic calculations, you will want to embark on your strategy for the flip. This, of course, needs to be done very early on in the process, preferably before you even make the offer. You need to have some general ideas on strategy because while your buy and sell numbers are fairly fixed, there are many variables in between to consider. The tighter your parameters, the more accurate your forecast and profit projections will be. This phase involves experience, good taste, market awareness, and sound business philosophy. The basic idea in the improvement phase is that you want to bring the property up to the standards of the surrounding homes or even slightly better. It is a mistake to go on the overly cheap side and make minimal improvements or use less expensive materials. For example, if the other homes in the area have tile flooring in the laundry area and bathrooms but you decide to install linoleum to cut costs, you might also expect to be overlooked or receive a lower offer because those materials are perceived as inferior to the rest of the neighborhood. Conversely, it may be a mistake to do what is called overbuilding, which is where the quality and amount of upgrades are way above the surrounding homes. If the surrounding homes have above ground circular pools and you decide to have an in-ground infinity edge pool with cascading waterfalls, grotto, slide, and raised hot tub that cost $130,000, you may price yourself right out of the neighborhood.

You want to hit a sweet spot of providing an updated home that is attractive but blends in with the rest of the neighborhood. My personal business philosophy on this is that I believe people like nice things. I think if they have the choice they would like something nicer with slightly more expensive features than not. Again, I'm not talking about trying to sell a Ferrari in a Volkswagen neighborhood. I'm talking about improving the property in a way that makes a significant impression while not being ostentatious. After all the whole idea of a flip is to get in and get out in the least amount of time. The more the home just pops when potential buyers see it, the faster your home will sell.

Where to spend your money

Beyond obvious repairs and updating obsolete or ugly features, I am often asked where the best place to invest money is. You want to spend money on the area that will have the biggest wow factor. In other words, you don't just want to waste money on insignificant things that make no impression. You want your dollars to make people stop and admire, and give you a strong offer. In my opinion the first place you spend money is on landscaping. Many people ignore this to their own peril. It's called curb appeal, plain and simple. If people aren't even attracted from the outside, you won't be able to entice them to look inside. Think about birds that fluff their feathers and display beautiful colors to attract a suitable mate. The landscaping is the first thing people see, and it creates the first impression of desirability.

Now as a former landscape architect and owner of a landscaping company, I may be partial, but I truly believe this to be the case. Compare a home done right with a rich deep-green lawn cut at a diagonal complimented by perfectly pruned shrubs, appropriately sized trees, and blossoming flowers to a home with a mediocre lawn with weeds and three half-dead bushes that look like they've never been pruned. Which home do you think will get attention? It's super logical. You have to catch them at the curb in order to get them inside. The great thing is landscaping doesn't have to cost that much, but it has in my opinion the greatest return for your dollar. Now that we have an attractive home that entices people to come inside, you have to focus on the kitchen. The kitchen is the central hub of the home. It is where people socialize, prepare and eat meals, do homework, and enjoy a good cup of coffee with a friend.

Again compare one kitchen with dated fluorescent rectangular lighting, Formica counters, linoleum floors, and cheap white appliances with a kitchen that has recessed lighting, five inch distressed pecan floors, granite counters, and top-of-the-line stainless steel appliances. One has people go "ho hum," and the other makes people go "wow"! If you are trying to sell your investment quickly and for maximum dollar, you clearly want the wow factor on your side. Let the cheap and greedy investor have his home on the market for six months while people haggle over the price. My properties always sell for top dollar and in short order. Why? Because my wife and I have good taste, and we know that people like nice things. We like nice things. Why would any potential buyer be any different? We give people nice things. It's not that complicated. You can get rid of the cheap builder grade hallway light that costs ten dollars and put in recessed canned lights for superior lighting and better aesthetics. Brighter is always better. Maybe it costs you a little more, but you get it back because people are always willing to pay more for quality.

We always paint the interior of our investments with nice vibrant but soft colors. You want the home to feel warm, and nothing creates warmth like a buttery cream paint and great lighting. Unless you feel risky or have tremendous design experience, I would suggest you avoid dramatic paint schemes. You want to appeal the masses. This isn't the time to be overly creative or artsy. Beyond landscaping and the kitchen, the bathrooms need to stand out. I usually use the same granite for the bathroom counters that I use in the kitchen. That way the home has a cohesive feel to it. I get rid of the ugly thirty-six-inch bar light above the mirror with those hideous opaque round light bulbs and put in a nice lighting feature. I also make sure the floors in the bathroom are tiled. Carpet in bathrooms is gross. Tile is best for cleaning and potential water drippings after showering.

Another place I always focus on is bedroom closets. There is one common complaint with most American homes: not enough storage. This overlooked component can really separate you from other homes on the market. Compare a standard bedroom closet with just a bar and shelf with a closet that has been completely re-imagined with a closet organizer that utilizes every square inch. There is no comparison. Yet another overlooked place is the garage. A light color epoxy coat on the garage floor makes a huge impression. This not only brightens things up, but it's also easier to clean. We install shelving and work benches if possible. We also add extra electrical outlets. Why? Haven't you ever lived somewhere and you try to vacuum out your car, for example, but the dumb garage only has one outlet, and its way in the back? That's why. Then to brighten things up a bit, we always install recessed canned lights. Garages are always notoriously dim and feel like a cave. With a clean floor and bright lights, I have seen where a nicely appointed garage got the home sold for full asking price. Like other things, it doesn't take that much work or that much money, but it makes a huge impact.

I can't overemphasize quality. People can tell if you buy cheap carpet and a thin pad versus a nice thick pad and lush carpet. They can tell the difference between standard two-inch outdated oak floor planks versus trendy five-inch pecan or dark wood. While some people may be gullible, they are not stupid. We all like nice things. I always improve my properties as if I was going to live in them. That's how I make my decisions on what to improve and what quality of materials to use. It's important to have good taste and know what is trendy, current, and attractive to buyers. It's important to spend money on places where the wow factor will potentially increase your profit. You also have to know when to stop. Some people endlessly tinker. If you're a tinkerer, stay in your garage and whittle wood. If you're a serious investor who wants to profit from flipping houses, make the improvements, stay within your carefully calculated budget, and then be done with it. It's time to put the for sale sign in the ground.

The sale
Now that you have done your homework, purchased the home, and made the needed improvements, it's time to sell. As I cover selling strategies in other parts of the book, I won't expand much here. However, I will touch on some things that are unique to flips. The first priority will be security. You've put a lot of effort into this flip and you want to protect your investment. Your property will be vacant so make sure you keep an eye on the home or have someone do that for you. Depending on the neighborhood, vacant homes can be susceptible to vandalism, break ins, and theft. You don't want to discover your stainless steel appliances have vanished or that the copper pipes in the basement have been removed. If you are concerned, it is not a bad idea to install wireless security cameras that feed you real time video through Wi-Fi. This is an easy fix as you can purchase and install a Wi-Fi unit in the home and then program it through an app on your smart phone. Anybody with bad intentions snooping around your property will be less inclined to do something stupid if they spot cameras on the outside of the home. The Wi-Fi unit and cameras should cost $400 to $700 depending on which model you purchase. You may

think $500 or so is a lot to spend, but in reality if it's protecting $50,000 of profit plus your time and efforts that's a small price to pay. After you're done, you can remove it and take it with you or even sell it with the home as an added feature.

Beyond security issues you want to make sure the appearance is always first class and that the home looks lived in and cared for. What is the point of spending all that money and doing all that work if you don't have someone cut the lawn regularly? If you live in an area where it snows, make sure the driveway and walkways are always clear. Sometimes advertisers throw promotional newspapers at every driveway or hang flyers on the front door. You want to make sure such things are picked up and are not lying around or piling up. In addition, you need to be sure that weeds are pulled, leaves are raked, dead branches are picked up, bushes are trimmed, and the landscaping always looks fresh and well maintained. On the inside, stay on top of vacuuming and dusting. Empty houses have a way of really showing dust. The tile or wood floors may need a mopping as buyers and agents can make tracks with dirty shoes. You can supply surgical booties that go over shoes and leave a box at the door to help cut down on the dirt.

Regarding showings, vacant homes do have some peculiar characteristics. Some people are huge fans of staging an empty home. This can be merely a kitchen table and a couch or two, but it can also be a full staging complete with decor and artwork. For me personally I have never staged a home. I think it is an unnecessary expense and effort and have never felt the need. I know great agents who stage homes all the time. I personally have never felt the additional cost was necessary let alone the risk of damaging walls, flooring, and doors moving furniture in and out of the property. I think most people like to see open spaces and imagine what their furniture would look like in every room. I also feel that an empty home shows off the improvements better and feels larger. In any case, one thing I always do is make sure the lights are all turned on in the morning and turned off at night. A bright home shows best, even in daylight hours. Also, just because it's empty doesn't mean the climate doesn't need to be controlled. Depending on season, make sure the AC or heat is on. Nobody likes to look at a home while they're either sweating or shivering!

As I've stated before, either you have to stay on top of it or somebody else does. Just make sure the home is looked after. A vacant home can become ignored quite easily and look neglected. Many investors make the mistake of checking out and going on the next flip once the sale sign is in the ground. Remember, this is still your property, and you have invested time, effort, and money into it. It is not sold yet, and you have not been reimbursed yet. Stay engaged and stay involved until you hand over the keys.

Real estate buyers, sellers, or investors in Denver, Castle Pines, Castle Rock, Colorado Springs, and surrounding areas:
If you are local in Colorado and would like to meet Johan and have him represent you in your next real estate transaction, contact him today to schedule an appointment!

Real estate buyers, sellers, or investors in other parts of the United States:
If you reside anywhere else in the United States but would like to have Johan speak with you regarding your next real estate transaction, please call or e-mail him to schedule a complimentary fifteen-minute, over-the-phone consultation. After your conversation, Johan will connect you with a top producing local agent from his national network.

Whether you live in Getzville, New York; Coupeville, Washington; Clearwater, Florida; or Valencia, California, we want to be your trusted resource for all things real estate. We look forward to speaking with you and we appreciate the opportunity to connect you with a top producing agent in your local area!

Seminars, conferences, and media appearances:
If you would like to have P. Johan Sekovski speak at your event, please call or e-mail us to discuss how we can customize a presentation or training event for your specific needs. Johan is also available for interviews, TV, and radio engagements. In addition, please contact us if you would like to replicate any portion of this book or have Johan write an article for your website, newspaper, or magazine.

Thanks, and we look forward to serving you!

info@pjohan.com
(888) 937-3846.

22901881R00178

Made in the USA
San Bernardino, CA
19 January 2019